MEDIA, STATE AND NATION

The Media, Culture & Society Series

Series editors: John Corner, Nicholas Garnham, Paddy Scannell, Philip Schlesinger, Colin Sparks, Nancy Wood

The Economics of Television
The UK Case

Richard Collins, Nicholas Garnham and Gareth Locksley

Media, Culture and Society
A Critical Reader

edited by
Richard Collins, James Curran, Nicholas Garnham,
Paddy Scannell, Philip Schlesinger and Colin Sparks

Capitalism and Communication
Global Culture and the Economics
of Information

Nicholas Garnham, edited by Fred Inglis

MEDIA, STATE AND NATION

Political Violence and Collective Identities

Philip Schlesinger

SAGE Publications
London • Newbury Park • New Delhi

SAGE Publications Ltd
6 Bonhill Street
London EC2A 4PU

SAGE Publications Inc
2455 Teller Road
Newbury Park, California 91320

SAGE Publications India Pvt Ltd
32, M-Block Market
Greater Kailash – I
New Delhi 110 048

British Library Cataloguing in Publication data
Schlesinger, Philip
  Media, state and nation: Political violence and collective
  identities. – (Media, culture and society series)
  I. Title II. Series
  320

  ISBN 0–8039–8503–7
  ISBN 0–8039–8504–5 pbk

Library of Congress catalog card number 90–053695

Typeset by The Word Shop, Bury, Lancs
Printed in Great Britain by Billing and Sons Ltd, Worcester

Contents

For Sharon

Preface

In various ways, the chapters in this book engage with key issues that have marked our political life in recent years: the use of political violence within the liberal-democratic state; the Cold War and its profound impact on our thinking; the presently resurgent questions of national and cultural identity. Given my long-standing interest in the sociology of the media, it is inevitable that my line of attack on these questions often begins with an analysis of communication. But I do not by any means see that as a limitation, merely as a starting-point for a broader discussion.

Although this book is certainly not a seamless whole, what does unify it is a recognition of the crucial importance of the contested processes of definition and interpretation in political culture. Or, in an idiom which is now out of fashion, of ideological struggle and its contexts.

Where I have edited the original pieces this has been largely to eliminate repetition. The passage of time has meant that in some cases additional background discussion and updating of key references are required. Here, the choice of how much – or how little – to say is always a compromise between rewriting completely and offering a sketch of some key developments. For obvious reasons, I have chosen the latter course of action.

In Part I, I have grouped chapters that deal with the role of the media in reporting political violence, and debates about this issue. Of these, Chapter 1, published for the first time in English, offers a general point of entry by considering the problems of conceptualizing the category of 'violence' and its relationship to legitimacy and the state. This provides the background to Chapter 2, which offers a critical assessment of official arguments in liberal democracies for censoring the reporting of 'terrorism'. These are to be understood within the context of competing propaganda strategies by the state and its enemies. If I put 'terrorism' in quotation marks it is because, like 'violence', 'terrorism' is a contested term in political discourse. To seek to control its application is to seek to control public understanding of contemporary struggles. In Chapter 3, we move from the analysis of doctrine to the practice of censorship in a detailed case study of the celebrated Iranian Embassy siege in London. The questions posed then about both the causes of such hostage-takings and about the state's use of force have not disappeared.

Part I offers one kind of discussion of the enemies of state and society in relation to the problem of violence, whereas Part II considers a key aspect of this theme more fully. Until the end of the Cold War was officially declared in the wake of the revolutions in Eastern Europe in 1989, we had lived within a Manichaean mental universe. If we did not accept it, we were nevertheless obliged to argue with it, or otherwise confront its compelling presence.

This brings us to Chapter 4 and an examination of the ways in which the war against domestic terrorism has been linked to the recently ended Cold War. The demise of communism as the old ideological enemy is going to have little impact upon the practice of counter-insurgency or the flourishing field of terrorism studies which has grown alongside it. Chapters 5 and 6 were written with my late friend, Philip Elliott, from whom I learned so much. Had his life not ended so tragically early, they would have been developed into a book. (That idea has not been abandoned, although it would inevitably look different now.) In Chapter 5, the way communism is represented in popular media discourse and the way it is analysed in political science are juxtaposed and connected. This is to illustrate an argument, more fully developed elsewhere, that political discourse is complexly structured and nuanced. It links into the fight over the meaning of 'Eurocommunism' (the Old Red Wolf newly decked out in unconvincing disguise or the Lamb of Peace challenging the integrity of the blocs, both East and West?) which was part of the wider ideological Cold War, and is analysed in Chapter 6. It was because of their general need for relatively unambiguous political classifications in ideological struggles that the label of 'Eurocommunism' proved so unacceptable to dominant groups on both sides. In a case study, the competing communicative strategies are laid out. Whilst that particular episode now lies firmly in the past, many of the questions it raised – not least what kind of politico-economic system should prevail in Europe, and elsewhere in the advanced capitalist world – remain on the political agenda, if anything, much less predictably than before.

We now come to Part III. Another way of thinking about the construction of images of friends and enemies, and the part these play in the framing of our imagined political world, is to talk about the identities of social and cultural collectivities. This is the final theme, and represents the most recent line of development in my work. It has strongly autobiographical roots and was begun when working in Italy at a 'European' institution. This provoked me to begin a line of interrogation that seems likely to persist. Chapters 7 and 8 were originally one continuous text but are now divided into two for the reader's convenience, and in any case this was my initial intention. In Chapter 7, a survey of recent media theory leads me to conclude that the theoretical issues that underlie our thinking about such collective forms of identity as the 'nation' and the 'culture' have been crassly side-stepped. Worse still, serious questions about the impact of communication on cultural collectivities have been begged. In Chapter 8, I have begun to address these questions by coming at them from the direction of various strands of contemporary social theory where, conversely, concern with processes of communication tends to be rather rudimentary. Clearly, there is work to be done. In a small gesture towards this need, Chapter 9, published for the first time in English, addresses the dynamic field of contemporary debate about 'Europeanness.'

In various ways, then, these chapters deal with the national state and political violence, with political legitimacy and the representation of friends and enemies, and with the ways in which struggles involving media might connect with the currently pressing question of collective identity. I have little doubt that as the various relations concerned continue to develop, we shall need to think about them afresh. But that is for another time and place.

Philip Schlesinger
Stirling, September 1990

Acknowledgements

Chapter 1 was specially written for the conference on 'The Future of Violence and the Violence of the Future', held in Lugano in November 1987 and organized by Professor Luigi Bonanate of the University of Turin. It first appeared in longer form in German as 'Die Intepretation von Gewalt' in *Innovation* (Vienna), 1. Jahrgang, Heft 4/5, 'Konflikt und Kooperation: Henrik Kreutz zum 50. Geburtstag', November 1988, pp. 435–53; and in Italian as 'Quanto è violenta la società contemporanea? Alcuni problemi di interpretazione', in L. Bonanate (ed.), *Il Futuro della Pace e la Violenza del Futuro: Atti del Simposio Internazionale Città di Lugano* (Lugano: Edizioni Città di Lugano, 1989), pp. 165–80.

Chapter 2 was originally published in a longer version in *Social Research*, vol. 48, no.1, Spring 1981, pp.74–99; and in Y. Alexander and A. O'Day (eds), *Terrorism in Ireland* (London and Canberra: Croom Helm, 1984), pp. 213–32; also published in Italian as 'Il "terrorismo", i media e lo Stato liberal-democratico: una critica dell'ortodossia', in R. Grandi, M. Pavarini and M. Simondi (eds), *I Segni di Caino: L'Immagine della Devianza nella Comunicazione di Massa* (Napoli: Edizioni Scientifiche Italiane, 1985), pp. 289–308.

Chapter 3 was originally published in *Screen Education*, Winter 1980–1, No. 37, 'The State and the Law: Images and Narrativity', pp. 29–54; it also appeared in J. L. Curry and J. R. Dassin (eds), *Press Control around the World* (New York: Praeger, 1982), pp.27–61; and in E. Wartella and D. C. Whitney (eds), *Mass Communication Research Yearbook*, Vol. 4 (Beverly Hills, Calif.: Sage, 1983), pp. 463–88.

Chapter 4 was originally published in G. Littlejohn, B. Smart, J. Wakeford and N. Yuval-Davis (eds), *Power and the State* (London: Croom Helm, 1978), pp. 98–127.

Chapter 5 was originally published in *Media, Culture and Society*, vol. 1, no. 2, April 1979, 'Political Economy', pp. 195–210.

Chapter 6 is a substantially revised and extended version of a paper first published in *The Sociological Review*, vol. 27, no. 1, February 1979, pp. 55–81, under the title 'On the Stratification of Political Knowledge: Studying "Eurocommunism", an Unfolding Ideology'. In its present form it appeared in D. Childs (ed.), *The Changing Face of Western Communism* (London: Croom Helm, 1980), pp. 37–73.

Chapters 7 and 8 were originally published as 'On National Identity: Some Conceptions and Misconceptions Criticized' in *Social Science Information*, vol. 26, no. 2, June 1987, pp. 219–64; and in Spanish as 'Identidad nacional: Una critica de lo que se entiende y malentiende sobre este concepto' in *Estudios sobre las Culturas Contemporáneas* (Colima, Mexico), vol. II, no. 6, pp. 39–98.

Chapter 9 was specially written for the *Telos*/FUNDESCO international conference on 'Europe and the Single Market: New Scenarios for the Media', held in Madrid in May 1990 and organized by Professor Enrique Bustamante, editor of *Telos*. It was originally published in a slightly shorter version in Spanish as 'Identidad europea y cambios en la communicación: de la politica a la cultura y los medios' in *Telos: Cuadernos de Comunicación, Tecnología y Sociedad* (Madrid), no. 22, Septiembre–Noviembre 1990, pp. 105–16.

The author thanks Mrs Wendy Elliott and the various editors and publishers for their permission to reprint.

Introduction to Part I

Part I is concerned with the relations between news media and the use of political violence within the capitalist, liberal-democratic, national state. My work on this question was first provoked by observing the impact on British media politics of the armed conflict in Northern Ireland. This has led on to much broader issues of theory and analysis that go well beyond the particularities of any single national case.

In order to raise some of these wider questions, Chapter 1 begins by examining some of the complexities of the category of 'violence'. Without doubt, the analysis of violence ought to be central in social and political analysis, for we cannot discuss the ultimate foundations of state power without recognizing how coercion and the use of force articulate with political consent. In the opening chapter I have sought to reflect relevant aspects of today's continuing and unresolved theoretical debate on these matters.

Ultimately, we all have to make judgements about the legitimacy or otherwise of acts of violence on the basis of the ethical and political values to which we adhere. I would argue that central to any such consideration is the question of whether or not we assess violence, in the social anthropologist David Riches' words, as 'a strategically, consciously employed resource' (1986: 11). Or, to put it more simply, should we start off by thinking that violent acts have purposes and intentions behind them? I would not wish to argue that *all* violence is of this kind, but that a starting-point for the analysis of politically motivated violence would do well to begin with this assumption. There would seem to be growing acceptance of this position. For instance, the sociologists Robert Slater and Michael Stohl have observed a recent shift of approach in the specific case of terrorism. They note:

> Terrorism is purposeful. A consensus appears to be emerging that abandons the more traditional view of terrorism as predominantly irrational behaviour . . . there is a set of beliefs or justification system which in some senses guides the actions. Thus, in our definition of terrorism, we assume that terrorism is a purposeful act which is intended to affect an audience either directly or indirectly. (1988: 4)

In short, to look for a rationale for acts of violence is a point of departure for further investigation; it is there to be tested in given situations, by empirical analysis, not to be understood as a dogmatic article of faith (cf. Miller, 1984: 414–19).

Many acts of violence, whatever their causes, are easily recognized as violent across divergent systems of interpretation and belief. It is this quality that has made the communicative or symbolic and expressive dimensions of violence so interesting and pertinent for contemporary debate. However, to acknowledge frequent ease of recognition of acts of physical force or material destruction (such as assassinations or bombings) is but to offer a starting-point. It is to say nothing at all about the ways in which they may be interpreted. As David Riches further observes: 'From the standpoint of witnesses on one side of a divide (ethnic or otherwise), the violence perpetrated and displayed by people on the other side comes to symbolize the existence of an alternative way of life' (1986: 14). Putting it differently, the interpretation of violence may work as a way of codifying the world into 'friends' and 'enemies', of separating 'us' from 'them', the 'national' from the 'alien'. It is such questions that are considered in this section.

The guiding thread is to ask how communicative strategies may be linked with political violence in contemporary liberal democracies. In this connection, it is impossible to ignore the major role that media may play in constructing our perceptions of the public domain and the legitimacy or illegitimacy of those who act within it. It is precisely the *conflict* over communicative strategies that provides the theme of Chapters 2 and 3, which were originally written in parallel with one another and which deal with related questions at different levels of analysis.

Following on from the more general opening discussion of 'violence' as a contested category in political discourse, my principal concern in Chapter 2 is to criticize the assumptions of official thinking on the control of media reporting of 'terrorism'. The debate about this question has developed very unevenly. Although it has certainly had an international dimension – which continues, given the various trans-border uses of politically motivated violence – it nevertheless has been most acute within given states when perceptions of national crisis have been at their most intense. For instance, whereas in the early 1980s one could hardly find any discussion of terrorism in France, towards the end of the decade, after a spate of violent incidents, debate was in full flow (cf. Wieviorka and Wolton, 1987). In Italy, to take a further example, debate reached its high water mark during the 'years of lead' (cf. Lumley and Schlesinger, 1982; Wagner-Pacifici, 1988).

The critique presented in Chapter 2 remains just as pertinent today as at the begining of the 1980s, for official thinking has not changed significant-ly. From the point of view of those who rule through the liberal-democratic state, the problem remains the same – namely, how to ensure 'responsible' media coverage and self-limitation without recourse to obvious acts of delegitimizing censorship. Consequently there has been no need for a shift in the basic doctrines of officialdom. Some insight into the current international consensus in governmental and parliamentary circles may be gained from a recent report by the North Atlantic Assembly's Sub-Committee on Terrorism, where it is argued that 'The practical answer to media coverage problems lies in closer media-to-government working relations [rather] than government-imposed restraint.' This is the essence of the doctrines examined in Chapter 2. Furthermore, it is recognized that

> apart from freedom of the press and free enterprise considerations, restrictions would be difficult to enforce and would not necessarily affect foreign media. Moreover, censorship could prove counter-productive in a crisis in that failure to comply with terrorist demands for coverage could result in hostage deaths or other violence. It should also be borne in mind that journalists are often a better source of information than government, and may obtain freer access to terrorists during incidents . . . More broadly, it would be most illusory to believe that but for media coverage terrorism would somehow disappear. (Nunes and Smith, 1989: 20–1)

These highly pragmatic arguments, which stress the system-sustaining potentialities of journalism rather than its boat-rocking qualities, may well be aired in some official quarters. However, they are heard much less frequently during the public rows that more usually characterize relations between media and state when the media are judged to have transgressed the acceptable limits. At any given time, the implementation of government communicative strategies in this field will, of course, vary considerably and be conditioned by the national political culture and the specific institutional links between media and state (cf. Crelinsten, 1987a). However this works itself out, at the heart of the matter lies the persistent effort to control the media's use of language, sounds, images and frameworks of interpretation, whether by agencies of the state or, alternatively, by those insurgents who use violence against the established order. The consequent problems raised by the 'semantics of political violence' have been noted by the BBC journalist Peter Taylor, who in surveying the terminology used by press and broadcasting has emphasized the 'difficult path one treads in working within a political framework which is itself under strain from the events one is reporting' (1986: 221). This is hardly likely to change, as shifting boundaries of political tolerance are inherent in the relations between media and state in liberal democracies.

In Chapter 3, a case study of the Iranian Embassy siege of 1980 shows competing communicative strategies at work which are to be found elsewhere. For example, in a comparable study of the reporting of two kidnappings by the FLQ in Canada, Ronald Crelinsten (1987b) has demonstrated how the insurgents lost their initiative when the Federal government invoked its emergency powers. On a much more detailed level, Robin Wagner-Pacifici (1988) has studied the strategies employed by political forces and media during the kidnapping of the Italian politician Aldo Moro. Although a dominant interpretation of the political meaning of the kidnapping and its outcome was eventually achieved, this was not without enormous struggles in a media and political system in which consensus is difficult to reach. For their part, although focusing most upon the French experience of recent years, Michel Wieviorka and Dominique Wolton (1987) have also argued for a comparative examination of the broader political contexts in which the media, authorities and terrorists pursue their objectives.

Perhaps unusually, Chapter 3 offers a detailed example of the kind of state–media collaboration called for by the North Atlantic Assembly's Sub-Committee on Terrorism. More commonly, it is the great set-piece rows over the media's alleged tendency to give terrorism the 'oxygen of publicity' (as the British Prime Minister, Mrs Margaret Thatcher, has memorably put it) that tend to dominate public discussion, rather than the instances of collaboration with the security forces. But both are equally interesting and analytically important, as they offer insights into the range of constraints that media coverage faces. Certainly, in the British case, as I have argued in *Televising 'Terrorism'* (Schlesinger et al., 1983), we should not see broadcasting either as a simple instrument of the state or as the terrorists' friend; nor should we buy the argument that it is a fearless part of the mythic Fourth Estate. The reality is actually more complex, and, as is documented below, the scope for reporting at any given time is in many respects conditioned by the contradictory communicative strategies of the state and its armed enemies.

References

Crelinsten, R.D. (1987a) 'Terrorism as Political Communication: The Relationship between the Controller and the Controlled', in P. Wilkinson and A.M. Stewart (eds), *Contemporary Research on Terrorism*. Aberdeen: Aberdeen University Press. pp. 3–23.

Crelinsten, R.D. (1987b) 'Power and Meaning: Terrorism as a Struggle over Access to the Communication Structure', in P. Wilkinson and A.M. Stewart (eds), *Contemporary Research on Terrorism*. Aberdeen: Aberdeen University Press. pp. 419–50.

Lumley, B. and Schlesinger, P. (1982) 'The Press, the State and its Enemies: The Italian Case', *The Sociological Review*, 30 (4) (November): 603–26.

Miller, D. (1984) 'The Use and Abuse of Political Violence', *Political Studies*, xxxi: 401–19.

Nunes, J.L. and Smith, L.J. (co-rapporteurs) (1989) *Terrorism*. North Atlantic Assembly Papers, Sub-Committee on Terrorism, International Secretariat, Brussels, January.

Riches, D. (1986) 'Introduction' to *The Anthropology of Violence*. Oxford: Blackwell.

Schlesinger, P., Murdock, G. and Elliott, P. (1983) *Televising 'Terrorism': Political Violence in Popular Culture*. London: Comedia.

Slater, R.O. and Stohl, M. (eds) (1988) *Current Perspectives on International Terrorism*. Basingstoke and London: Macmillan.

Taylor, P. (1986) 'The Semantics of Political Violence', in P. Golding. G. Murdock and P. Schlesinger (eds), *Communicating Politics: Mass Communications and the Political Process*. Leicester: Leicester University Press; New York: Holmes & Meier. pp. 211–21.

Wagner-Pacifici, R.E. (1988) *The Moro Morality Play: Terrorism as Social Drama*. Chicago and London: University of Chicago Press.

Wieviorka, M. and Wolton, D. (1987) *Terrorisme à la Une: Media, Terrorisme et Démocratie*. Paris: Gallimard.

1

The Interpretation of Violence

How do frameworks of interpretation affect how we think about the question of violence in contemporary liberal democracies? It is obvious that we have to address questions of definition and categorization. I shall therefore begin by commenting briefly upon some theoretical perspectives in the social and human sciences. This leads me to consider the importance of control over the operation of social memory for contemporary perceptions of violence and sets the stage for a discussion of current official concern about the mass media and political violence in the chapters that follow.

The problem

There is no well-demarcated, widely accepted concept of violence. On the contrary, as many contemporary commentators have pointed out, 'violence' is a term that suffers from conceptual devaluation or semantic entropy. It is used as part of a discourse of social pathology in which we are perpetually threatened with disorder and decline, a discourse which is 'more than alarmist; it is catastrophist' (Chesnais, 1981: 8). As the historian Eric Hobsbawm has observed, for most citizens of liberal democracies such dark imaginings are not connected with the realities of everyday life, for physical violence narrowly understood is still a remote experience:

> Directly, it is omnipresent in the form of the traffic accident – casual, unintended, unpredictable and uncontrollable by most of its victims . . . Indirectly, it is omnipresent in the mass media and entertainment . . . Even more remotely, we are aware both of the existence in our time of vast, concretely unimaginable mass destruction . . . and also of the sectors and situations of society in which physical violence is common and probably, increasing. Tranquillity and violence coexist. (Hobsbawm, 1977: 209–10)

But is our *sense* of the present tranquil? Probably, since Hobsbawm wrote the passage quoted, some two decades ago, consciousness of the balance of terror has become more acute in many sectors of the populations of Europe, and in the post-Chernobyl years to be aware of what the aftermath of nuclear war would mean is surely vividly present to all who think. The past two decades have also seen the growth of various forms of political violence, often nationalist in origin, sometimes anti-systemic, used both within national confines and across them. This has gone under the label of 'terrorism' and has contributed to a sense of instability out of all proportion to its material, as opposed to its symbolic, importance. In the case of 'transnational terrorism', deriving from theatres of conflict such as the Middle East, physical violence is often transported from one context to another. The same could be said when sectoral conflicts such as that in Northern Ireland are fought out on the British mainland. But these are only the best-publicized faces of terrorist violence, the internal repression practised by states against their own citizens on the whole receiving much less attention.

To talk of contemporary violence, then, carries with it the risk of being all-embracing, of aggregating many diverse manifestations of the use of force and their effects: these might include all or any of criminal violence, public disorder and military actions. How can we make the issue intelligible? A starting-point, I suggest, is to look at practices of interpretation and to point to some of the problems involved in these. This does not make violent phenomena disappear by any means. But it can, at the very least, make us think more clearly about what we are doing and the underlying choices that are being made by opting for one or other evaluative framework.

One necessary step in considering the place of violence in contemporary society is to consider its relationship to the modern state. This, in turn, requires us to distinguish between types of state. But before dealing with either of these points let us briefly consider what might be meant by 'violence'.

The limits of defining

It needs but the slightest acquaintance with the literature on violence and terrorism to recognize the hazards of definition. Of course the process of defining and classifying acts and processes is far from neutral in this connection, for it is closely tied up with the question of legitimation and delegitimation. The well-known slogan that one man's terrorist is another man's freedom-fighter is perhaps the most simplistic way of making this point, directing us as it does to underlying frameworks for evaluating a given use of force and the status of the agent who uses it.

If there is a stand to be taken for the purposes of rational analysis, then it is surely with those who argue for restricting the scope of the term 'violence'. This may give us a sense of proportion about just how violent our times actually are and counter the inflationary effect of treating violence indiscriminately. There is little to be gained by lumping together such diverse manifestations as symbolic protest, the damaging effects on the poor of inegalitarian economic decision-making, the injustices of the routine and impersonal workings of bureaucracy, and the killing and maiming of persons. Although to take such a conceptually conservative stand is easy in principle it is difficult in practice. I have selected several restrictive definitions of violence, almost arbitrarily, in order to illustrate the analytical problems involved.

To take one recent example, Alain Chesnais, author of a study of violence during the past two centuries, proposes that: 'Violence in the strict sense, the only violence which is measurable and indisputable is *physical* violence. It is direct injury to persons; it has three characteristics: it is brutal, external and painful. It is defined by the material use of force' (Chesnais, 1981: 12). Much along the same lines is this formulation by the sociologist Robin Williams (1981: 26): 'the clearest cases of violence are those which cause physical damage, are intentional, are active rather than passive, and are direct in their effects.' Yet a further attempt to circumscribe what is meant by violence comes from the philosopher Ted Honderich (1980: 153), who suggests that 'An *act of violence* . . . is a use of considerable or destroying force against people or things, a use of force that offends against a norm.'

There would be little difficulty in compiling an entire volume of such definitions, and indeed this has been done (cf. Schmid, 1984, ch. 1). We could, moreover, attempt to classify them in various ways. For instance, in our three illustrative cases the 'basic' meaning of violence is stipulatively proposed (a) as physical violence to persons alone; *or* (b) as causing physical damage to unspecified categories of object, whether animate or inanimate, plus restrictive conditions about intentionality, directness and so forth; *or* (c) as involving both persons and things, together with a clause that locates the discussion of violence within a normative framework.

It could be said, fairly enough, that there is no great distance between these various definitions, and that some compromise reformulation could incorporate the essential elements of all three to the satisfaction of all concerned. However, the problem goes deeper. For to define 'violence' is not by any means to offer a protocol for its study and analysis. We might agree on a definition but still disagree about the details of subsequent categorization and what is to count as an adequate method for assembling evidence.

Thus, Chesnais categorizes violence as either 'private' or 'collective'. Under 'private' comes crime, suicide and accident. Under 'collective' come Soviet state terrorism and Western anti-state terrorism. Williams (1981: 28, 31) distinguishes collective from individual violence. In the first category come 'internal wars, revolutions, guerrilla wars, insurrections, rebellions, political purges, genocide, strikes with violence, vigilante actions, pogroms, riots, sabotage, political executions and assassinations'. In the second category come homicide, manslaughter, rape, assault, vandalism and attacks on persons and property. For his part, Honderich is concerned pre-eminently with examining the principle of violence from below directed towards changing a democratic political system.

Faced with such divergent strategies, it is tempting to abandon the rationalist road of definition and to say, as does the political scientist W.J.M. Mackenzie (1975: 160, 117), that the problem may be 'better stated by myth than definition', given his view that violence is 'itself symbol and metaphor'. Undoubtedly, when discussing whether our times are more or less violent than others we cannot fail to address how communication in its broadest sense constructs our perceptions of present dangers for us, and the role which violence as everyday drama plays in our lives.

This, however, is merely one intellectual line to be pursued. The broader question of how violent contemporary societies are can only be made intelligible in empirical terms by a process of rigorous comparison across space and time, a strategy that raises enormous problems of data collection, as Alex Schmid (1984: ch. 3) has pointed out in the case of political violence and terrorism. Ideally, this would require us to meet the following conditions: that (i) an agreed categorization of types of violence is employed during (ii) a clear-cut period in which (iii) comparable social formations are investigated (iv) using evidence or data adequate to support theoretically informed generalizations.

I do not wish to labour the point. But it is clear that even where we are being explicit and go to the lengths of enumerating given types of action within a society to be categorized as violent, this is an area in which normative assumptions are going to affect what we select in a major way. For example, when Britain mobilized for the recent war in the Falklands in the dominant view this was a legitimate use of force where diplomacy had failed. If we then refer to official concern about violence in the United Kingdom during the past decade, this 'small war' and its dead and wounded would scarcely register as something to be counted in (somehow) together with football hooliganism, terrorist bombings and fighting on the picket line during the miners' strike.

A second obvious point concerns the most conventional 'objective' measure of violence in society, namely crime statistics, which are frequently used as the basis for international comparison (cf., for example, Chesnais, 1981). As is well known, however, not only do categories of violent crime and understandings of motivation differ as between cultures, but the reporting of crimes, stringency of enforcement, success in apprehending criminals, sentencing policy, and so forth, all vary across time even within a single society. Such difficulties do not, of course, make comparative discussion of violence impossible. But it is always going to be problematic.

Power, violence and the state

As W.J.M. Mackenzie rightly observes, one route into the problem 'is to relate the problem of violence to that of political power, treating political power as a necessary basis for collective decision-making' (1975: 117). Our concern with the extent of violence in a society has to consider the ways in which it is inherently bound up with a system of rule.

According to Max Weber, control of the means of violence is an essential feature of the modern state – though not by any means the only one – and holds the key to the exercise of power within the political order: 'the state is a human community that (successfully) claims the *monopoly of the legitimate use of physical force within a given territory* . . . The state is considered the sole source of the "right" to use violence' (Weber, 1948: 78). A later eminent historical sociologist, Norbert Elias, also contends that the formation of the centralized, national state has brought with it the creation of territorially based monopolies of force, observing that 'When a monopoly of force is formed, pacified social spaces are created which are normally free from acts of violence' (Elias, 1982: 235). By violence in this context Elias means the exercise of physical force by non-authorized individuals or groups. In the modern era, 'physical torture, imprisonment and the radical humiliation of individuals has become the monopoly of a central authority, hardly to be found in normal life. With this monopolization, the physical threat to the individual is slowly depersonalized' (Elias, 1982: 237).

The 'right' to monopolize violence results in the depersonalization of its exercise through the decision-making processes of judicial authorities and law-enforcement bodies. This has been described by René Girard (1977: ch. 1 *passim*) as, in effect, the rationalization of revenge – an 'interminable, infinitely repetitive process' – from which the 'resounding authority' of the state is there to protect us (Girard, 1977: 15, 22). But those who claim to be in the business of social protection must in turn protect themselves from attacks upon their monopoly of force by invoking the mystique of legality and legitimacy: this then permits them to use violence in ways accepted as different in kind from the ways of those who act against the state. For, as Eugene Walter has pointed out in his study of political terror:

> When a violent process is socially prescribed and defined as a legitimate means of control or punishment, according to practices familiar to us, the destructive harm is measured and the limits made clear. Social definition as an authorized method often extracts it from the category of violence – at least from the standpoint of the society – and places in it the same domain with other socially approved coercive techniques. (Walter, 1969: 23)

If one accepts this broad line of argument, therefore, one of the immanent possibilities of the state's monopoly of violence is the transgression of those very legal frameworks which in theory act to limit its arbitrariness. It is at this point that we talk of states becoming terroristic, or of employing unacceptable techniques (such as torture) whose use they themselves would wish to deny, dissimulate or euphemize.

Forms of state

Throughout the period of the Cold War – now officially dead – we tended to differentiate between types of state and the place of violence within them. At its most simple, at least until the revolutions of 1989–90 in the former Communist bloc, the dominant world-picture was of a capitalist (democratic) West confronted by a socialist (totalitarian) East. Although by the time the Berlin Wall had collapsed it was widely conceded that state socialism was not in most places a regime of Stalinist terror, it was nonetheless still rightly seen as inherently repressive and authoritarian, with violent origins that still continued to exert influence upon the policing of dissent (Curtis, 1979; Friedrich et al., 1969). By contrast, however, the violent origins of most liberal democracies tended (and still continue) to be conveniently forgotten. But we will return to this point.

Liberal democracy, therefore, has stood, and still stands, as the contrast case to totalitarianism. As Ted Honderich (1980: 157) has pointed out, it is widely assumed 'that democracy and violence somehow conflict'. However, such a view does need to be tempered by a good dose of realism. If the Weberian view of the state is correct, it applies as much to liberal democracy as it does to totalitarianism: the differences are a matter of degree rather than of kind. This line of argument has recently been pursued to its logical conclusion by the social theorist Anthony Giddens (1985: 301), who has argued that ' "totalitarian" is not an adjective that can be fruitfully applied to a type of state, let alone to soviet-style states generally. It refers rather to a *type of rule*.' For Giddens all nation-states are potentially subject to the implementation of totalitarian rule, whose primary element, he suggests, involves 'an extreme focusing of surveillance, devoted to the securing of political ends deemed by the state authorities to demand urgent political mobilization' (1985: 303). To this he adds the more usual characteristics of moral totalism, terror and prominence of a leader figure.

We are not obliged to accept the view that all contemporary regimes are immanently totalitarian in this sense. A less far-reaching position is this: that *in extremis*, the liberal-democratic state may suspend all civil rights in defence of the social order itself. Pertinent here are the hard-nosed insights of Carl Schmitt (1985: 8, 12), who, anticipating the transition from the Weimar Republic to the Third Reich, said:

> Sovereign is he who decides on the exception . . . What characterizes an exception is principally unlimited authority, which means the suspension of the entire existing order. In such a situation it is clear that the state remains, whereas law recedes. Because the exception is different from anarchy and chaos, order in the juristic sense prevails even if it is not of the ordinary kind.

That is as blunt a recognition as one could wish that 'law and order', usually spoken of as an indissoluble couple, can pull in opposed directions.

The *état d'exception* in such a far-reaching sense is not unknown to us: Greece and Turkey, for instance, have both offered examples of the suspension of democracy in recent years. And exceptional measures have been taken in combating insurgency, as for instance in Northern Ireland, which offers an intermediate, sectoral, case: it is a not entirely successful attempt to insulate the wider polity from the effects of suspending business as usual in one province (cf. Faligot, 1980; Pistoi, 1981).

Nor is the democratic state a guarantee against a use of force that no one

– anywhere – willingly admits to: namely, torture. As the historian Edward Peters remarks in his study of this form of political violence, with the emergence of the nation-state, conceptions of treason have expanded. From *lèse-majesté*, focused on royal persons and households, we have moved to *lèse-nation*, in which the threat to 'a people or a state' has become 'both a larger and less specific offence'. Peters goes on to say: 'Paradoxically, in an age of vast state strength, ability to mobilize resources, and possession of virtually infinite means of coercion, much of state policy has been based on the concept of extreme vulnerability to enemies, external or internal' (Peters, 1985: 105, 7). Moreover, although in the twentieth century torture first appeared in the Soviet Union and the Third Reich and under Spanish and Italian fascism, it has also been found 'in some circumstances, under ordinary legal authority' (Peters, 1985: 105).

The classic example which crystallized post-war debate was the use of torture by the French administration during the Algerian independence struggle, a fact concealed for as long as possible (cf. Vidal-Naquet, 1972). In the case of Northern Ireland, 'counter-terrorist' operations involving the use of sensory deprivation and violent interrogation have been well-documented; instead of being labelled 'torture' it has been euphemized as 'ill-treatment' (McGuffin, 1974: Taylor, 1980). We are not obliged to say, as does Anthony Giddens, that all states tend towards totalitarianism to recognize the force of Peters' argument that the increasing salience of the nation-state as the basis of moral–political judgement, together with the growth of state security apparatuses, 'is perhaps the ultimate cause of the reappearance of torture in the twentieth century' (1985: 114).

Hence, the euphemization of a particular form of violence in the context, say, of a counter-insurgency campaign opens up a struggle over forms of classification, and consequently over the perception and measurement of 'violence'. The same arguments have been central to the debate about the origins of current terrorism in the West. In this connection, one can hardly forget the major efforts made by the first Reagan administration, at the beginning of the 1980s, to forge the ideological connections between international terrorism and Soviet communism. One decade on, and the post-Cold War climate has rendered this irrelevant. It is the Middle Eastern bogyman of 'Islam' that occupies centre stage at this time of writing.

The ideological argument against communism has been linked with US support for repressive regimes, in particular in Latin America and South-East Asia. The disappearance of the Soviet Union as chief ideological adversary will not render this redundant elsewhere. It was at the outset of the 1980s that so much was made of the distinction between 'authoritarianism' and 'totalitarianism', the former label being attributed to politically acceptable regimes of the right. It has also been the key to the running of what Edward Herman and Frank Brodhead (1984) have called 'demonstration elections' in places such as the Dominican Republic, South Vietnam and El Salvador. Given the association of democracy with consent, to make regimes look democratic is also to make them look legitimate and therefore to bring about the recodification of state terror as acceptable force.

Political frameworks and social memory

But it is not the current scene alone that poses problems of analysis. One theme too little explored in much contemporary discussion, given its fixation with the immediate, is the role of what we might call received social memory in structuring perceptions of the kind of society in which we live. Every eruption of violent political conflict, each 'crime wave', is heralded as though it were unprecedented, and an index of novel social pathology. This directs our attention to the ways in which frameworks of interpretation are created, sustained and contested by the activities of those acting for diverse political interests, intellectuals cast in the role of moralists or commentators and the journalistic imperatives of mass media.

Various commentators have noted how manifestations of political violence and 'crime waves' are greeted with surprise, as though they were novel events alien to the democratic political culture of the nation in question, and a telling index of unprecedented decline in civil conduct. The foreshortened temporal perspective at work has major consequences for the way in which the role of violence in the democratic order may be popularly conceived.

One pertinent example comes from the United States of the late 1960s in the wake of the urban riots in the black ghettos, student protest about the Vietnam War and the political assassinations of the Kennedys and Martin Luther King. As is well known, the Kerner Commission was appointed by the Johnson administration to investigate the 'civil disorders' in 1967, and the Eisenhower Commission to consider the 'causes and prevention of violence' was set up the following year.

One product of the latter commission's work was some historical research on violence in America in comparative perspective. One of the themes which emerged clearly from many of the studies conducted was the extent to which collective violence was a central part of American political culture, whether in the form of vigilantism, urban rioting, racial violence or violence on the industrial front. (Interestingly, and very tellingly, genocide is not one of the categories used.) Noting the parallels with Europe, the book's editors comment that 'group violence has been chronic and pervasive in the European and American past' and that 'both Europeans and Americans have a noteworthy capacity to forget or deny its commonality' (Graham and Gurr, 1969: xxxi).

In his survey of major Western European countries, the historical sociologist Charles Tilly has likewise observed that 'The collective memory machine has a tremendous capacity for destruction of the facts' and that the amnesia in question centres on the well-established finding that

'Historically, collective violence has flowed regularly out of the central political processes of western countries' (Tilly, 1969: 8, 4). Tilly, who considers the transformation of countries such as Britain, France, Germany, Italy and Spain into urban and industrial national states and economies, argues for a political interpretation of collective violence. Central to the various types which he identifies – whether primitive, reactionary or modern – is a 'struggle for established places in the structure of power' (Tilly, 1969: 10). In the contemporary context, argues Tilly, violent collective action tends to be organizationally based in forms of association such as political parties, unions and special interest groups and ought to be seen as interacting with the continual effort of authorities to 'monopolize, control, or at least contain' it (Tilly. 1969: 41). What Tilly calls the 'repertoire of collective action' has changed over long periods of time as social relations have changed with the advance of capitalism and the centralizing tendencies of the national state. Nevertheless, typical nineteenth-century forms such as demonstrations, strikes and armed actions – albeit with different protagonists – are still used today (Tilly, 1983: 73–8). The essential point is the *normality* of collective violence in political life, in the democratic era as before it.

These points about the social memory of historical development also apply to a different type of concern with violence. Whereas Tilly concerns himself with collective forms that might be considered 'political', the sociologist Geoffrey Pearson has examined what he calls the history of respectable fears about criminal violence. Taking the British example, which could undoubtedly be extended to other cases, Pearson (1983: 207) points to a history which is 'a seamless tapestry of fears and complaints about the deteriorated present' in which the leitmotiv is the moral decline of the British people.

One of the dominant themes of British political life, particularly accentuated under Mrs Thatcher's successive administrations, has been 'law and order', in which fighting the country's crime wave and its supposed decline into lawlessness has figured large. The pronouncements of conservative politicians, top policemen and the bulk of the press all share assumptions about the essentially pacific nature of the British nation and project a pre-war idyll of tranquillity and good behaviour. It is worth underlining the importance of images (indeed myths) of the nation in forming such debates. As Pearson (1983: 227) observes: 'Viewed in this light, culture is to be seen not so much as a control upon violence, but as an incitement to violence: a form of regulation to be sure, but a regulation that defines, promotes, organizes and channels violence.' This directs our attention to the role of the mass media which will be discussed in Chapters 2 and 3.

Antisocial forms of violence, such as gang warfare on the streets, vandalism, football hooliganism, street crime, Pearson convincingly argues, are perceived by each generation as a malaise of the present, when in fact they have an unbroken history. This, he contends, is rooted in 'the social reproduction of an under-class of the most poor and dispossessed' which 'is the material foundation to these hooligan continuities' (1983: 236). A further element, again paralleled elsewhere (as for instance in France, Italy and Germany today) is the way in which successive waves of immigrants or aliens are held responsible for violent crime: in Britain, this is particularly noticeable in the case of the black community which is seen as the principal source of 'mugging'. However, this label was imported from the United States, with the effect of disowning as '"unBritish" the old-fashioned crime of street robbery', the history of which long predates World War II (Pearson, 1983: 20; cf. Hall et al., 1978: ch. 1).

To say all this is not in any way to belittle justifiable public concern about contemporary forms of violence. It is however, to place such anxieties in a broader context in which historical continuities put the crises of the present into perspective.

Symbolic violence?

To appeal to historical analyses of the place of violence in collectivities is but to invoke one more cultural practice of interpretation. It is obvious that rational reconstructions cannot easily avoid consideration of the symbolic dimension of violence. In conclusion, it is now time to address this issue more explicitly.

One relevant line of argument conjoins the symbolic and the violent in the concept of 'symbolic violence' which the German communication theorist Harry Pross (1981: 69; his emphases) has defined as 'the power to make so effective the *validity* of meaning through *signs* that others *identify* themselves with it . . . Symbolic violence is bound up with the materiality of signs.' For the French sociologist Pierre Bourdieu (1977: 196), who coined the term, 'symbolic violence is the gentle, hidden form which violence takes when overt violence is impossible'.

I would question whether we should conceive the effects of symbols as more than *metaphorically* violent, although it is easy to see the attraction of the analogy between the regulation of mental life within hierarchical social relations and control over human bodies through the exercise of physical power. However, to go further and insist seriously that symbolic violence and physical violence are variants of a single phenomenon opens up the whole question of scope and definition once more. How, if at all, we might apply a calculus to symbolic effects is one of the unresolved issues of contemporary media theory, and has been the object of repeated reconceptualizations and operationalizations throughout the era of mass communication (cf. McQuail, 1987: chs 8, 9; Wolf, 1985: chs 1, 2).

'Symbolic violence' may be deconstructed into two analytically useful ideas: (i) that the symbolic domain *is* coercive with respect to those who live within a collectivity (although differently according to social location and endowment with cultural capital); and (ii) that symbolic violence offers an alternative to physical coercion where political circumstances permit, and that under some conditions it may also be complementary to it. This question is central to the influential work of Antonio Gramsci, whose analysis of the relations between coercion and consent by a ruling class in the pursuit of hegemony has shaped much contemporary debate.

At the heart of these concerns is the notion that the symbolic domain is a locus in which struggles for ideological domination – for hearts and minds – takes place. This is widely accepted across the political spectrum (although not always honestly stated) as witness the quest in regimes of all colours, using a variety of means, for control over propaganda, the imposition of censorship and state secrecy, and the management of information.

The symbolic and the violent come together in another way, namely the obsessive interest in whether the mass media – today, television in particular – cause political and criminal violence and forms of antisocial behaviour that threaten the stability of liberal-democratic states. Although substantial research has been conducted with approaches ranging from behaviourist psychology to ethnography, the results remain inconclusive (cf. Gerbner, 1987). As the next chapter shows, the arguments are bound to continue, fuelled by the strong conviction amongst politicians, counter-insurgents and moral entrepreneurs that mass-mediated violence must somehow have deleterious effects, even if they cannot be pinned down decisively. Hence the common assumption that it is crucial to control the symbolic domain of communication in fighting enemies of the state.

References

Bourdieu, P. (1977) *Outline of a Theory of Practice*. Cambridge: Cambridge University Press.

Chesnais, J.C. (1981) *Histoire de la Violence en Occident de 1800 à Nos Jours*. Paris: Laffont.

Curtis, M. (1979) *Totalitarianism*. New Brunswick, NJ: Transaction Books.

Elias, N. (1982) *The Civilizing Process (Vol. 2): State Formation and Civilization*. Oxford: Blackwell.

Faligot, R. (1980) *Guerre Spéciale en Europe: Le Laboratoire Irlandais*. Paris: Flammarion.

Friedrich C.J., Curtis, M. and Barber, B.R. (1969) *Totalitarianism in Perspective: Three Views*. London: Pall Mall Press.

Gerbner, G., with the assistance of Signorielli, N. (1987) 'Violence and Terror in the Mass Media: A Consolidated Report of Existing Research'. University of Philadelphia. Unpublished paper.

Giddens A. (1985) *The Nation-State and Violence: Volume Two of a Contemporary Critique of Historical Materialism*. Cambridge : Polity Press.

Girard, R. (1977) *Violence and the Sacred*. Baltimore, Md, and London: Johns Hopkins University Press.

Graham, H.D. and Gurr, T.R. (eds) (1969) *The History of Violence in America: Historical and Comparative Perspectives. A Report Submitted to the National Commission on the Causes and Prevention of Violence*. New York, Washington and London: Praeger.

Hall, S., Critcher, C., Jefferson, T., Clarke, J. and Roberts, B. (1978) *Policing the Crisis: Mugging, the State, and Law and Order*. London: MacMillan.

Herman, E.S. and Brodhead, F. (1984) *Demonstration Elections: US-Staged Elections in the Dominican Republic, Vietnam, and El Salvador*. Boston, Mass: South End Press.

Hobsbawm, E.J. (1977) 'The Rules of Violence', in *Revolutionaries: Contemporary Essays*. London: Quartet.

Honderich, T. (1980) *Violence for Equality: Inquiries in Political Philosophy*. Harmondsworth: Penguin.

McGuffin, J. (1974) *The Guineapigs*. Harmondsworth: Penguin.

Mackenzie, W.J.M. (1975) *Power, Violence, Decision*. Harmondsworth: Penguin.

McQuail, D. (1987) *Mass Communication Theory: An Introduction*, 2nd edn. London: Sage.

Pearson, G. (1983) *Hooligan: A History of Respectable Fears*. Basingstoke and London: Macmillan.

Peters, E. (1985) *Torture*. Oxford: Blackwell.

Pistoi, P. (1981) *Una Comunità sotto Controllo: Operazioni Contro-Insurrezionali delle Forze di Sicurezza Britanniche nel Quartiere Cattolico di Ballymurphy, Belfast*. Milan: Franco Angeli.

Pross, H. (1981) *Zwänge: Essay über Symbolische Gewalt*. Berlin: Kramer.

Schmid, A.P. (1984) *Political Terrorism: A Research Guide to Concepts, Theories, Data Bases and Literature*. Amsterdam: North-Holland; New Brunswick, NJ: Transaction Books.

Schmitt, C. (1985) *Political Theology: Four Chapters on the Concept of Sovereignty*. Cambridge, Mass: MIT Press.

Taylor, P. (1980) *Beating the Terrorists? Interrogation in Omagh, Gough and Castlereagh*. Harmondsworth: Penguin.

Tilly, C. (1969) 'Collective Violence in European Perspective', in Graham and Gurr (1969). pp. 4–45.

Tilly, C. (1983) 'Violenza e azione collettiva in Europa: riflessioni storico-comparate', in D. Della Porta and G. Pasquino (eds), *Terrorismo e Violenza Politica*. Bologna: Il Mulino. pp. 51–87.

Vidal-Naquet, P. (1972) *La Torture dans la République: Essai d'Histoire et de la Politique Contemporaines (1954–1962)*. Paris: Editions de Minuit.

Walter, E.V. (1969) *Terror and Resistance: A Study of Political Violence with Case Studies of Some Primitive African Communities*. London, Oxford and New York: Oxford University Press.

Weber, M. (1948) 'Politics as a Vocation', in H.H. Gerth and C. Wright Mills (eds), *From Max Weber: Essays in Sociology*. London: Routledge & Kegan Paul. pp. 77–128.

Williams Jr, R.M. (1981) 'Legitimate and Illegitimate Uses of Violence: A Review of Ideas and Literature', in W. Gaylin, R. Macklin and T.M. Powledge (eds), *Violence and the Politics of Research*. New York and London: Plenum Press. pp. 23–45.

Wolf, M. (1985) *Teorie delle Comunicazioni di Massa*. Milan: Bompiani.

2

'Terrorism', the Media and the Liberal-Democratic State: A Critique of the Orthodoxy

The government must promote its own cause and undermine that of the enemy by disseminating its view of the situation, and this involves a carefully planned and co-ordinated campaign of what for want of a better word must regrettably be called psychological operations. (Kitson, 1971: 78)

The Conference succeeded in bringing about a better understanding of the respective problems faced by newsmen and government officials in dealing with terrorism. Most participants agreed that a postponement of information for a few days was acceptable if either human life or national security were at stake. While there will always be some degree of mutual suspicion between press and government in a democratic system, mutual co-operation and proper working procedures in times of crisis can produce an acceptable balance between the interests of the state and the press. (Galliner, 1980)

This chapter explores an issue which has received little systematic attention within the sociological literature: the media reporting of terrorism in Western democracies. First, I will indicate how the term 'terrorism' is conventionally related to the question of legitimate political activity and to the concept of practical rationality. Such a semantic dimension is relevant for understanding how media discourse may routinely reproduce dominant meanings. Next, to illustrate the quest to control the process of mass communication, I examine official and semi-official orthodox views on the role of the media in reporting terrorism. This sets the scene for the case study that follows in Chapter 3, which shows how official doctrine may be translated into practice.

Terrorism: official and unofficial

The language used by the media in describing acts of political violence is of crucial importance in the eyes of state agencies. The standard official view was clearly stated at the International Press Institute's 1978 conference on 'Terrorism and the Media.'[1] by Lord Harris, then Minister of State in the British Home Office. In an 'off-the-record' contribution he is reported to have said that 'the Italian media allowed themselves to be caught up in the language of the Red Brigades which had kidnapped and murdered Aldo Moro. The so-called communiqués of the Red Brigades were just an example of *play-acting* staged for the benefit of the *media*, which accepted them with too little caution. "Terrorists . . . are common criminals: they do not have courts, they do not issue communiqués and they do not have the status of public servants"' (cited in Pontello, 1980).

The rest of Lord Harris' views are, unfortunately, not publicly available. However, Dr Conor Cruise O'Brien provides a reasoned elaboration of this position, one which is not without interest given his former post as Minister for Posts and Telegraphs in the Irish government and his advocacy of censoring broadcast interviews with IRA spokesmen. Dr O'Brien states a central axiom which stands neatly for virtually all the thinking done on this subject: 'The force used by a democratic state is legitimate while the violence of the terrorist is not legitimate' (O'Brien, 1977: 38). Thus a controlled political discourse is an essential part of the liberal-democratic state's fight against its enemies: 'The terms, "force", and "violence", are . . . like, "terrorist", and "freedom-fighter", largely emotive propaganda terms; which we use about a given act depends, not on the degree of force or violence, but on a view of its justification' (O'Brien, 1977: 35). Talking principally about the IRA, Dr O'Brien argues that as both the British and Irish states pursue rational procedures for solving political problems they are legitimate, and the IRA's campaign of violence is not justified. In this view, liberal democracies are embodiments of rationality, while terrorists, being violent, are quintessentially irrational. Their notions of liberation, whether universal or nationalistic, are but quasi-millennarian; they concern articles of faith, not practical reason. Hence, political debate with a terrorist should be refused, for 'though he can argue fluently from his own peculiar premises, he is not accessible to rational argument on premises other than his own' (O'Brien, 1977: 38). Terrorists should receive no publicity and should be dealt with by military rather than political means.

Whatever their undoubted advantages, liberal democracies are not embodiments of rationality. For one, proper adherence to democratic practices, coupled with widespread inequality and suffering, and the anarchy of production, might, on other criteria, be thought less than fully rational, if not positively irrational. Moreover, Dr O'Brien fails to question the use of force in the pursuit of national security. Must it invariably be above suspicion? On his view, yes, for he engages in a definitional sleight of hand in which rationality and democratic institutions mutually imply one another. It is, furthermore, important to recognize that political violence employed against the liberal-democratic state is not *inherently* irrational. It depends upon the likelihood of a successful outcome, which may be a morally unappealing view but is none the less attuned to current political realities. In short, the use of political violence by those opposed to the state is prima facie evidence neither of rationality nor of irrationality (cf. Honderich, 1980).

Lord Harris and Dr O'Brien propose a form of linguistic surgery in order to effect an ideological closure in which the good elements within the polity are radically distinguished from the bad, the orderly from the chaotic. This rigorous drawing of the conceptual lines has attendant dangers. By being overwhelmed by moral repulsion and by criminalizing politics, one is apt to overlook the possible political rationale of those acts which one rejects. A general presumption of political rationality would seem to be an important precondition for analyzing a 'terrorist problem'. Moreover, the dehumanization of the state's enemies endangers civil liberties. These positions have been eloquently argued by Professors Sir Edmund Leach and Franco Ferrarotti.

Leach observes that there are problems when divergent concepts of rationality, order and criminality coexist 'within the matrix of a single political domain'. Although real consensus may be absent, the legal apparatus is obliged to produce a consensual view which identifies and treats criminals not merely as unheroic but also as inhuman. Thus:

> according to the value system which is taken for granted by the press and radio, anyone who refuses to accept the prevailing conventions of how hostilities should be conducted should automatically be categorized as a criminal, lawless, barbarian, terrorist, a savage who can properly be likened to a reptile or a wild beast. (Leach, 1977: 26)

In the cast of mind of those who engage in indiscriminate terrorism, thinks Leach (1977: 30), potential victims are thought of as '"people quite unlike us", sub-human others, people to whom *my* rules of morality do not apply'. This refers both to agents of the state and to its opponents. For states engaged in counter-terror there is the peril of mounting 'crusades of reprisal' and of obscuring the sources of political violence: 'However incomprehensible the acts of the terrorists seem to be, our judges, our policemen, and our politicians must never be allowed to forget that terrorism is an activity of our fellow human beings and *not* of dog-headed cannibals' (Leach, 1977: 30). This humanistic caution would seem to be well made at a time when liberal-democratic states such as Britain, Italy and West Germany have acquired 'exceptional' legal powers such as the Prevention of Terrorism Act, the *Berufsverbote* and the *Legge Reale* (cf. Cobler, 1978; Cowan, 1980; Rose-Smith, 1979).

Franco Ferrarotti has gone further than Leach in trying to outline a set of humanistic assumptions within which violence, including political terrorism, should be evaluated. First, in terms redolent of Leach, he argues that 'the violent are not "mad wolves" but fully human beings.' Second, he suggests that violence has a 'specific historical determination' and that its causes require empirical exploration. Last, he proposes that violence is the 'perversion of a virtue' and a search for meaning in order to escape the straitjacket imposed by a rational, bureaucratic society. It is this deeper metaphysic which leads him to be sceptical of those who would treat violence as the symptom of a 'sickness'. Mere repression, he suggests, is a theoretical error with the likely consequence of eventually increasing violence rather than abating it (Ferrarotti, 1980: ch. 7). One might add that the manipulation of the media by states pursuing short-term 'psywar' goals will also come home to roost.

As Professors Noam Chomsky and Edward Herman (1979a and b) have pointed out, the dominant assumptions about order, legitimacy and rationality embed themselves in a 'semantics of "terror"'. Like Dr O'Brien they recognize the importance of language in propaganda battles. But rather than endorse the liberal-democratic state as perfectly rational, they are concerned to point to US support for repression in the Third World and the ideological function of 'human rights' rhetoric. While the substance of their study extends well beyond the performance of Western media reporting of violence, it is their focus upon this theme which makes it relevant here.

Chomsky and Herman argue that US policy towards Third World states provides, at any given time, an ideological framework within which 'the spectrum of acceptable and unacceptable bloodshed' may be defined. Central to this framework are 'the words "terror" and "terrorism"' which 'have become semantic tools of the powerful in the Western world' (1979a: 85). These terms, they rightly contend, 'have generally been confined to the use of violence by individuals and marginal groups. Official violence which is far more extensive in both scale and destructiveness is placed in a different category altogether (1979a: 6). In the public discourse of the West, those who oppose established orders are the terrorists, while state terrorism is a category virtually never employed, unless it refers to the Communist bloc. In the course of their analysis Chomsky and Herman develop a provocative distinction. They talk, on the one hand, of 'official violence' as resulting in 'wholesale terror' and, on the other, of 'unofficial violence' as producing 'retail terror'. If adopted, this quantitative criterion would doubtless lead to a transvaluation of present values about terrorism in Western democracies. But it is unlikely to be persuasive either to the Western media or to the 'accredited spokesmen', in Stuart Hall's apt phrase, who provide the primary definitions of social reality which the media largely reproduce. Instead, as Chomsky and Herman argue, the Western media have for the most part fallen in with the officially endorsed usage, which, in 'the 1970s has been institutionalized as a device to facilitate the exclusive preoccupation with the lesser terror of the alienated and the dispossessed, serving virtually as a disguised form of apologetics for state terror and client fascism' (1979a: 87).

A caveat is in order, lest in acknowledging the justice of Chomsky's and Herman's critique we uncritically go overboard for the 'alienated and dispossessed'. An acceptance of the quantitative critique and its implications for linguistic reform does not mean abandoning the need for moral and political opposition to indiscriminate political violence by the repressed. E.P. Thompson (1980: 171) puts it well when he observes that

in conditions of extreme repression, democrats and socialists may be forced to take arms in self-defence or in a strategy of insurrection. And in such conditions they merit our solidarity. But where other measures of organization and agitation remain open, the recourse to terrorism is at best romantic, self-defeating and profoundly elitist (people who cannot be moved by arguments must be terrorized by guns), and at worst merely sick and villainous.

Although this chapter is concerned with, in Chomsky's and Herman's terms, 'retail terrorism', one should bear in mind the integral links between the *internal* policing of dissent through mechanisms of control such as the media and the *international* dimension. Chomsky and Herman make some relevant points here. First, and most Northern Ireland coverage in the British media has taken this form, by commonly representing revolutionary terrorism as the initiating force, state violence may be seen as purely 'responsive' and states therefore as justified in riding roughshod over civil liberties. Second, official violence in, for instance, Latin American states such as Brazil and Uruguay is redefined in the Western media and thus implicitly endorsed. Again, to take an 'internal' example, in Northern Ireland state-sanctioned torture of prisoners was redefined first by a judicial inquiry, and then by the media, as 'inhuman and degrading treatment'. Third, retail terrorism is presented as an irrational activity, and its seeming irrationality the more persuasively presented in virtue of inadequate contextualization. Finally, they note, in the United States supporters of the anti-Vietnam War movement were effectively discredited by being labelled as 'terrorists'. Again, in Britain and elsewhere, the expanded category of 'subversion' elides the distinction between legitimate and illegitimate dissent in much the same way.

The orthodox consensus and its limitations

The debate about the media reporting of unofficial terrorism in Western capitalist democracies has primarily developed within the compass of the psychological warfare aims of the state. In this respect there are significant parallels with the way in which information policy is located in Latin American states governed according to an ideology of 'national security' which is fixated upon the 'enemy within' (Mattelart and Mattelart, 1979). During the past decade, and especially since the mid-1970s, an international conventional wisdom has been elaborated within official and semi-official circles in which the media are conceived of pragmatically, as instruments which can contribute to, or impede, final victory. Although mere expediency might seem to dictate outright censorship in order to deny violent opponents of the state the supposedly clear-cut advantages of publicity, matters are not so simple. Overt censorship threatens the legitimacy of the liberal-democratic order, one in which the received conception of press freedom is that the media are completely separate from the state. Hence, it is advantageous for the state to set in train an information policy which integrates the media into a national-security design while, at the same time, preserving the necessary appearance of separation. The dominant view in the current orthodoxy has been succinctly expressed by Major-General Richard Clutterbuck, the British counter-insurgency expert:

The television camera is like a weapon lying in the street. Either side can pick it

up and use it. If governments use it in this way – encouraging their officials,
policemen and soldiers to help the media-men, and to answer their questions – it
is far more effective than any kind of censorship or government control.
(Clutterbuck, 1975: 147)

Aside from seeking media co-operation, there would seem to be two
possible options. First, there is overt censorship. But this is rarely argued
for in an across-the-board manner – except when 'news freezes' are sought,
and even then media compliance is usually forthcoming. In general, open
censorship is advocated for broadcasting rather than the press, and in such
limited contexts as refusing to allow interviews with spokesmen of illegal
organizations engaged in political violence. Dr O'Brien has persistently
pursued this line in Britain and the Irish Republic as part of his wider
argument that 'a liberalism relevant to the dangers of the day should be
concerned to support and strengthen the principle of authority under the
law (1979: 9). It has also been advocated by some counter-insurgency
theorists and the London-based right-wing Institute for the Study of
Conflict (ISC, 1978; Wilkinson, 1977: 169).

Falling outside the orthodoxy is the much less frequently stated
libertarian case as proposed, for instance, by the US political scientist
Bernard Johnpoll (1977: 160): 'It is useless to discuss what the media can
do about terror. The media are not judicial institutions; their role in
modern society is to transmit information. How to erase terror is a judicial
and ethical question; not a question of the media.' Perhaps this could be
seriously argued only in the United States and, moreover, by a confirmed
believer in the separation-of-powers doctrine both as reality and as ideal.

In US law-enforcement circles different grounds are advanced for
non-interference. Patrick Murphy (1980), a New York police chief, offers
three reasons: censorship 'concedes a victory to terrorists' by suppressing
freedoms; the media 'can and do play an important and positive role' by
stilling rumours and speculation; and the government does not have the
expertise to 'fine tune' the media. The last point is particularly disingenuous, and the other two are plainly informed by a long-term psywar
outlook. H.H.A. Cooper (1977) of the Task Force on Disorders and
Terrorism also argues for non-censorship in news reporting, but advocates
'care' in commentaries and investigations, suggesting that the media should
recognize the possibility of their being abused and therefore be 'responsible'.

This argument for 'socially responsible' media is developed against the
background of some highly questionable assumptions about the nature of
the contemporary liberal-democratic state and the operation of the media
within it. These are: that liberal democracies are very vulnerable and they
do not censor news; that the media are willing victims of terrorist
propaganda and function as open conduits for such views; that media
coverage has a 'contagion effect'. As noted, Conor Cruise O'Brien has
argued, in effect, that liberal democracies need to take on an 'exceptional'
character, 'relevant to the dangers of the day'. This is but an extension of

the view that such states are presently highly vulnerable, especially when confronted by publicity-seeking terrorists. They are presumed to lack an effective repressive apparatus and to be perfectly open. This line has been canvassed by Professor Walter Laqueur of the Center for Strategic and International Studies, Washington, DC, and Dr J. Bowyer Bell of the Institute for War and Peace Studies, Columbia University, both of whom are prominent writers on political violence (Bowyer Bell, 1978: 78; Laqueur, 1977: 109–10).

However, this assumption needs to be critically evaluated by reference to the recent growth of research suggesting that there have been significant alterations within the liberal democracies in the direction of what is variously termed a 'strong state', 'authoritarian statism' or the 'national security state'. The development of European anti-terrorism legislation and police and military co-operation for 'internal defence', the weakening of the rights of defendants in both criminal and political trials, the growth of high-technology police surveillance of whole populations, the expanded category of 'subversion', restrictions upon the rights of trade unions and of political demonstrations, the use of repressive technology in civil policing are all manifestations of this shift (cf., for example, Ackroyd et al., 1980; Bunyan, 1976; Enzensberger, 1979; Poulantzas, 1978; Thompson, 1980). Against such a background, which, to be sure, in part represents a response to unofficial political violence, it is difficult to concur with the picture of present vulnerability which is drawn in the writings of the 'terrorism studies' experts – where, indeed, one rarely finds any analysis at all of the operations of the present advanced capitalist state.

But where the vulnerability-of-liberal-democracy thesis is retained it is but a small step to promote the role of the media of communication in exacerbating that weakness to one of crucial significance. Thus Professor Laqueur remarks:

> Terrorists have learned that the media are of paramount importance in their campaign, that the terrorist act by itself is next to nothing, whereas publicity is all. But the media, constantly in need of diversity and new angles, make fickle friends. Terrorists will always have to be innovative. They are, in some respects, the super-entertainers of our time. (1977: 223)

These few remarks command widespread assent. Bowyer Bell links the centrality of the media to subversive strategies for publicity: hence 'it matters a great deal not only why and how a rebel kills, but also where and when. The television terrorist understands prime time, the need to escalate his deed, to manipulate the media, to reach the masses. He goes on to argue that manipulation of the media by terrorists requires that several conditions be satisfied. First, there should be a good locale with communications facilities, such as the Munich Olympics in 1972. Second, the media need to be enticed by the prospect or actuality of violence. And finally, in order to hold the media's attention a terrorist 'spectacular' should contain frequent shifts of scene, as in, say, an aircraft hijack (Bowyer Bell, 1978: 110–16).

For Bowyer Bell the terrorist is a publicist or showman. This dramaturgical perspective is present throughout similar writings. So Laqueur talks of 'super-entertainers', while Brian Jenkins (1980), the Rand Corporation's expert on international terrorism, likewise observes: 'Terrorists choreograph their violence. Terrorism is theatre.' In a perspective which sees political violence as unambiguously effective drama it is not surprising that media coverage is accorded such importance. Assuming the simple convergence of terrorist actions and the values and needs of capitalist media, it is no great step to the view that the media are the willing victims of the superstars of violence. However, Laqueur does qualify this by noting that they are 'fickle'.

In the orthodox view, then, liberal democracies are seen as uncensored with media engaging in the untrammelled pursuit of news values stressing violence and drama, the result being disproportionately great publicity. But this argument runs against actual developments where some liberal-democratic regimes, in strengthening their repressive apparatuses, have also developed sophisticated policies for the management of publicity. State strategies towards the media in West Germany are a case in point.

Armin Grünewald (1980), the West German government's official spokesman, has observed that the media 'play a substantial part in the terrorists' logistic organization' and that the state therefore has a right to insist on collaboration from the press and broadcasting. In the 1970s 'information policy has become a stable component of every consultative moment of the situation', and principles of collaboration between the media and state have been developed involving centralized channelling of information. He has illustrated this process of control revealingly. During the month-long 'news freeze' during the kidnapping of Hanns Martin Schleyer, head of the West German industrialists' organization,

> the Secretary of State, Herr Bölling, granted dozens of interviews, made statements and took part in a series of debates almost entirely centring round the meaning and legitimacy of these restraints. *This was not only a quest for understanding but a conscious calculation. Self-restraint by the media, the most important element of the news operation, is feasible only if they are urged to deal with questions that are not dangerous for police tactics.* (Grünewald, 1980, emphasis added)

Successful control of media coverage was achieved without legal compulsion, for such powers did not exist.

The vice-chairman of the Bonn Criminal Police, Reinhard Rupprecht (1980), has given a similarly frank account of the control of news during the Schleyer kidnapping. Preferring the more euphemistic 'deferment of news' to 'news freeze', Mr Rupprecht argues that the media were of crucial importance in achieving public co-operation in the hunt for those suspected of the kidnapping. A few minutes after Schleyer's body had been found, a police information film was broadcast, and the entire press carried a

> whole-page insert with photos and distinctive characteristics of the 16 wanted terrorists, together with summaries of certain pieces of evidence and details

which would on the one hand arouse suspicion should the terrorists rent flats that could be used as meeting or hiding places or purchase used cars, and on the other be useful in recognizing any forgery of passports, identity cards and driving licences.

Other aspects of this public mobilization for 'national security' included a further nine police films broadcast on television at prime time on nine consecutive days 'with no need to have recourse to the right of divulgation on radio and television which was reserved to the Federal government'. Special research on the use of pictures and graphics was commissioned in order to make this 'search operation' more effective. When one considers evidence such as this of the effectiveness with which the media may be subject to state direction at times, it is hard to accept the general picture of limp-wristed liberal democracy current in the orthodox view. Nevertheless, it is important to recognize that not all states have had such effective systems of control. The continual leaking of information to the Italian press during the Aldo Moro kidnapping led to calls for news freezes and for a code of practice (cf. Solé, 1979: 221–30).

Let us now turn to the last standard assumption – that the media, by reporting terrorist acts, have 'contagious effects'. This has been advanced, for one, by Professor Yonah Alexander of the State University of New York. But while he says that publicity legitimizes terrorism, he provides no sound evidence to support this contention. For instance, he cites the results of two US public opinion polls which indicated 'greater awareness' of the PLO during 1974–5, years when that organization was attracting lots of media attention. However, he seems not to realize that public recognition of a group's existence does not indicate that its goals are now publicly favoured. Nor, indeed, does recognition mean that the public necessarily understands the political aims of the group in question in terms that it itself would wish. For the media treatment of sieges, bombings and hijackings may well result in their ostensible rationale being either excluded entirely, ridiculed, challenged, distorted or played down as occurred for instance with the 'Angry Brigade' in Britain (cf. Chibnall, 1977: 95ff.).

A further variant of this naïve 'effects' argument is Alexander's suggestion that publicity for terrorism leads to the exportation of violent techniques which are taken up elsewhere. Yet the evidence cited is exiguous indeed: we are merely told that Nelson Rockefeller, Andrew Young and Major-General Clutterbuck believe this to be so. The following illustration is offered: 'Several weeks after Argentina's Montoneros removed the body of ex-president Pedro Aramburu to secure the return of Eva Peron's body from Spain, Burmese terrorists stole the body of U Thant for the purpose of using it in negotiations with the Burmese government' (Alexander, 1978: 47). But surely a particular technique, body-snatching, cannot be considered in total isolation from the social relations in which it occurs. One must specify the mediating conditions which explain *why* such acts occur. It is not enough to assert loose correspondences between actions in Latin America and in Asia with the supposed explanation that terrorism is a 'world-wide theatrical attraction [which] tends to encourage angry and frustrated groups beyond a particular country to undertake similar acts out of their helplessness and frustration (Alexander, 1978: 48). Which angry groups? Why them especially? In which societies and in which circumstances do they use such techniques? Do they have alternatives? Such basic questions for research cannot be made to vanish by the magical invocation of media effects.

In fact, Professor Alexander's argument is yet another variant of the venerable and quite unproven contention that the portrayal of violence on television, or in the cinema, or before that in the nineteenth-century theatre, has had deleterious effects, especially upon impressionable children. There has been a long-standing debate on this question in cultural criticism and mass-communication research which makes it plain that no simple cause–effect relationship between the portrayal of violence in the media and a given social response has so far been established. Indeed, to conceptualize the problem in those terms at all is to leave out any study of popular attitudes, their production by given social relations and the highly complex process of the mediation of meaning which communicative activities entail (cf. Hall, 1977; Halloran, 1978). When Alexander (1978: 51) asserts that 'by providing extensive coverage of incidents the media give the impression that they sympathize with the terrorist cause, thereby creating a climate congenial to further violence', he is actually posing a problem for future research into the reporting of political violence and its public interpretations, not stating an established proposition.

Where now?

The 'terrorism studies' experts' views on the media reporting of political violence are therefore entirely innocent of any serious analysis of the process of news production and the constraints it faces in a liberal democracy shifting to an 'exceptional' modality of rule armed for psychological warfare. From the early 1970s until the mid-1980s the British model of media control provided a particularly good illustration of how crass overt censorship by the state may be avoided and instead be substituted by indirect control coupled with media self-censorship. The appeals of this solution are international. At the 1978 IPI conference on 'Terrorism and the Media' it was widely hailed as an example worth following. One can readily see why. For by avoiding evident censorship the state's ideological capital remains intact, and the media, by being socially responsible and by pursuing 'voluntary self-restraint', also retain their public credibility. And yet the solution does have its costs for the state, for, at given moments, the institutional imperatives of the media supervene over the doctrine of national security, and so they rock the boat.

The orthodox arguments considered here, which derive from the instrumental preoccupations of a national-security-minded officialdom, point in the perilous direction of increased censorship and enhanced secrecy. Before further progress is made down that restrictive road, some dispassionate analysis, addressed to the widest possible public, of the real significance of publicity in present struggles to 'suppress terrorism' would seem to be called for.

Unquestionably, we need to pay careful attention to the specific forms of political violence within a given state and to their causation. Detailed attention needs to be given to the organization of national media systems and the ways in which they articulate with the state. A comparative approach would have the merit of highlighting how national peculiarities have affected the evolution of psychological-warfare strategies. Such a systematic study of the dialectical interplay between media, political violence and the state has hardly begun.

Notes

1 Reference is made throughout this chapter to the proceedings of this international seminar, held in Florence in 1978. The meeting was organized by the International Press Institute and the Rome-based foreign affairs journal *Affari Esteri*. As the book (IPI, 1980) is unpaged, all references are to given articles.

References

Ackroyd, C., Margolis, K., Rosenhead, J. and Shallice, T. (1980) *The Technology of Political Control*, 2nd edn. London: Pluto Press.
Alexander, Y. (1978) 'Terrorism, the Media and the Police', *Police Studies*, June: 45–52.
Bowyer Bell, J. (1978) *A Time of Terror: How Democratic Societies Respond to Revolutionary Violence*. New York: Basic Books.
Bunyan, T. (1976) *The History and Practice of the Political Police in Britain*. London: J. Friedmann.
Chibnall, S. (1977) *Law-and-Order News*. London: Tavistock.
Chomsky, N. and Herman, E. (1979a) *The Washington Connection and Third World Fascism; The Political Economy of Human Rights, Vol. 1*. Nottingham: Spokesman Books.
Chomsky, N. and Herman, E. (1979b) *After the Cataclysm: The Political Economy of Human Rights, Vol. 2*. Nottingham: Spokesman Books.
Clutterbuck, Maj.-Gen. R. (1975) *Living with Terrorism*. London: Faber.
Cobler, S. (1978) *Law, Order and Politics in West Germany*. Harmondsworth: Penguin.
Cooper, H.H.A. (1977) 'Terrorism and the Media', in Y. Alexander and S.M. Finger (eds), *Terrorism: Interdisciplinary Perspectives*. New York: John Jay Press. pp. 141–46.
Cowan, S. (1980) 'Terrorism and the Italian Left', in C. Boggs and D. Plotke (eds), *The Politics of Eurocommunism: Socialism in Transition*. London: Macmillan. pp. 171–96.
Enzensberger, H.–M. (1979) 'An Address on German Democracy to the Citizens of New York', *New Left Review*, 118, November–December: 3–14.
Ferrarotti, F. (1977) 'Anche i terroristi sono esseri umani', *La Critica Sociologica*, 43, Autumn: 184.
Ferrarotti, F. (1980) *L'Ipnosi della Violenza*. Milan: Rizzoli.
Galliner, P. (1980) 'Introduction', in IPI (1980).
Grünewald, A. (1980) 'Government and the Press: National Security and the Public's Right to Know', in IPI (1980).
Hall, S. (1977) 'Culture, the Media, and the "Ideological Effect",' in J. Curran, M. Gurevitch and J. Woollacott (eds), *Mass Communication and Society*. London: Edward Arnold. pp. 315–48.

Halloran, J.D. (1978) 'Mass Communication: Symptom or Cause of Violence?' *International Social Science Journal*, 30 (4): 816–33.

Honderich, T. (1980) *Violence for Equality: Inquiries in Political Philosophy*. Harmondsworth: Penguin.

Institute for the Study of Conflict (ISC) (ed.) (1978) *Television and Conflict*. London: ISC.

International Press Institute (IPI) (ed.) (1980) *Terrorism and the Media*. London: IPI (unpaged).

Jenkins, B. (1980) 'Responsibilities of the News Media – I', in IPI (1980).

Johnpoll, B. (1977) 'Terrorism and the Mass Media in the United States', in Y. Alexander and S.M. Finger (1977) (eds), *Terrorism: Interdisciplinary Perspectives*. New York: John Jay Press. pp. 157–165.

Kitson, Maj.-Gen. Sir F. (1971) *Low-Intensity Operations*. London: Faber.

Laqueur, W. (1977) *Terrorism*. London: Weidenfeld & Nicolson.

Leach, Sir E. (1977) *Custom, Law, and Terrorist Violence*. Edinburgh: Edinburgh University Press.

Mattelart, A. and Mattelart, M. (1979) 'Information et état d'exception', in *De l'usage des Médias en Temps de Crise*. Paris: Alain Moreau. pp. 243–89.

Murphy, P. (1980) 'The Case of the United States', in IPI (1980).

O'Brien, C.C. (1977) 'Liberty and Terror: Illusions of Violence, Delusions of Liberation', *Encounter*, 49, (4) October: 34–41.

O'Brien, C.C. (1979) 'Freedom and Censorship'. Lecture at the Independent Broadcasting Authority, London, 28 March.

Pontello, C. (1980) 'Terrorism and the Media', in IPI (1980).

Poulantzas, N. (1978) *Power, State, Socialism*. London: New Left Books.

Rose-Smith, B. (1979) 'Police Powers and Terrorism Legislation', in P. Hain (ed) *Policing the Police*, Vol. 1. London: John Calder. pp. 107–56.

Rupprecht, R. (1980) 'The Case of Federal Germany – I', in IPI (1980).

Solé, R. (1979) *Le Défi Terroriste: Leçons Italiennes à l'Usage de l'Europe*. Paris: Seuil.

Thompson, E.P. (1980) *Writing by Candlelight*. London: Merlin.

Wilkinson, P. (1977) *Terrorism and the Liberal State*. London: Macmillan.

3

The Media Politics of Siege Management: The Case of the Iranian Embassy Siege

Now that the euphoria following the Iranian Embassy siege has abated, the doubters step in. But where you ask? In the letter columns of the *Guardian*, we answer. Yesterday that newspaper published a fascinating array of letters which pose some very proper questions. One complains his televised snooker was interrupted by the *coup de grâce* of the siege, and we sympathize; another grumbles about the role of television in the affair, and here there must be at least one embryonic thesis. (Leader, *Daily Telegraph*, 10 May 1980)

The siege at the Iranian Embassy in Prince's Gate, Kensington, between 30 April and 5 May 1980 was a media event *par excellence*, covered from the outset by a veritable circus of newsmen. It had a bloody conclusion: for the first time the élite Special Air Services regiment (SAS) was used in an overt police action on the British mainland and killed five of the six hostage-taking gunmen. Millions of British television viewers watched the denouement live. For many media professionals, such as Alan Protheroe, the BBC's Editor of Television News, it was one of television's 'finest hours' (BBC TV, *The Editors* 16 June 1980)[1] and a 'definitive example of just how high standards of broadcasting journalism really are in this country' (Protheroe, 1980: 641). Others were less enchanted, and had serious doubts about the value of the television reporting. The novelist John Le Carré, eschewing Protheroe's sub-Churchillian rhetoric, pointed out that both television channels actually failed to interpret correctly what was going on during the busting of the siege, and that

the ITN commentator risked a most perilous theory about what was going on: a disaster theory, a theory of total ignominious failure on the part of the authorities. Assuming – as many of us benighted viewers *did* assume – that the explosions had been set off by the captors, he floated the idea that the captors had been panicked by the sight of masked men on the outside of the building. (Le Carré, 1980: 2)[2]

The BBC's commentary was even less informative. Indeed, the moment of the siege-busting made the limitations of television actuality programming plain for all to see. In the excitement of seeing it 'for real', one is apt to forget how important was the absence of interpretation.

John Le Carré puts television's communication failure down to the confusion of the reporters, a fact which needs some explanation. The available evidence suggests that the broadcasters were actually in a position to know broadly what was going on *at the time it was happening*. It also seems that they – at least senior editors, particularly in the BBC – had received briefings on government policy and were aware of the likely outcome of the siege. These contentions are documented below. Commenting on the television coverage, *Broadcast* (the television and radio industry's journal) observed how both ITN and BBC news 'went live from the scene only *after* SAS men stormed the building, amidst fire and explosions'. The moment of entry was videotaped, and ITN's report began four and a half minutes after this, and the BBC's only after eight minutes. *Broadcast* (1980) speculated:

> Given the close links between the broadcasters and the security forces during the siege, and bearing in mind that the hostages' captors may have had access to a television set inside the embassy, it is likely that the broadcasting organizations were actually warned off going live during this period for fear of giving the game away.

The suggestion that the transmission time was subject to consultation seems well founded. But I am doubtful that the authorities were worried at *this* stage of the siege about television coverage 'giving the game away'. There is no evidence from any of the accounts of the siege that *television* played any significant role in the hostage-takers' monitoring of the responses to their demands. All references to their concern with broadcasting mention radio coverage exclusively. Given the sophisticated monitoring devices being used by the security forces, it would have been known if the captors and their captives had also been watching television. Neither reports so far nor the reconstruction based on hostages' accounts have mentioned this possibility. It therefore seems reasonable to assume that control of television coverage of the siege-busting was as much concerned with the information available to the mass audience as to those inside the embassy. (Had they been watching television, they would have known about activities on the roof and the presence of monitoring equipment from the start, as these were disclosed by ITN on *News at Ten* on 30 April, the first night of the siege.)

These introductory points raise crucial questions about the extent of state control over the media during the siege. They also raise the question of what role was played by the media, and by broadcasting in particular. I shall try to answer these questions, in so far as published sources permit. My aim is not to chart in detail the media coverage of the siege but to bring out the process of control and set this in the context of the British state's strategies for the control of 'news about terrorism' during the past decade.

Using the media

In the siege at the Iranian Embassy, both the state and the hostage-takers had conscious strategies for making use of the media. The six gunmen who held twenty-six persons as prisoners in the embassy were members of an autonomist guerrilla movement from the predominantly ethnically Arab area of Iran. This region is called 'Khuzistan' by the Iranian central government and 'Arabistan' by the autonomists. The group's central goal was to draw attention to the oppression and exploitation of their area – the principal source of Iran's oil wealth – by the Khomeini regime. As it is frequently argued that acts of terrorism are inherently irrational, it is worth pointing out that the seizure of the embassy had a clear political rationale. This was explained by 'Oan', the leader of the hostage-takers, in an interview conducted by the journalists Moustafa Karkouti and Mohammed Hashir Faruqi, who were also among the hostages:

> *Question*: What is the immediate goal you think you will achieve by carrying out this operation here and now?
> *Oan*: It will be publicity, propaganda and information outside. I realize that this operation or any similar operation which might happen in the future will not achieve our legitimate rights and might not force the Iranian government to grant Arabistan its autonomy, but what we can achieve from this kind of operation is to make our voice heard by world public opinion, especially in the light of the information blockade which the central government in Tehran is encircling us with, in addition to most of the Arab countries as well as the world media.[3]

Apart from this conscious and evidently rational intention to communicate a grievance by using extreme means, the guerrilla group also held certain assumptions about the British media – apparently not realizing that 'information blockades' are not the sole prerogative of the Iranian government. Moustafa Karkouti, interviewed after the siege, recalled one of his conversations with the gunmen thus:

> They talked about the freedom of speech and said they thought it was more respected in Britain than in the rest of the world. They made it clear that they thought the media here are stronger than anywhere else in the Western world – they believed the British media and the British population would give their cause a fair hearing. (*Obs*: 76–7)

But their conception of the media, in particular during the exceptional circumstances of siege coverage, was naïve in the extreme – hardly surprising as they appear to have had virtually no real knowledge of British politics and society. As the British media were, in effect, absorbed into the siege-breaking operations of the state, the Arabistan autonomists did not find it easy to get their message across. For the control of communications is one of the key weapons in the struggle between the security forces and those who challenge the authority of the state by actions of this kind. The account which follows, therefore, necessarily has psychological warfare as one of its central themes. Aside from these two contradictory communicative strategies, there is another way in which the siege is especially illuminating about points of connection between the media and the state. The capture of two BBC television newsmen, Chris Cramer, a news organizer, and Sim Harris, a sound technician, meant that the BBC was not just a reporter of the action at Prince's Gate, but also an actor of some significance, as I show below. With its own men on the inside, the Corporation's existing special significance to the state was enhanced. The presence of British journalists inside the embassy probably also had a more general effect on the media, encouraging the already considerable co-operation which had been built up in previous years.

The press and broadcasting were subject to general guidelines issued by the police on the second day of the siege. The request for self-censorship by the press went as thus:

> During the course of the current hostage situation at the Iranian Embassy, the Commissioner seeks your co-operation in refraining from publishing or broadcasting details of the deployment of personnel in the immediate vicinity of the Embassy or the use of specialist equipment. The publication or broadcast of such information can provide valuable intelligence to the hostage-takers and by so alerting them could seriously jeopardize the safety of the hostages and the success of the operation. This memo will be cancelled as soon as operational circumstances permit. (*ST*: 42)

The insistence that newspapers should not publish such details seems odd, given that the police were not going to allow them into the embassy. It could presumably be justified on the ground that the police wished to control all publicity in case foreign radios picked up information which could assist the gunmen, or alternatively, to prevent press stories from being developed which the British broadcasting media would feel compelled to follow. Broadcasting seems to have been controlled more precisely than the press:

> 'We worked more than closely with the authorities throughout the siege,' an ITN spokesman said. And the BBC's involvement with the security forces became inevitable as soon as it became clear that two BBC men were actually among the hostages at the beginning. (*Broadcast*, 1980)[4]

After the siege, William Whitelaw, then Home Secretary, expressed his satisfaction at the broadcasting media's self-censorship:

> Inevitably events such as these are a matter of major public concern. They are bound to be covered by TV and radio. Had there been a moment when it was necessary to ask the authorities to exercise restraint then that restraint would have been asked for. But . . . such an occasion did not in the final event arise. (cited in *Broadcast*, 1980)

Such co-operativeness did not emerge out of the blue. There had been a long build-up.

The state security background

The handling of the Iranian Embassy siege cannot be understood in isolation. As the journal *State Research* (1980a: 117) has pointed out, it reflects the state's current rethinking of 'administrative, policing and military aspects of internal security. Considerations of terrorism and those of demonstrations and strikes have both influenced the outcome.' We should therefore look briefly at some recent observations on the emergence of a 'strong state' in Britain.

The development of what Nicos Poulantzas (1978) has termed an 'authoritarian statist' form of rule derives from at least two key intractable problems. First, there is the continuing economic crisis, with its concomitant industrial relations struggles. The current 'monetarist experiment' of the Thatcher government involves the restructuring of capital by following the path of mass unemployment. Given this policy, as Andrew Gamble (1979: 15) has observed, 'if the economy is to remain free, the state has to become strong; and nowhere stronger than in its dealings with organized labour'. But although it is under the present administration that the armed forces and the police have been given a more overtly prominent role in countering 'subversion', their strengthening began in the not-too-distant Keynesian days, when other economic policies were being pursued. The second key problem is the persisting failure to achieve a solution to the socio-political problems of Northern Ireland. Against this backdrop, the outlines of Britain's 'secret state' (in E.P. Thompson's telling phrase) have become clearer during the past decade. Its significant features include:

- the refurbishing of a 'parallel' emergency state apparatus for use against external attack and internal disorder;
- major shifts in the practice of policing including the emergence of a paramilitary 'third force' and the strengthening of the political police;
- the increased use of high-technology surveillance against loosely defined 'subversives' involving, for instance, uncontrolled data-banks and bugging devices;
- the use of official secrecy legislation against journalists;
- jury-vetting in political trials;
- restrictions upon, and aggressive policing of, demonstrations and picketing; and
- the trial use of repressive technology and special forces in Northern Ireland and the gradual application of the lessons learned in Britain itself (cf. Ackroyd et al., 1980; Bowden, 1978; Bunyan, 1977; Hain, 1979–80; Leigh, 1980; Thompson, 1980).

Although I cannot survey all the relevant material here, it is worth mentioning in passing that such evidently accelerating repressive tendencies within the liberal-democratic state-form should not be assumed necessarily to be irreversible (cf. Kettle, 1980; Wolfe, 1971). But it is certain that without an effort to defend against such encroachments of existing political space, democratic freedoms eventually will be seriously imperilled.

Most relevant for my argument here are some of the changes in the state's emergency apparatus, the increased role of 'military aid to the civil power', and the unceasing efforts to control the media, especially broadcasting, in the reporting of political violence. Control of the Iranian Embassy siege was vested in the Civil Contingencies Committee (CCC). This body, called the National Security Committee (NSC) until 1975, was created in 1972 after the government's failure to break the miners' strike.

The NSC drew together military, intelligence, police, Home Office and Department of Trade and Industry personnel, and was serviced by a full-time staff. Its tasks were twofold: 'to prepare short-term contingency plans for emergency situations, and to redraw the standing "War Plan" to meet a possible internal threat to the security of the state' (Bunyan, 1977: 293). From 1972 to 1975 a National Security Plan was worked out, involving the military, in which preparations for interventions were made for situations ranging from limited strikes to civil war or invasion. As Tony Bunyan (1977: 277) points out, this plan is actually 'directed at an internal rather than an external enemy' and is basically concerned with effective counter-revolution. The NSC/CCC drew up new guidelines about the occasions on which the Ministry of Defence could assist the police and the civil power. During the Iranian Embassy siege the SAS were brought in under the rubric of 'military aid to the civil power' (MACP), an arrangement which had been used on previous occasions against armed terrorists.

Although the SAS action at Prince's Gate may have been unprecedented, the use of an élite military unit in an urban action represents no more than the latest stage in the growing co-operation between police and army. The police have become increasingly prominent and vociferous over recent years as they have become involved in confrontations with political demonstrators, trade unionists and racial minorities, and as various forms of political violence have been encountered and have required suppression. The political imperative to control such 'law-and-order' problems has led to the construction of the 'third force' which has lately emerged to take up the paramilitary ground between the army and the more traditional functions of civil policing. Most controversial, probably, has been the activity of the Special Patrol Groups; despite official denials, these are armed paramilitary units, highly mobile and trained in riot control. But the SPGs are only the most visible part of the new 'third force'. According to *State Research*, there are now over 12,000 riot-trained police organized as Police Support Units and there has also been a growth in specialist units such as the anti-terrorism squad and the diplomatic protection group:

> The police's answer to providing a 'third force' in the UK has been double edged. The anti-terrorist role is carried out by SPGs, newly formed Tactical Firearms Units . . . *and, as a last resort, by the army's Special Air Service (SAS)*. The public order role of a 'third force' is undertaken by the Police Support Units and the SPG. Taken together this means that a qualitative change in the role of the police has . . . occurred. (*State Research*, 1980b: 152)

It is clear from this analysis that the use of the SAS *in extremis* should be seen in the context of a drift towards tougher policing in the era of the 'technological cop'. The higher profile largely forced on the police by social change has created an atmosphere in which the deployment of troops becomes acceptable.

During the past decade, both Labour and Conservative governments have brought the SAS into operations, first in Northern Ireland, and now on the British mainland. The SAS's post-war role was primarily in the field of counter-insurgency actions during the gradual dissolution of the Empire. It became a bogyman in Northern Ireland, where it was important both in combat against the IRA and in intelligence work (cf. Geraghty, 1980: ch. 6). The SAS's specific anti-terrorist role on the home front dates back to 1972, when the British government, like other Western European administrations, became concerned about the growth of political violence in the aftermath of the Munich Olympics. A special 'counter-revolutionary warfare' (CRW) team was developed within the SAS. This was first deployed in Britain during the hijack of an aeroplane from Manchester in January 1975 (Geraghty, 1980: 168–9). In December 1975, the SAS were present during the Balcombe Street Siege; the mere announcement of their presence was apparently sufficient to make the cornered IRA men surrender. In that same month, the 'Europeanization' of the anti-terrorist campaign gathered steam when, at a European Council meeting in Paris, it was decided that the European interior ministers should discuss how to combat terrorism. Meetings were held in June 1976 and in May 1977, and agreement was reached on the exchange of information about terrorism and techniques for dealing with terrorist incidents. The exchange of information and personnel between national security forces was also agreed. The first occasion on which this arrangement came into operation was in October 1977, when an SAS liaison team assisted the West German anti-terrorist unit GSG-9 to bring an end to the Lufthansa aircraft hijack at Mogadishu. Joint military co-operation of this kind would seem to be well established now. A further instance was the SAS's involvement in the hunt for Aldo Moro, the kidnapped Italian Christian Democratic leader; the West German police also assisted in this.[5] Although it went unreported by the British media, the head of GSG-9, Ulrich Wegener, came to London during the Iranian Embassy siege.[6]

The full-scale commitment of the SAS to a domestic policing role resulted from a decision by the Callaghan government, after the successful military action at Mogadishu, to increase the CRW force substantially. 'From now on, each squadron was committed in turn to the CRW role on rotation, between tours in Northern Ireland and training sessions abroad. The implication of the decision was that *Britain was now a potential SAS operational zone in a way not previously contemplated*' (Geraghty 1980: 173, emphasis added). The commitment of resources has been significant, with the SAS receiving sophisticated weaponry, more training facilities (such as the 'killing house' where close-quarter battle is practised) and the specialization of CRW units in 'assault' and 'perimeter containment' (Geraghty, 1980: 174–5). These developments lie behind the dramatic eleven-minute SAS action which took place on 5 May 1980.

'Law-and-order' news and the state

State security actions such as the breaking of the Iranian Embassy siege are reported within a specific ideological framework, that of 'law-and-order' news. Stuart Hall and his colleagues have pointed out how this form of news has developed during the past decade within the context of a growing 'crisis of hegemony' in the British state. The continuing inability of governments to discipline labour and restore adequate profitability to capital has led towards a more authoritarian structure of rule, aspects of which were outlined earlier. The role of the media in winning consent for this shift from the social democratic consensus to the 'exceptional' law-and-order state has been crucial (cf. Hall et al., 1978: chs 8, 9; Hall, 1978). In a convergent analysis, Steve Chibnall (1977) has demonstrated the especial significance of the focus upon 'violence' in media discourse – in particular, the way in which it is used to police the boundaries of legitimate dissent. Within the media-created artefact of 'the violent society' wildly differing activities, with quite distinct causes, have come to be classified as fundamentally the same, as 'violent'. Thus 'mugging', the Angry Brigade bombings, IRA terror campaigns, criminal shootings of the police, football hooliganism, picketing and political demonstrations are represented within the dominant media discourse as the symptoms of an underlying social malaise – one for which the big stick of coercion becomes an increasingly attractive policy option.

Winning consent for actions like those taken by the SAS at Prince's Gate involves an exceedingly complex process which is by no means just a cognitive one. Hijacks, assassinations, sieges and bombings – especially where they are directed against prominent people like Lord Mountbatten or Airey Neave – can provoke a sense that the entire society is under threat; and, as Philip Elliott (1980) has pointed out, they evoke ritualized responses from the media. For instance, where IRA activities have taken place on the British mainland, Elliott argues, the press and broadcasting have carried out 'affirmatory rituals' which emphasize the integrity of the social order. In Britain itself, it has been possible to presume adherence to a common symbolic order articulated by those in authority, whereas in Northern Ireland, given the social divisions there, such a mobilization of common sentiment has proven impossible. Similarly, Yves Lavoinne (1979) has argued that in cases of hostage-taking the dominant discourse emanating from the state and reproduced by the media stresses social consensus. Like Elliott, he points to the utilization of a discourse which is quasi-religious, through which assaults on hostages are taken as affronts to the social collectivity, requiring terrorism to be evaluated as inhuman and irrational, as the very embodiment of chaos.

Although knowledge of how audiences perceive accounts of violence and terrorism remains fragmentary, the evidence is stronger when it comes to the efforts made by state agencies to control media coverage. This suggests the background to the stratagems adopted during the course of the

Prince's Gate siege: the long-term efforts to control the flow of information and to secure a privileged place in media representations for the agents of the state. Two instances are briefly covered here: Sir Robert Mark's media strategy and the *de facto* partial censorship of broadcast news and current affairs coverage of Northern Ireland.

The Mark strategy

The degree of compliance shown by the British media during the Iranian Embassy siege derives in part from an initiative taken in 1972 by Sir Robert Mark, then Commissioner of the Metropolitan Police. Mark decided that his force should be more accessible to journalists, keeping back information 'subject only to *judicial restrictions, the right to individual privacy*, and the *security of the state*' (Mark, 1980; original emphasis). The Metropolitan Police and the national media agreed upon the new terms of reference, and the Home Office ratified them. Mark's objective, as he later said in a general memorandum issued on 24 May 1973, was to improve the police's relationship with the news media and 'consequently a better understanding on their part and that of the public of the force's problems and policies' (Mark, 1977: 123–9). But the new 'openness' was coupled with a determined effort to secure a measure of control over journalists. The general memorandum made reference to a new press identity card. This enabled the police to sift the accredited journalists who hold the card from among the non-accredited, and so to identify those they deemed unhelpful, in particular members of the radical press. Efforts by the National Union of Journalists to ensure that its card alone should constitute acceptable accreditation have so far been unsuccessful. In September 1975, Mark organized a conference at Scotland Yard for the editors of the national media aiming to work out agreed procedures for 'mutual aid in dealing with kidnapping'. It was stressed that the lives of victims should be the principal concern and that 'any self-denying measures adopted by the press should apply to all' (Mark, 1980). A distinction was made between 'commercial' and 'political' kidnappings and hijackings, 'political' offences being excluded from the agreement (Harland, 1977: 5–7). Hardly had this initiative been taken when Sir Robert's media policy was tested on three occasions with results that evidently satisfied him greatly. Two of the incidents were sieges and the third involved the news blackout of a kidnapping.

The sieges are obviously of greater interest here: what were their continuities with, and differences from, Prince's Gate? Unlike the latter, both the 1975 sieges were under the sole operational control of the Metropolitan Police. At the Spaghetti House in Knightsbridge, a group of three gunmen held up the managers of a restaurant chain as they were about to bank the day's takings. The gunmen and their hostages were cooped up in the basement for the duration of the siege. The police put into operation a plan devised over the previous two years. The area was sealed off; the Home Office supplied liaison officers and psychiatrists to assist in the bargaining. The liaison officers were present in case troops were required and because some Italian nationals had been taken hostage. The police refused to bargain over the gunmen's demands, but provided them with a radio to help 'make clear to them, not only in shouted conversation, but through the news broadcasts, that they were going nowhere except to a cell, or by implication, to a mortuary, if they preferred that' (Mark, 1979: 199). The police were able to monitor activities inside the basement, first through sound recordings and later through a television picture supplied by surveillance devices developed by C7, Scotland Yard's technical support branch. The police found the media exceedingly co-operative. The editor of the *Daily Mail*, David English, agreed to kill a scoop about the arrest of one of the gunmen's accomplices. Mark sought the suppression of this information as he did not want it broadcast over the radio. Although Scotland Yard thanked the *Mail* and the rest of the press this was not published, provoking from Mark the disingenuous comment that 'It was almost as if they felt that there was something wrong in suppression of news in the interest of saving human life' (Mark, 1979: 201).

The Balcombe Street siege in December 1975 was a more clearly political event. The successful conclusion at the Spaghetti House – where no one was killed – gave the police added confidence in dealing with it. This siege was the climax to a bombing and shooting campaign by the IRA in Britain. The police had set an ambush for the Provisional IRA active service unit involved, and after a chase from Mayfair four of its members were cornered in a private flat in Balcombe Street. The siege was handled according to the principles established a mere two months earlier. Once again, the Home Office sent a liaison officer, this time the SAS were moved in, and a team of psychiatrists was organized. The police controlled communications by cutting off the telephone and sending in a field telephone. The police strategy was, again, to play a waiting game, using time to wear down the resistance of the gunmen. Sir Robert Mark noted the important role played by the media: 'They asked, at our prompting loaded questions such as "What about the safety of the hostages?" which enabled me to reply, "The best guarantee of their safety is the swift and ruthless retribution that will follow any harm that befalls them"' (Mark, 1979: 193).

As the siege wore on, and the likelihood of sending in the SAS to shoot things out increased, the ambiguities of the media presence became obvious. On the one hand, the police did not want any 'gory end to the siege' shown on the screen, and so they blocked off the view of the cameras. On the other hand, the media were again open to manipulation. As the flat was blocked off from the cameras, 'coincidentally, both the *Daily Express* and the BBC disclosed that the SAS were there. This was, of course, broadcast on radio for the encouragement of the terrorists. Thereafter they could hardly surrender fast enough' (Mark, 1979: 194). In another account Mark says quite bluntly that the presence of the SAS was 'leaked' to the media – so there was little that was 'coincidental' about the disclosure (Mark, 1980).

The police scored a further success in their relations with the media over the kidnapping for ransom of a Greek Cypriot girl, Aloi Kaloghirou, in November 1975, when Mark described their behaviour as 'opening a new era in police–press relations' (Mark, 1980). Editors were requested not to publish the story in the public interest. In order to maintain the media's compliance, the police gave daily news conferences at Scotland Yard to inform journalists of progress. This news blackout was sustained for ten days until the girl was released unharmed. Chibnall has noted that many journalists were disenchanted by their end of the bargain. He also makes the point that such 'stops' are common practice in Britain, the only unusual feature being the extent of co-operation on this occasion (Chibnall, 1977: 186–7). After the Met's success with 'voluntary co-operation', the Home Office extended the London model of 'guidelines' to editors of the provincial press. However, these guidelines make no distinction between 'political' and 'commercial' terrorism, and had in some cases been very widely interpreted by chief constables to mean that they can ask for a news blackout whenever publicity might endanger life (Harland, 1977: 7). Clearly, the establishment of such common procedures helped the authorities in their eventual handling of the Prince's Gate siege.

Northern Ireland

The prime focus of 'news about terrorism' in recent years has been Northern Ireland (cf. Belfast Workers' Research Unit, 1979; Campaign for Free Speech on Ireland, 1979; Dunkley, 1978; Howkins, 1978; Schlesinger, 1978: ch.8; Smith, 1972). Coverage in the British media, as Philip Elliott (1977) has pointed out, has tended to simplify violent incidents, to avoid historical background, to concentrate upon human-interest stories and to rely upon official sources. Even during periods of intense political activity, the story has been pre-eminently one of violence – and irrational, inexplicable violence at that. Apart from weaknesses in the journalistic practice of the British media, there can be little doubt that the one-dimensional coverage reflects, at least in part, the effective long-term strategy of attrition waged by the state in its psychological warfare campaign. Most critical attention has been focused upon the British state's repeated efforts to control broadcast news and current affairs coverage without stepping over that fatefully delegitimizing line into overt censorship. It is a struggle which has been waged patiently and with skill, despite an orchestrated series of apparently intemperate rows. On the other hand, there are indications that the pitch of intimidatory rhetoric has risen of late, and overt intervention looks more likely than ever.

The immediate relevance of this Northern Ireland coverage to the Iranian Embassy siege is that it had led to strained relations between the BBC and the Thatcher government. Two incidents involving the television reporting of political violence were the cause. The first was a *Tonight* interview in July 1979 with a representative of the Irish National Liberation Army, the group which assassinated the Tory Northern Ireland spokesman, Airey Neave. This resulted in representations to the BBC from the Northern Ireland Secretary, Humphrey Atkins, questions in the House of Commons, shocked reaction from Neave's widow, criticism from the Opposition Northern Ireland spokesman Merlyn Rees and Mrs Thatcher's comment that she was 'appalled'. The BBC's Director-General defended its action as responsible, in part by arguing that 'We believe that this was an exercise in exposing the enemies of democracy, not condoning them' and by pointing out that this was only the fourth member of a proscribed organization to be interviewed in ten years (Trethowan, 1979). Mrs Thatcher asked the Attorney-General to consider taking legal action. Later, reference was made to Section 11 of the Prevention of Terrorism Act – a new departure in English jurisprudence (Connell, 1980). Under Section 11 it is a criminal act not to disclose information to the police about suspected terrorism, with the attendant possibility of five years' imprisonment or an unlimited fine, or both.

The reverberations had hardly died away before the second incident in which the BBC disgraced itself in the government's eyes, this time by filming an IRA road-block in Carrickmore. Again, this led to frenzied declamations in Parliament against the BBC, which had not even transmitted the film, and which invariably gives painstaking attention to any decision to screen manifestations of IRA strength. On this occasion, after saying that it was time the BBC 'put its house in order', Mrs Thatcher said that the film would not be shown. The police – for the first time – seized an untransmitted copy of the film under the Prevention of Terrorism Act. The threat of a prosecution under the PTA hung over the BBC until July 1980. One immediate response was to tighten up further the guidelines on Northern Ireland reporting: there is little doubt that the exemplary intimidation of the BBC raised widespread anxiety among journalists about the legality of contacts with paramilitary organizations. The government's views became clear in August 1980, when in a letter to the BBC's Chairman, Sir Michael Swann, the Attorney-General, Sir Michael Havers, said that he thought both incidents constituted offences under Section 11 of the Prevention of Terrorism Act 1976. While denying any intent to censor, Havers accused the BBC of aiding terrorist propaganda and decried the fact that BBC personnel had not attempted to 'contact the appropriate authorities to pass on the information required' to apprehend or prosecute terrorists (*Guardian*, 2 August 1980). As the government has not chosen to test its arguments in the courts, the legal standing of its view remains obscure. Nevertheless, this pressure on the BBC to 'behave' forms part of the background to the period of the Iranian Embassy siege, and may have influenced the BBC in its eventual interpretation of its proper role as that of a model corporate citizen.[7]

The role of the media during the siege

> It is perhaps unreasonable to expect the police to think first of the press, though in this case they thought very carefully about the press because . . . they realized . . . that they were part of the game. (Professor John Gunn)[8]

How, in detail, did the state authorities and the gunmen pursue their respective communicative strategies? In what ways was publicity a crucial factor in the management of the siege? My analysis is provisional; I merely seek to clarify the role of news broadcasting and of BBC personnel. It is also restricted by being based largely upon the accounts provided by the *Observer* and *Sunday Times* 'instant' books,[9] which are obviously incomplete. A good deal more of the 'story' of the siege has yet to come out. None the less, the books do provide a great deal of material which illuminates, in particular, the importance attached to broadcasting. As I pointed out in the introduction, radio reporting seems to have been of paramount significance, as the gunmen and the hostages had receivers. There is no clear evidence whether any television viewing went on, but it seems reasonable to suppose that it did not. Newspapers were not allowed into the embassy (*ST*: 115).

The growth of the Civil Contingencies Committee (CCC) as part of the emergent 'strong state', which I noted earlier, is of especial importance here, since, unlike at the Spaghetti House and Balcombe Street sieges, operational control was vested in the Civil Contingencies Committee rather than in the police. It is also worth recalling that since the early 1970s the British government has refused to countenance the escape of hijackers and hostage-takers – a policy in keeping with the emergent European position on anti-terrorism – and has increasingly made the SAS a part of domestic policing under the formula of 'military aid to the civil power'. In the present case, the unit used was the Special Air Services' Special Operations Group, SAS-SOG (*State Research*, 1980a: 118). The deployment required the formal request of the Metropolitan Police Commissioner, Sir David McNee. The police decision eventually to call on these crack troops, however, can only be understood by recognizing the guiding framework of constraints which emanated from the Civil Contingencies Committee, or 'COBRA', as it was labelled by the media. From the start the siege was correctly perceived to be political in character. It was a calculated gesture aimed at the Iranian government, and, given the complex international ramifications, this meant that direct British government involvement was inevitable. The CCC was chaired by William Whitelaw, the Home Secretary, and had fifteen staff members drawn from relevant Departments of State, the Civil Service and the security and intelligence forces. The Foreign and Commonwealth Office was represented by Douglas Hurd, and the Ministry of Defence by Barney Heyhoe (*Obs.* 23; *ST*: 43).

Day 1: Wednesday 30 April   The embassy was seized at 11.32 a.m. At noon, commercial radio's IRN broadcast a report about the seizure; shortly afterwards, they indicated in an eyewitness report from the scene that the police were on the embassy roof (*ST*: 20). The gunmen's leader, Oan, was evidently upset by a BBC report early in the afternoon which suggested that he and his group were Iraqis (*ST*: 30). He wished to correct this view. At this point, the *Guardian* made contact through the embassy's telex and managed to establish that the group were Arabistan autonomists before Oan terminated the interview (*Obs*: 25; *ST*: 31). It was the *journalists* among the hostages who suggested that their captors make contact with the media. At 2.45 p.m. the Syrian journalist Moustafa Karkouti managed to get in touch with the BBC's External Services at Bush House, and explained that 'he was a hostage acting under orders to pass on a message. The men holding him wanted ninety-one prisoners in Arabistan to be released. And the BBC should also note that the hostage-takers were from Iran – not Iraq'. (*Obs*: 25; *ST*: 31)

This was the first time this demand was transmitted. The Metropolitan Police received details of the demands at 3.15 p.m. according to their log. Either they were already tapping the line, or alternatively the BBC made them available (*ST*: 32). At 3.45 p.m. Karkouti spoke to the BBC's External Services again, and Oan relayed his demand that the ninety-one prisoners be released the next day or the embassy and the hostages would be blown up. Some fifteen minutes earlier, Chris Cramer, the captured BBC news organizer, had telephoned or telexed BBC Television Centre listing the gunmen's demands. Apart from the threat to blow up the embassy, there was a request for Arab ambassadors to mediate between the gunmen and the British government and a promise that the non-Iranian hostages would not be harmed. The request for mediation was suppressed, at the request of the police, for three days (*Obs*: 26–7, 137–8; *ST*: 33). Before the first day ended, the telephone links had been used to make several personal calls, and in addition the gunmen had spoken to the Iranian Foreign Minister, Sadeq Ghotzbadeh, who had refused any compromise (*ST*: 33).

Although the gunmen were able to make use of their access to the media to put across their aims during this first day, these were not relayed in full detail at the request of the police. According to the editor of BBC Television News, the telex from Cramer was immediately made available to the police.[10] The contacts with Bush House probably were as well – given the position of its two men inside the embassy, the BBC had assumed a crucial role. Even without this chance the Corporation was apparently considered important by the gunmen. In his account of the siege, Chris Cramer (1980) notes:

> Barely a matter of minutes after the firing and the shouting had stopped, I chose to identify myself to the gunmen as a BBC journalist . . . On reflection, I was taking a stupid risk by singling myself out as representing what, to many worldwide, is a less than perfect organization. The crazy thing is that it actually

worked. The BBC's credibility rating is obviously high with terrorists . . . They seemed to know the time of every bulletin in English, Persian and Arabic. Without that kind of worldwide publicity things might have got very nasty.

Day 2: Thursday 1 May Only some of the press acceded to the police request not to mention the noon deadline for the release of the prisoners in Iran – namely *The Times*, the *Guardian* and the *Daily Telegraph* (*Obs*: 44). But this was of little note; once again, the BBC was of paramount importance. At 6.20 a.m., at Oan's request, Karkouti again telephoned Bush House to remind the British public that the noon deadline stood, but that the non-Iranian hostages would not be harmed in the meantime. The duty editor of *Radio Newsreel* managed to engage Oan in a lengthy interview which was subsequently broadcast on early-morning domestic bulletins (*Obs*: 45–7, 138; *ST*: 35–9). Alan Protheroe has surmised, presumably on an informed basis, that this recording was made available to police before it was broadcast. The gunmen evidently kept listening to the radio, because they heard Karkouti's voice on the BBC, and also mentioned that Tehran radio had broadcast the rejection of their demands (*Obs*: 48). Chris Cramer, who had been taken ill overnight, was released by the gunmen at 11.20 a.m. He was evidently an important source of information for the police; for instance, he told them that PC Lock, the Diplomatic Protection Squad officer held captive, still had his gun (*Obs*: 52; *ST*: 41). Cramer says nothing about what he told the police. He had promised the gunmen, obviously under duress, not to reveal anything.[11] However, his unconstrained attitude is revealed in this comment:

> After my release, lying in a hospital bed, I mentally pleaded with all the broadcasters to do exactly what the gunmen wanted, to co-operate fully with the police and the Home Office . . . if necessary to broadcast complete lies. Anything to get the remaining hostages out and to safety. That thought process is completely alien to all my professional beliefs. But, as one of my close BBC friends said last week, professional beliefs don't save lives. (Cramer, 1980)

By the afternoon of the second day, the gunmen had modified their position. They dropped the demand for the release of the prisoners, and asked instead that their demands be broadcast and that three Arab ambassadors arrange for a plane to fly them out. Such a solution was closed off by the security policy of the British state. The government, operating through the CCC, did not want any Arab mediators it could not control. It was worried about the requested use of the Iraqi ambassador, given Iran–Iraq tensions. And it did not want to seem to be endorsing the seizure by taking a soft line (*Obs*:58–9; *ST*: 43, 45). Karkouti, an astute observer, is quoted as noting retrospectively that 'from the second evening, I felt it was being treated by those outside the Embassy as a security problem and it was going to end in a critical situation. It was no longer a political situation and that was very frightening' (*Obs*: 57). In truth, it had been defined as a security situation *from the very beginning*, in line with the developments in anti-terrorist policy since the early 1970s. During the second day the police cut off the telex and telephone links, and the gunmen were entirely dependent upon the police field telephone or conversations through the window for communications (*Obs*: 50; *ST*: 46). By the end of the day, therefore, the media had no direct access to informants inside the embassy, and could reveal nothing of the changing intentions of the gunmen.

Day 3: Friday 2 May It was on this day that the BBC became directly involved as an intermediary between the gunmen and the police, although much is not yet known about the precise role of its personnel. Cutting off communications caused the gunmen intense frustration, and led to the first death threat against a particular hostage. However, despite the plea of PC Lock that there was 'a man about to be killed' unless Oan was allowed to talk to the media by telephone or telex, again this request was refused. Oan modified his demand, and asked to speak to someone at the BBC known to Sim Harris. Apparently, this idea originated with Sim Harris, the BBC sound recordist, who had suggested the previous night that his captors speak to a senior BBC executive to find out why their demands had not been broadcast.[12] The police had then said no one was available, which was false.

After the death threat, however, the police did contact the BBC, asking for the Television Home News Editor, John Exelby. As it turned out, the Managing Editor of Television News, Tony Crabb, took his place and departed for the embassy at 9 a.m. (*Obs*: 73–4; *ST*: 47). By 9.30 Crabb was talking to Harris at the embassy (*Obs*: 74; *ST*: 51 differs, and presumably wrongly says this conversation did not take place until the afternoon).[13] Harris asked why the gunmen's demands had not been broadcast. Crabb asked 'what demands?' This seems odd, as Cramer had telexed them through to Television Centre on the first day. Although the *Observer* team comments that 'it was never clear why the police decided to keep from the Press the fact that gunmen had demanded the presence of Arab ambassadors to act as mediators' (*Obs*: 74) their own evidence indicates that the BBC *did* have this information (*Obs*: 27, 131). *So the BBC alone of all the media colluded with the police in keeping this crucial demand secret.*[14]

Crabb had been told by the police that he could offer nothing, and that he should keep the content of the conversation to himself. At the centre of this request was the suppression of the key demand for the intervention of the Arab ambassadors; this apparently 'neither surprised nor particularly upset' Crabb (*Obs*: 74–5). He took notes of the gunmen's demands:

Oan said he wanted:
1) a coach to take gunmen, hostages, and one Arab ambassador – unnamed – to Heathrow;
2) the non-Iranian hostages to be released at Heathrow;
3) an aircraft to take the remaining hostages, gunmen, and ambassador to a Middle East country – again unspecified – and there released. (*ST*: 52)

It appears that the communication of their aims now obsessed the gunmen, who did not doubt that they would be allowed a safe passage. It was only at 11.30 that night that a BBC bulletin referred to the new demands. 'But, to Oan's fury, the BBC not only truncated his statement, but got it wrong. The broadcast said that the gunmen wanted the three Arab ambassadors to negotiate not with the *British* government, which was the fact, but with Iran' (*ST*: 52). This error seems quite extraordinary, unless, of course, it was an intentional one. But the two books differ about this incident. The *Observer* account contains no reference to a BBC bulletin late on Day 3, but reports that at the beginning of Day 4 Oan 'was listening, as ever, to what the radio had to say about the siege, preoccupied with the demand for three ambassadors which the police had not yet made public. He heard Radio Tehran say that the ambassadors were needed to negotiate with the Iranian government, not the British' (*Obs*: 81).[15] This indicates that, rather than getting the demands wrong, the BBC did not report them at all – a point which merits further inquiry.

Day 4: Saturday 3 May   By the late morning, the gunmen were evidently getting edgy about the non-broadcasting of their demands, as well as the non-appearance of any ambassadors. They demanded to see Crabb once more. As tension mounted, the police realized that something had to be done about a public statement, and made urgent efforts to find Crabb, who was unavailable until the afternoon (*Obs*: 82–3). The bugging of the embassy was obviously important in providing intelligence, not least in allowing the police to monitor the gunmen's reactions to the radio reporting. The police apparently knew 'how disastrous the previous night's inaccuracies had been' (*ST*: 56), whether these are attributed to the BBC or Tehran radio.

Tony Crabb reappeared at the embassy just before 2 p.m. He was clearly an intermediary for police demands, and, during the hour before he again spoke to the gunmen, seems to have received a briefing. 'The police asked me to stress that anything they did for the gunmen had to be reciprocated by an act of goodwill from them. I was asked to emphasize that my own presence at the embassy was a concession from the police.' To Harris' question about why the statement had not been broadcast, Crabb replied that there had been a 'misunderstanding'. Given the evident anger of the gunmen's leader, the police negotiator on the spot said that the statement would be taken down correctly. Either the police officer or Crabb took down the statement (*Obs*: 84; *ST*: 56); the accounts conflict. The gunmen demanded that the statement be broadcast accurately. Crabb hesitated, but the police agreed the terms, provided that two hostages were released (*Obs*: 84; *ST*: 56). There were delays before the statement was broadcast, caused by the time taken by the CCC in evaluating its consequences. Oan threatened to kill a hostage unless the statement was published, but was prevailed upon to release one instead. 'Almost immediately, the police rang back to say thank you and told Oan that the statement would be released in full on the BBC World Service at 9.00' (*Obs*: 84–5; *ST*: 56–7). This formulation suggests very close co-operation.

At 8.35 p.m. Deputy Assistant Commissioner Peter Neivens, the police spokesman, read the statement at a press conference. He prefaced it with a comment that: 'It is very important, and I stress very important, that it is given maximum amount of coverage' (*Obs*: 85).

In addition to this, according to Alan Protheroe (1980: 641), even as the statement was being read to the assembled newsmen,

> there came one high-level call to me, underlining just how urgent the broadcasting of those demands was . . . In the event everybody ran the story – but it was run because it was a good story-development. Little had come out of the siege; here was a top cop spelling out the newest demands, and again asking for the maximum publicity for it. There was, frankly, no need to stress the urgency; a journalistic assessment had already been made concerning the story, and TV News, BBC Radio News, ITN and IRN/LBC were in there, running the story as a news flash.

Inside the embassy, the radios were tuned in to IRN and the BBC World Service. IRN broadcast the statement at seven minutes to nine. The captors and their captives also listened to BBC Radio 4 and the BBC World Service. Both the books and Sim Harris' diary describe the immense relief inside the embassy as the gunmen's objective was realized. Subsequently a further hostage was released. The statement assured the British government and people that no harm was intended towards the hostages; that three Arab ambassadors were required for the purposes of negotiating the safety of all concerned; and that the reason for the siezure of the embassy was to draw attention to the plight of Arabistan (*ST*: 85–7).

Day 5: Sunday 4 May   The highwater mark of media involvement had been reached on the previous day. The early news bulletins spoke of the Arab ambassadors being willing to assist and of the Red Cross standing by (*Obs*: 88). The British government stuck to its policy, however, and could not reach a working agreement with any of the Arab ambassadors. It refused to permit the gunmen to go free, and was not prepared to let the ambassadors negotiate. It wished them merely to convey the terms of surrender. That evening a further hostage was released, and now the gunmen demanded one ambassador and a safe conduct (*ST*: 76). During the day, the Iranian Foreign Minister had suggested that thousands of Iranians were ready to storm the embassy. Although the BBC's engineers had decided after studying its aerials that the embassy was capable of receiving Tehran radio, no reference was made to Ghotzbadeh's speech. Alan Protheroe (1980: 641) has commented that this was 'to avoid provoking the gunmen' and has added that there had been 'requests not to broadcast things' which he had known were on Tehran radio.

Day 6: Monday 5 May   This day began with anxiety about the non-appearance of the Arab ambassadors and with the gunmen's intense awareness that security preparations were going on all round the embassy. Both Harris and PC Lock pleaded with the police negotiators to make some progress over the ambassadors, which they could hardly do as the issue was out of their hands. One of the negotiators assured them that discussions were still going on and that they should listen to the BBC World Service at 12 o'clock for confirmation (*Obs*: 108; *ST*: 82). This news broadcast reported meetings at the Foreign Office, but nothing about any decisions being reached.[16] The stalemate produced a decisive action from the gunmen: they shot a hostage. This ensured the eventual entry of the SAS.

What emerges from this reading of the best existing accounts of the siege is that the BBC was of especial significance. Two aspects of its role need to be considered further: the use of its personnel for mediation, and the extent to which the corporation may have received special briefings.

The role of Tony Crabb was obviously important, and it is worth noting the ways in which it was described. According to *Broadcast*, he 'at one stage acted as go-between for security authorities. (He later explained, "At no time did I act as a negotiator, but I willingly abstained from taking any journalistic advantage of my involvement in order to be of some help to the negotiators").'

Alan Protheroe (1980: 641) echoes this formula in his article on the siege:

> Crabb, for three days, deliberately and honourably stopped working as a journalist and remained at the disposal of the police. He had at no time acted as a negotiator, but his presence may have been helpful in defusing a tense situation, and the advice he was able to give the negotiators was crucial in the resolution of the siege.

Crabb himself is quoted elsewhere as commenting that 'although the gunmen felt that I was a journalist, I didn't feel that I was there in that capacity' (*Obs*: 83).

All these statements reveal an anxiety to play down the BBC's involvement. The way in which Crabb took no journalistic advantage of the situation was presumably by deciding not to broadcast the demands on Day 3. But the BBC was already in possession of the crucial demand for mediation, although not, of course, the specific demands about the arrangements for the safe conduct. In any case, Crabb could not himself have taken journalistic advantage. He would have had to refer the matter upwards, at least to the Director of News and Current Affairs, if not the Director-General. The suppression of the information must have been a policy decision. If Crabb was not there as a journalist, then what was his role? Protheroe suggests that his advice was crucial to the police, but does not say how. The *Guardian* (6.5.80) suggests that the use of Crabb as 'an independent, non-police representative' was important in securing the gunmen's trust, and indeed that would seem to be so. Similar suggestions were made in television broadcasts during the siege. *Nationwide* (2.5.80) described Crabb as 'a recognizable BBC figure', but added that he had 'joined the police team'. *News at Ten* (2.5.80) reported on the arrival at the embassy of John Exelby, the BBC Television Home News Editor who was there 'to prove that not everyone surrounding the embassy are police'. *Newsnight* (2.5.80) said that Crabb had established rapport with the hostage-takers. These characterizations suggest the importance of the role played by the BBC's quasi-negotiator – delaying tactics on the third and fourth days were clearly assisted by his presence. The cautious descriptions of Crabb's role probably reflect anxiety within the BBC over its entanglement with state agencies, and about the effect on its credibility in the future. Looking back the day after the ending of the siege, *Newsnight* insisted that Crabb was not involved in the negotiations. But although Crabb was not a fully fledged negotiator in that he was not empowered to offer anything, he did help to secure the release of two hostages as a trade-off for broadcasting the gunmen's demands on Day 4. His self-ascribed role, if not journalistic, must have been that of a responsible citizen assisting the state in the maintainance of law and order. This setting aside of journalistic professionalism *in extremis* echoes Chris Cramer's sentiment in the quotation cited earlier.

The other noteworthy aspect of the BBC's role concerns the extent of its contacts with the state. Speaking on the BBC television programme *The Editors* (16.6.80), Alan Protheroe has deplored 'the reluctance of the Authorities to trust the media, and to recognize that we are, actually, immensely experienced and honourable individuals'. The whole tenor of his argument is that the authorities ought to trust the media more, and that there might be 'some kind of system where much more information can be given to editors' (Protheroe, 1980: 641). He denies that there was a 'hot line' by which instructions from 'higher authority' caused the suppression of information, stressing instead the ability of journalists to work out the state's strategies for themselves.

> It was possible, for example, by deduction from hints and straight information, to establish that the gunmen were infinitely more professional than, say, the 'hoods' of the Spaghetti House, or the IRA men of Balcombe Street. Our assessment, made at the earliest stage, turned out to be absolutely correct: *we were sure that this siege could not be resolved without the intervention of the SAS or a similar group.* (*The Editors*, 16.6.80; emphasis added)

How could they be so sure? Undoubtedly, there is something to be said for journalistic experience. Many of the reporters at Prince's Gate had been at the previous London sieges, and from the beginning there was speculation about the SAS being brought in. Reporters were suspicious of the 'gasmen' digging up the road near the embassy. But what Protheroe says seems to go beyond this reportorial conventional wisdom, for he has amplified his opaque reference to 'hints' by talking on *The Editors* of 'certain briefings which I had received as an individual' which made him conclude that the siege would result in violence. This seems pretty incontrovertible evidence of top-level links between the BBC and the security forces, and calls into question the argument that journalistic experience alone produced the right decisions.

Also puzzling is Protheroe's confident assertion that he knew the television coverage of the final intervention could not damage the operation. Indeed, he seems to have had a good idea that the SAS were going to be used when he says: 'I don't think there was any possibility of bodies coming out . . . I am utterly convinced from the dispositions of troops and policemen that it was extremely unlikely that anybody would walk out of there unless he was surrendering.' If detailed briefings were not available, Protheroe's own military intelligence background could have led him to such inferences, along with contributory assessments from other BBC defence experts like Peter Snow and Christopher Wain.

The BBC has frequent informal consultations with members of the military and police establishments. One occurred some six months before the Prince's Gate siege at the closed Abingdon Conference on *'Politics Extremism, the Media and the Law'*, held on 16–18 November 1979. This brought together top media personnel, civil servants, soldiers, policemen and politicians from Israel, West Germany, the USA and Britain. It was sponsored by the BBC together with the International Press Institute and the Ford Foundation. Amongst the participants were the BBC's Director of News and Current Affairs, Richard Francis, and Kate Adie, the reporter who covered the SAS's taking of the embassy. Another participant was Deputy Assistant Commissioner John Dellow, the officer in charge of operations during the siege. According to *State Research* (1980a: 119):

> One of the case studies in which those present participated concerned the seizure of hostages in a Western capital by a dissident movement from the Middle East. The denouement of this case study was a shoot out, organized by the Government, which, although it had carried on talking throughout never intended to allow the hostage-takers to escape. Discussion centred on whether a newspaper, which had been told that the hostage-takers were in the end to be ambushed and shot rather than any deal being struck, should release the information.[17]

Knowledge of such scenarios, coupled with Protheroe's 'certain briefings' and 'hints', suggests that top broadcasters could hardly have been unaware of the government's intentions on the occasion of the Prince's Gate siege, and that some of these expectations must have been transmitted, via briefings, to the reporting teams.

But if this is so, then why was the actual live coverage so incoherent? The trade magazine *Broadcast* (1980) has noted that it was

> obvious for at least half an hour before the assault took place that a turning-point had been reached in the siege. Both ITN and BBC News had broadcast news flashes at 19.14 and 19.11 respectively, announcing that the body of a man, probably a hostage, had been pushed out of the embassy. Newspaper reports speak of increased police activity toward 19.18.

On the fact of it, well-briefed reporters familiar with previous anti-hijack and anti-siege actions should have been able to interpret the event more adequately than they did. Admittedly, the 'frame charges' used by the SAS to blow out the windows were a new element, but the 'stun grenades' were familiar from the Mogadishu hijack rescue in 1977. Also unclear is the significance of ITN's camera at the rear of the embassy, ingeniously smuggled in on the last day of the siege in defiance of the police, who had wanted the preparations round the back to be unobserved. Oddly enough, no reports of police or Home Office displeasure at this have emerged. The ITN director in the field was aware of the immediate build-up to the SAS attack three minutes before it happened (*ST*: 116).

A final point about the television coverage is that the most complete programme available is undoubtedly that in the hands of the security forces. Throughout the siege, events at Prince's Gate were continuously monitored by police cameras. Television viewers who knew what to look for could see them, and in the 'aftermath' coverage there was film of the cameras being dismantled. A police helicopter was flying overhead throughout the ending of the siege. Such helicopters are generally fitted out with television cameras, and six months after the siege viewers of the BBC's *Nine O'Clock News* saw some of the pictures taken from this vantage point. A further source of televised material is the BBC. It is reliably reported that videotapes of the SAS action have been made available to the regiment. On previous occasions, the BBC has been rather sensitive about such co-operation. For instance, there was concern in top editorial circles about the Royal Ulster Constabulary having 'pirated' a videotaped recording of a controversial programme about 'The Republicans' shown in December 1977, as this could give the appearance of collusion with the security forces. The BBC's News and Current Affairs minute number 115 of 7 March 1978 noted that the 'BBC must respond to any formal legal requests for access to transmitted material but in all other cases it always considered most carefully the consequences of making it available, both in relation to the BBC's own position and to that of individual members of staff.' During the same meeting Alan Protheroe said that the BBC had given film for 'instructional purposes' to the Ministry of Defence and the Metropolitan Police.

It is unclear at present whether ITN also co-operated by releasing film of the siege, but it is known that they would not have raised objections had they been asked. Such requests are largely a matter of form as television coverage can anyway be monitored and taped by the police. Evidently the SAS had their own videotape of the rescue. Mrs Thatcher, who was visiting their tactical headquarters for a celebration party on the night of the action, was invited to watch a recording (Geraghty, 1980: 181). Of special interest to the authorities would be the pictures not being transmitted, especially those from ITN, which switched between cameras at the front and the rear of the Embassy. Somewhere there must exist a fascinatingly detailed compilation tape of the way the SAS stormed the Prince's Gate Embassy – one which will never receive a public showing.

Some conclusions

Sieges, hijacks and hostage-takings raise major problems for the media. There is strong pressure on them from the state, supported by public opinion, to act 'responsibly' in order to save life. Such pressure is perhaps most intense on radio and television, whose transmissions may be directly monitored by the gunmen. In the Iranian Embassy siege, radio news was of unquestionable importance as the gunmen were aiming to obtain airtime for their views: the broadcasting of their demands undoubtedly saved several lives. The BBC became particularly involved in the bargaining process on two days of the siege, and although its representatives have played down their contradictory position, the Corporation seems to have put the demands of safeguarding law and order before any journalistic imperatives. The presence of two BBC men among the hostages gave them good institutional reasons for this; less clear is whether there will be any future consequences of such close compliance with the security forces' aims. Alan Protheroe's plea for greater 'trust' from the authorities could surely result in an even greater absorption into the crisis-management apparatus of the state. A somewhat different position has been taken by the editor of the *Observer*, Donald Trelford, who suggested in *The Editors* on BBC TV that 'better communication' was needed between the police and journalists, but reserved the right of editors to decide what to use. Such a position is plainly more tenable for newspapers which are not so proximate to the state as broadcasting.

It would be dangerous to accept too readily the public rhetoric of state officials about the need to save life. Without being too cynical – such humanitarian concerns are certainly not totally absent – they do have other priorities. Foremost among them are state security and the maintenance of political credibility by stamping firmly on any manifestation of 'terrorism'. The duality of official attitudes is well illustrated by some remarks from Sir Robert Mark. When agreeing procedures for covering kidnapping with editors in 1975, he 'emphasized at the outset that *the safety of the victims should be the primary concern* of the police and, hopefully, of the Press' (Mark, 1980: emphasis added). Compare this with his reflections on the Balcombe Street siege:

> Though we were deeply concerned about the safety of the hostages I did not consider for one moment that they were not expendable. I felt heartfelt sympathy for Mr and Mrs Matthews but felt that *human life was of little importance when balanced against the principle that violence must not be allowed to succeed.* (Mark, 1979: 193, emphasis added)

Raison d'état thus guides the actions of state agencies; it would therefore seem appropriate to evaluate carefully all requests for total co-operation. Otherwise the media are apt to become tools of a given 'psywar operation', and this would foreclose any basis for criticism of the deficiencies in the state's conduct.

Although it is not my purpose here to raise detailed questions about the conduct of the Iranian Embassy siege, it is worth noting that it was not an unmitigated success. Most obviously, there was loss of life – five gunmen killed by the SAS and two hostages killed by the gunmen. The eventual shoot-out stemmed from the British government's determination not to allow the gunmen to go free. As the *Sunday Times* team comment: 'in the final analysis, the Government was prepared to sacrifice the lives of the hostages if necessary rather than give in' (*ST*: 71). The deaths were politically acceptable, because, to be blunt, they did not involve any of the British hostages. Indeed, this 'invisibility' of the non-British hostages characterized the handling of the story, coupled with the adulation for the undoubted bravery of PC Lock.

To their credit, several newspapers – the *Observer*, the *Sunday Times* and the *Guardian* – did raise questions about the circumstances in which the SAS killed the gunmen, and about the wisdom of the government's policy in not bringing in the ambassadors earlier. On the first question, using hostages' accounts, both the *Observer* and the *Sunday Times* revealed that after killing a second hostage, and attempting to kill two more, three of the gunmen threw away their arms and surrendered (*Obs*: 119–20; *ST*: 124–8). Two of these gunmen, having been identified by the hostages, were shot by the SAS. Both the *Sunday Times* and *Observer* writers expressed unease about the circumstances in which this took place, but both papers argued that there was little else the SAS could have done, given the uncertainty about whether the men were still armed or whether they could blow up the embassy. Tony Geraghty (1980: 180), the *Sunday Times*'s defence correspondent (and historian of the SAS), had no reservations: 'The only way of saving the hostages' lives . . . was to kill the terrorists unless it was unequivocally clear that they were identifying themselves for what they were and were very plainly surrendering. This was far from clear at the time.'

Nevertheless, questions do remain. The *Observer* team asked, 'Did the SAS team have orders to take no prisoners – and if so who issued them?' (*Obs*: 119). This question obviously runs across the purely situational explanation offered for the SAS's action – that in the battleground which was the embassy they had no choice but to eliminate the enemy. The *Sunday Times* investigators were at odds with their defence correspondent: 'The crucial question is, had the gunmen dropped all of their weapons and genuinely surrendered before they were shot? And if so, can their killings possibly be justified on any legal and moral basis?' (*ST*: 127). Tony Geraghty (1980: 169) has, in fact, suggested that there certainly was a strong legal basis for the action:

> the SAS is stringently subject to the rule of law, for which the police are responsible. The Army's CRW (counter-revolutionary warfare) teams are reminded of this by a litany of ground rules, more elaborate even than the 'Yellow Card' governing the rules of engagement for soldiers in Northern Ireland. It travels with the team for display in their tactical operations room near the scene of the siege.

This observation adds to our knowledge: when *State Research* (1980a: 118) tried to find out more about these regulations, the Ministry of Defence would not even comment on their existence. To know that they exist, however, is not to know what they detail. Nor does it reveal whether they were observed – it seems that they have not been on occasions in Northern Ireland. At the time of writing, some six months after the siege, these questions have not been pursued by the British media; at any rate, nothing has been published.

What of the FCO's refusal (at the behest of the CCC) to let the ambassadors mediate? Obviously, this was a matter of high-level political calculation, in which the possibility of a negotiated solution that allowed the gunmen to escape was rejected. The deterrent effect of a hard line seems a plausible enough argument if hostages' lives are not the top priority. It is surely a matter of public interest, though, that the BBC, which alone of the British media was privy to the demand for diplomatic intervention, aligned itself uncritically with government anti-terrorism policy. By keeping quiet about the Arab ambassadors, the Corporation played a crucial role in facilitating the pursuit of the government's strategy for three days. It is extraordinary that this has occasioned no comment – indeed, has eventually gone unnoticed. Did the Corporation have no doubts about the wisdom of the government's approach? Its unique status in the affair was also reinforced by the way in which the BBC's personnel – Tony Crabb on the outside and Sim Harris on the inside – assisted in the exchange of publicity for hostages, and in contributing to the attrition of the gunmen's will. The BBC was certainly in a difficult position: it *had* to co-operate extensively with the security operation and was rightly concerned for the safety of its personnel. At the same time, the siege undoubtedly represented a further milestone in the peacetime exercise of state control over broadcasting in a moment of crisis. Perhaps the configuration of circumstances was unique: equally, it could have enduring consequences.

No doubt from the siege-managers' point of view a partial censorship is better than none at all. But although successful in practice, the present British model has a paradoxical long-term consequence. The very absence of total censorship makes it possible for interested parties to reconstruct the details of siege operations, including the role of communication media – as I have done here. This means that the security forces have to think out a new 'game plan', at least on the most pessimistic assumption that future hostage-takers will be literate and will understand how things work in Britain. At the extensive debriefing of all those involved in the security side a week after the conclusion of the siege, the question of whether it would be 'necessary to change contingency plans to counter terrorist incidents because of the extensive television coverage of the siege including "blacked-up" SAS men storming the building' was considered (*Daily Telegraph*, 11.5.80). Although total censorship remains unlikely, and would anyway be utterly unacceptable to both media and public, a clear code of practice governing media–state relations on such occasions is needed. Fudging the reality of existing *ad hoc* agreements (as with the BBC in this case) is of course the preferred British way out. But it is hardly the most democratic: we have a right to know just how compliant the media propose to be at given moments, and why they choose (or are constrained) to be so.

Finally, the overall coverage of the siege does give cause for serious concern. The episode was generally treated in patriotic, even chauvinistic, terms. A violent solution was favoured, even glorified. From the point of view of civil liberties, this is worrying indeed. Will this mean that strong-arm tactics for dealing with political problems will become an accepted part of our political culture?

Notes

1 BBC Television's *The Editors* was a regular commentary programme on journalistic matters. Quotations are taken from the BFI Education Department's transcript of the programme broadcast on 16 June 1980.

2 John Le Carré's article introduces the *Observer* reporting team's book-length version of the events, titled *Siege*, published on 30 May 1980. Extensive use is made of this account below, hence referred to as *Obs*.

3 An interview quoted on pp. 61–2 of *Siege!*, the *Sunday Times* reporting team's account, also published in 1980 and also extensively used later: hence referred to as *ST*.

4 On 6 May 1980 the BBC's *Newsnight* programme revealed that the police had asked the television organizations not to show the plans of the embassy.

5 On this, cf. the following *State Research* Bulletins: no. 5, April–May 1978: 83–4; no 11, April–May 1979: 84–5. The convergence over policing has a legal dimension too. The UK has extended the grounds for political extradition by ratifying the Council of Europe's Convention on the Suppression of Terrorism, on which cf. *State Research* Bulletins no. 4, February–March 1978: 63–5; and no. 8, October–November 1978: 6–7.

6 This was reported by ABC Network News on 2 May 1980.

7 Perhaps the BBC's final expiation came when on 6 October 1980 it broadcast a eulogistic drama-documentary titled *Airey Neave: A Will of Steel*. The programme's title picked up a phrase of Mrs Thatcher's, who, suitably enough, had the last word too.

8 Professor Gunn was psychiatric adviser to the police during the siege. The quotation is taken from *The Editors* programme, referred to in note 1 above.

9 In the development of the argument that follows, I have tied particular statements to accounts given in the two 'siege' books. I have read them with particular questions in mind concerning the role of the media, whereas the books have been written with this as an important but nevertheless subordinate issue. The critical reading offered below points up some crucial moments which were left rather implicit in the books; and as it traverses controversial ground, especially concerning the relationship between broadcasting and the state, it is crucial to provide evidence for each turn in the argument.

10 On *The Editors*, the BBC's Alan Protheroe observed: 'In the case of the telex that was sent to us from Chris Cramer on the first day, the contents of that were, in fact, made immediately available to the police. The police had copies of the telex. They talked to the people who had received the telex at this end.'

11 A point he made during an interview on the BBC television programme *Newsnight*, 5 May 1980.

12 According to Harris' diary as published in *The Day of the SAS: The Inside Story of How Britain Ended the Siege of Prince's Gate*. This war comic was the *Daily Express*'s siege special. On the whole, its interest is iconographic rather than factual.

13 Sim Harris' diary supports the *Observer* version.
14 Given the importance of this point, the evidence for it should be quoted in full: 'At 5.30 Karkouti and Cramer were allowed to use the telephone again. Karkouti called the BBC World Service at Bush House and Cramer BBC Television at Shepherd's Bush, dictating the statement of the gunmen's demands, the threat to blow up the Embassy if they were not met, *a request for Arab ambassadors to mediate*, and a promise that the non-Iranian hostages would not be harmed . . . the demand for Arab ambassadors to mediate was concealed for three long days' (*Obs.*: 27). Astonishingly, even media pundits like Simon Jenkins (then of the *Economist*, now editor of the *Times*), who chaired the *Editors* discussion, seem not to have grasped this point. Jenkins said on the programme: 'There was an occasion when the police failed to communicate . . . with the media that the gunmen were demanding that their ambassadors act as liaison officers. Now, why didn't the police communicate that to the broadcasting authorities, even though they didn't want it to be broadcast?' Well, in one case at least they simply didn't need to.
15 This accords with Sim Harris' diary in the *Daily Express*'s special, p. 56, cited in note 12 above.
16 According to Sim Harris' diary, p. 60.
17 The other two scenarios discussed at the conference concerned the reporting of extreme Left and Right politics and the question of how to handle torture allegations against the security forces in Northern Ireland.

References

Ackroyd, C., Margolis, K., Rosenhead, J. and Shallice, T. (1980) *The Technology of Political Control*, 2nd edn. London: Pluto Press.
Belfast Workers' Research Unit (1979) *Media Misreport N. Ireland*. Belfast.
Bowden, T. (1978) *Beyond the Limits of the Law*. Harmondsworth: Penguin.
Broadcast (1980) 'After the Siege: How TV Covered the Kensington Gore', *Broadcast*, 12 May.
Bunyan, T. (1977) *The History and Practice of the Political Police in Britain*. London: Quartet.
Campaign for Free Speech on Ireland (1979) *The British Media and Ireland*. London.
Chibnall, S. (1977) *Law-and-Order News: An Analysis of Crime Reporting in the British Press*. London: Tavistock.
Connell, D. (1980) 'Reporting Northern Ireland, 1979–80', *Index on Censorship*, 9 (3), June.
Cramer, C. (1980) 'Inside the Embassy', *Broadcast*, 19 May.
Dunkley, C. (1978) 'Programmes on Northern Ireland', in *Official Programme of the Edinburgh International Television Festival 1978*. pp. 58–61.
Elliott, P. (1977) 'Reporting Northern Ireland', in *Ethnicity and the Media*. Paris: Unesco.
Elliott, P. (1980) 'Press Performance as Political Ritual', in H. Christian (ed.), *The Sociology of Journalism and the Press*. University of Keele: Sociological Review Monograph No. 29. pp. 141–77.
Gamble, A. (1979) 'The Free Economy and the Strong State', in *The Socialist Register 1979*. London: Merlin Press. pp. 1–25.
Geraghty, T. (1980) *Who Dares Wins: The Story of the Special Air Service*. London: Arms & Armour Press.
Hain, P. (ed.) (1979–80) *Policing the Police*, Vols 1 and 2. London: John Calder.
Hall, S. (1978) 'Drifting into a Law and Order Society'. Cobden Trust Human Rights Day Lecture.
Hall, S., Critcher, C., Jefferson, T., Clarke, J. and Roberts B. (1978) *Policing the Crisis: Mugging, the State and Law and Order*. London: Macmillan.
Harland, P. (1977) 'Terror and the Press. Politics and Greed: When Lives Are at Stake Where Is the Difference?' *IPI Report*, 26 (10), November: 5–7.

Howkins, J. (1978) 'Censorship, 1977–78', in *Official Programme of the Edinburgh International Television Festival 1978*. pp. 50–6.

Kettle, M. (1980) 'The Drift to Law and Order', *Marxism Today*, October: 20–7.

Lavoinne, Y. (1979) 'Presse et cohésion sociale: le cas des prises d'otages', *Revue Française de Communication*, 2, Winter: 35–41.

Le Carré, J. (1980) 'Introduction', in *Observer* (1980). pp. 1–7.

Leigh, D. (1980) *The Frontiers of Secrecy*. London: Junction Books.

Mark, Sir R. (1977) *Policing a Perplexed Society*. London: Allen & Unwin.

Mark, Sir R. (1979) *In the Office of Constable*. London: Fontana/Collins.

Mark, Sir R. (1980) 'The Case of Great Britain', in *Terrorism and the Media*. London: International Press Institute, unpaged.

Observer (1980) *Siege: Six Days at the Iranian Embassy*. London: Macmillan.

Poulantzas, N. (1978) *State, Power, Socialism*. London: New Left Books.

Protheroe, A. (1980) 'The Authorities Were Reluctant to Trust the Media: The Iranian Embassy Siege', *Listener*, 22 May: 641.

Schlesinger, P. (1978) *Putting 'Reality' Together: BBC News*. London: Constable.

Smith, A. (1972) 'Television Coverage of Northern Ireland', *Index on Censorship*, 9, June: 15–32.

State Research (1980a) 'How the SAS Ended the Prince's Gate Siege', Bulletin no. 18, June–July.

State Research (1980b) 'Policing the Eighties: The Iron Fist', Bulletin no. 19, August–September.

Sunday Times (1980) *Siege! Insight on the Great Embassy Rescue*. London: Hamlyn.

Thompson, E.P. (1980) *Writing by Candlelight*. London: Merlin Press.

Trethowan, I. (1979) Letter to the Editor, *Daily Telegraph*, 14 July.

Wolfe, A. (1971) 'Political Repression and the Liberal Democratic State', *Monthly Review*, December: 18–37.

Postscript 1990

Because of the powerful symbolic role of the SAS, the Prince's Gate siege became a kind of *locus classicus* for analytical discussion in media sociology and cultural studies (cf. Bazalgette and Paterson, 1980–1; Hartley, 1982; Knight and Dean, 1982; Newsinger, 1983; Paterson and Schlesinger, 1983). The mythic qualities of the SAS were further enhanced by their exploits during the 1982 Falklands campaign; and in retrospect, the patriotic rhetoric deployed after the siege bust may be seen to have been a pre-echo of the later 'small war'.

The present case study emphasizes the moment of censorship and complicity. It would be wrong to conclude that this offers a complete account of the coverage of terrorism. A broader look at the range of variation of television's output (such as that conducted in *Televising 'Terrorism'* (Schlesinger et al., 1983)) offers a much more complex picture: we need to be sensitive to variations in the type of programming, the channel on which a programme is transmitted, the formats used, the audience addressed, the political conjuncture, and so forth. Moreover, in Britain, there have been occasions of considerable resistance to pressure amongst broadcasters. Whether this will still hold good in a new and more complex broadcasting ecology in which satellite and cable are to play an increasing role, and in which the 'public service' remit of broadcasting is being heavily redefined, remains a question for future research.

In 1980, as outlined above, the reporting of the siege was conditioned by the overall national security background (in which the SAS had become part of the domestic counter-insurgency operations), the evolution of media strategies of state agencies such as the Metropolitan Police and, in particular, the troubled relations between the BBC and the Thatcher government over Northern Ireland. Ten years on, and the basic scenario remains largely unchanged: indeed, if we are to take seriously the arguments of civil-libertarian critics, if anything, the overall conditions for freedom of information generally have deteriorated (cf. Ewing and Gearty, 1990; Hillyard and Percy-Smith, 1988). Unhappily, too, the continued use of the SAS in counter-terrorist operations has continued to fuel controversy, most notoriously in the case of the Gibraltar shootings of 1988, discussed briefly below.

So far as broadcasting and the state are concerned the past decade has been peppered by a sequence of major disputes. These have been thoroughly documented elsewhere, so it will be sufficient to give the barest outlines of some key moments.

Since the rows referred to above (the INLA interview and Carrickmore affair of 1979), the British government's efforts to control the coverage of Northern Ireland have increasingly edged towards overt censorship. In 1985, the *Real Lives* affair (at the root of which was an interview with a senior Sinn Fein figure) involved intense pressure from the Home Secretary on the BBC to ban the programme concerned. This provoked a severe internal crisis at the Corporation, when the Board of Governors banned the programme and overruled the Corporation's top managers. Although the film in question was eventually screened, with changes, the incident badly dented the BBC's legitimacy and marked a new, highly interventive approach by the government (cf. Bolton, 1990: 160–76; Cockerell, 1989: 295–8; Schlesinger, 1987: xviii–xxi).

The other major dispute related to 'terrorism' also had its roots in the continuing crisis in Northern Ireland. It concerned the shooting dead in Gibraltar of three IRA personnel who were planning a bomb attack on British troops stationed there. When killed by the SAS they were unarmed, and the attendant circumstances gave rise to considerable public discussion (cf. Jack, 1989). So far as the British government was concerned (and this was the view subsequently taken by the Gibraltar inquest) the killing was lawful. However, as has been amply documented elsewhere, there were numerous questions to be answered. Thames Television's *This Week* investigated the story in March 1988, and on the basis of eyewitness evidence suggested that the three were shot by the SAS without warning and without making any of the alleged movements towards concealed weapons. The BBC's *Spotlight* programme, broadcast only in Northern Ireland, also raised similar questions. There was a disquieting echo of the unresolved questions concerning the shooting of the Prince's Gate gunmen (cf. Paterson and Schlesinger, 1983: 57–8).

This Week's coverage resulted in a further major row, with hostile interventions by the Prime Minister, Foreign Secretary and Conservative MPs, on this occasion focused on the IBA (then the commercial television regulatory body) and Thames TV. In order to establish its journalistic credentials, Thames TV asked a former Conservative minister Lord Windlesham, to investigate its journalistic probity, which he subsequently broadly vindicated – although without satisfying the government, which dismissed his findings (cf. Bolton, 1990: *passim*: Windlesham and Rampton, 1989: *passim*).

The most overt act of censorship to date, however, was to occur in October 1988, when the Home Secretary used his powers under the Licence and Agreement and the Broadcasting Act to ban the broadcasting of the voices of members of proscribed organizations by, respectively, the BBC and the commercial television and radio companies. Although this ban included both republican and loyalist organizations, it is widely recognized that its main purpose was to strike at Sinn Fein, which despite its connections with the proscribed IRA, is a legal political party (cf. Ewing and Gearty, 1990: 243–50; Miller, 1990). The new directive, which has led to such absurdities as the lip-synchronization of actors' voices with the television images of Sinn Fein representatives, has evidently had a further inhibiting impact on Irish coverage, and a very negative effect on the international standing of British broadcasting, without in any way contributing positively to a resolution of the Northern Ireland conflict.

However, the growth of overt government intervention over Northern Ireland should not be seen in isolation. There have been, successively, well-documented disputes over the BBC's coverage of the Falklands War in 1982, a Conservative campaign against the BBC in the run-up to the general election of 1987 (with a so far lower-level reprise in 1990) and repeated attacks on both press and broadcasting over the handling of official secrecy, such as the Special Branch raids to seize film and documentation from the BBC and *New Statesman* magazine over the making of the *Secret Society* series (cf. Cockerell, 1989; Morrison and Tumber, 1988).

Concerning the overall impact on civil liberties in Britain of these interventions, the academic lawyers K.D. Ewing and C.A. Gearty (1990: 129) have remarked that 'while all British governments this century have been obsessed by questions of secrecy and security, the last ten years have seen this obsession carried to remarkable lengths'. In the wake of a number of celebrated prosecutions for breaches of official secrecy, the most internationally notorious of which was the *Spycatcher* affair, there have been major revisions of security service and official secrecy legislation. These changes are intended to make investigation into the workings of the 'secret state' much more legally hazardous and succeed the widespread use of injunctions against newspaper coverage of the *Spycatcher* allegations of misconduct by the security service. Moreover, in 1989 the Prevention of Terrorism Act, a 'temporary' provision since 1974, assumed a permanency never originally intended. These various lines of development are continuous with those I noted during the Iranian Embassy siege, which continues to offer food for thought today.

References to postscript

Bazalgette, C. and Paterson, R. (1980–1) 'Real Entertainment', *Screen Education*, 37, Winter: 57–67.

Bolton, R. (1990) *Death on the Rock and Other Stories*. London: W.H. Allen.

Cockerell, M. (1989) *Live From Number 10: The Inside Story of Prime Ministers and Television*. London and Boston: Faber.

Ewing, K.D. and Gearty, C.A. (1990) *Freedom under Thatcher: Civil Liberties in Modern Britain*. Oxford: Clarendon Press.

Hartley, J. (1982) *Understanding News*. London: Methuen.

Hillyard, P. and Percy-Smith, J. (1988) *The Coercive State: The Decline of Democracy in Britain*. London: Fontana.

Jack, I. (1989) 'Gibraltar', *Granta*, 25: 13–86.

Knight, G. and Dean, T. (1982) 'Myth and the Structure of News', *Journal of Communication*, Spring: 145–61.

Miller, D. (1990) 'The History behind a Mistake', *British Journalism Review*, 1(2), Winter: 34–43.

Morrison, D. and Tumber, H. (1988) *Journalists at War: The Dynamics of News Reporting during the Falklands Conflict*. London: Sage.

Newsinger, J. (1983) 'The SAS and Popular Fiction', *Race and Class*, xxv, Summer: 81–7.

Paterson, R. and Schlesinger, P. (1983) 'State Heroes for the Eighties', *Screen*, 24, (3), May–June: 55–72.

Schlesinger, P. (1987) 'Ten Years On: An Introductory Essay', in *Putting 'Reality' Together: BBC News*, 2nd edn. London: Methuen. pp. xvi–xxi.

Schlesinger, P., Murdock, G. and Elliott, P. (1983) *Televising 'Terrorism': Political Violence in Popular Culture*. London: Comedia.

Windlesham, Lord and Rampton, R. (1989) *The Windelsham/Rampton Report on 'Death on the Rock'*. London: Faber.

Introduction to Part II

These next chapters may be read as a series of connected reflections on the political discourses of the Cold War, written when it was still very intense. We have only just emerged from that historical phase, and, no doubt, measured appraisals of its cultural consequences will be undertaken in due course. Looking back on these essays now, I am struck by how much they deal with an entire system of thinking, elaborated within a structured 'intellectual field' in Pierre Bourdieu's phrase (cf. Bourdieu, 1990: chs 8, 9). Oppositional or alternative points of view were developed perforce in relation to the dominant interpretations and shaped by unavoidable political imperatives as well as more academic ones.

If the Old Ideological Enemy in the Kremlin has been declared officially dead, and is being rapidly converted into a friend, there is still much work to be done in interpreting the world. Today, with the disintegration of the Soviet bloc, of course, one coherent 'Other' against which 'The West' could be defined has disappeared. However, the demise of the Cold War has bequeathed some quite convenient off-the-shelf ways of organizing our thinking. There are many threats that can be assembled in the pursuit of a comprehensive world-picture, depending upon one's vantage point. At this time of writing, 'Islam' (well supplied with demons such as Colonel Gaddafi, Saddam Hussein and the late Ayatollah Khomeini, and with large migrant communities throughout the West, whose loyalty and assimilability can be questioned) is the hot contender for succession. The debate about 'Orientalist' interpretations of the Muslim world and how these articulate themselves into common sense via the media of communication was put on to the agenda a decade ago by Edward Said (1981), and is likely to become ever more central.

As in Part I, we are concerned here with the ways in which images of the enemies of the national state and its underlying socio-economic system are constructed. We are also talking about the 'enemies of our bloc', of the purveyors of an alien creed and way of life. Chapter 4 provides a direct link with the previous essays, for it considers how domestic political violence and subversion have been interpreted as part of wider Soviet aims to dominate the world. Although it is centrally concerned with British counter-insurgency thinking, this is placed within a much broader international context in which US and French doctrines also figure. The instrumentalist conception of propaganda prevalent in counter-insurgency thought largely informs the official positions discussed in Part I. The role of political violence is also a common thread.

Any consideration of counter-insurgency thinking raises questions about the political role of intellectuals, a theme central to this section. Here, one can hardly avoid confronting the ambiguous position of military intellectuals who often bestraddle the academic institution and the government think-tank. To be noted, too, are the conceptual sleights of hand in which they may engage.

Although I have offered but a provisional sketch, I believe that it is still valid, providing many points of contact with current critical writing on counter-terrorist doctrine. The Australian political scientist Jenny Hocking (1988) has recently noted how, in the course of the 1980s, counter-terrorism in liberal democracies has gone well beyond the limited goal of fighting insurgencies to advocate the passage of exceptional legislation, to legitimize the build-up of internal surveillance of dissent, to blur distinctions between civil policing and military action and to attempt media management. For his part, the philosopher Alexander George (1991, forthcoming) has interrogated the underlying assumptions of what he labels 'the discipline of terrorology'. As I do here, he argues that by turning a blind eye to the involvement of the liberal-democratic West in directly supporting or acquiescing in atrocities when convenient, 'terrorism' is laid at the door of the West's enemies, and seen as antithetical to the practice of the democratic state. He, too, has noted the authoritarian tendencies inherent in 'terrorology' and how this plays into the ceaseless search for internal enemies.

Chapter 4 outlines the institutional organization of the intellectual field of terrorism studies in Britain in the late 1970s. It is clear that many of the key players publishing then remain active today. Despite the persistent lack of research in Britain itself on counter-insurgency doctrine and institutions, such critical work does exist elsewhere (cf. Schmid, 1984). The most comprehensive recent account – which, incidentally, does offer brief complementary analyses of two British institutes, the Institute for the Study of Conflict and the Institute for the Study of Terrorism – is to be found in Edward Herman and Gerry O'Sullivan's 1989 study of the enterprise of terrorism studies. Their overall approach to institutional analysis will undoubtedly stand as a model for future researchers, whatever differences one might have with some of its assumptions, which in my own case relate particularly to the analysis of the media (cf. Schlesinger, 1989b: 295–302; Schlesinger et al., 1983: 163–5).

Herman and O'Sullivan set out to describe and analyse the 'industry' that 'manufactures, refines, and packages for distribution information, analysis, and opinion on a topic called "terrorism"' (1989: 55). This leads them into a detailed investigation of the public sector of government agencies and officials as well as the private sector of think-tanks, research institutes, security firms and 'experts'. Their review deals mainly with the United States but also to a lesser extent with activities in Britain, Canada, South Africa and Israel. It shows convincingly that despite the nominal independence of the private sector, the bulk of its activities actually takes place in the service of the state, and as an integral part of a broadly rightist ideological conception of both domestic and international politics.

The struggle against terrorism and the fight against communism have been linked in Cold War thinking. It is the latter theme that occupies Chapters 5 and 6, which are closely related in conception and were originally written in parallel. The first of these chapters takes a broad canvas and considers how the threat of 'communism' has functioned to organize key aspects of our political culture. The second shows by means of a case study of the coining of a slogan, 'Eurocommunism', just how complicated and dynamic the conflict over political discourse may be. Underlying both is an analytical approach that lends itself to wider application.

'Anti-communism', both as a political project and as an ideological formation, dates back to the October Revolution of 1917. There are lines of continuity from the anti-Bolshevism of those days to the anti-Soviet struggles of just yesterday (cf. Miliband and Liebman, 1984). Looked at from the vantage point of the 1990s, one may discern two distinct stages since these chapters were originally written, in pre-*glasnost* days.

The first stage has been initiated with the onset of *glasnost* itself. The public relations skills of the Gorbachev team and their adoption of Western media management techniques have been noted by many commentators. Observing the growing impact of these new approaches on British television coverage of the Soviet Union in the mid- to late 1980s, Brian McNair (1988) found cause for cautious optimism about the growth of a more 'objective' form of reporting. The nascent reassessment of the Soviet threat he detected was more noticeable in the analytical current affairs field rather than in that of 'hard' news coverage. *Glasnost* has had an impact in facilitating Western newsgathering, thereby allowing a more rounded and complex picture of Soviet society to emerge. In addition, the use of more sophisticated Soviet media strategies to promote foreign affairs initiatives and publicize the activities of the reformers meant that even before the collapse of the Soviet bloc the traditional image of the Communist enemy was becoming less clear-cut for Western publics.

However, the second, decisive stage has come with the end of the Cold War itself. Formally declared terminated in 1990, this has involved an explicit official withdrawal of the label of enmity from the former Soviet bloc, and the rediscovery of a common, ostensibly transcendent 'European' heritage. At this time of writing, we are still in a transitional phase, and remain poised for the major work of redefining both the immediate European and wider global political cartography in terms of friendship and enmity, similarity and difference. Of course, such making of basic distinctions between 'us' and 'them' is meat and drink for any propaganda war, and such lines of division were central to the post-war experience. But, more fundamentally, it is also part of the continuous activity of socio-cultural categorization that all societies must engage in. So the gap left by the demise of communism is likely to be filled, in broadly analogous ways, by other enemies. 'Islam', as I have suggested, is now the principal candidate.

Chapter 5 charts how the interpretation of communism by Western news media and social theory relates to basic modes of differentiation between one type of society and another. The theory of totalitarianism, it is argued, has played a major role in denominating state socialism as the antithesis of capitalist democracies, one might term this the *external* critique of totalitarianism. By contrast, the *internal* critique of totalitarianism in the former East has differed from that in the West, as Jacques Rupnik (1988: 269) has cogently pointed out: the central objective has been to contest 'the supremacy of ideology as the institutionalized lie' and to resist the destruction of memory and the corruption of language. This battle from within has been concerned with keeping alive forms of identity and autonomy repressed by the party-state, and with developing an alternative morality to that of the regime. In the wake of the revolutions in East and Central Europe, the challenge now is to develop durable forms of civil society in the uncertainly emergent democracies of the former Eastern bloc.

My focus here is on the role of the *external* critique of totalitarianism as a form of boundary-maintenance. The analysis proceeds by applying concepts such as difference and similarity and threat and irrationality: taken together as part of a system of interpretation these organize a great deal of the political discourse on communism. The processes of interpretation concerned, moreover, despite taking place in different parts of the system of cultural production – popular media and academic studies – are demonstrably linked.

In Chapter 6, the level of analysis is different. So far as I know, this remains the only study to examine how the term 'Eurocommunism' emerged and evolved in meaning during the course of political debate.[1] Although 'Eurocommunism' has long been interred in the graveyard of the dead slogans society, many other Euro-terms are current today whose logic of development could be analysed along similar lines. The even more contested ground of 'European identity', for instance, presently dominates contemporary discussion and provides the central theme for the chapters in Part III.

The case study of how 'Eurocommunism' was fought over on the ideological plane applies an approach to the competing communicative strategies of politicians and intellectuals that can be applied to other fields of political and cultural conflict (cf., for example, Schlesinger and Lumley, 1985). It offers many insights into how the ideological boundaries of the political system are defended and challenged through political discourse. In the case of 'Eurocommunism', the threat of heterodoxy was faced within each of the blocs, making it especially intriguing because it hit at established – and mutually hostile – political identities, in East and West alike.

Chapter 6 is also highly relevant to the growing debate in media sociology about the concept of 'primary definition' (cf. Curran, 1989 and 1990; Schlesinger, 1989a and 1989b; Schudson, 1989). I have argued elsewhere against the classic formulation of 'primary definition' (cf. Hall et al., 1978) in which it is assumed that official sources' access to the media is largely secured by their places in the social structure, and that their privileged definitional power to dominate the public domain follows accordingly. This view tends to understate the amount of conflict amongst those who principally define the political agenda in 'polyarchic' political systems; it is largely atemporal; it ignores how new forces may reshape definitional space; and, finally, overstates the passivity of the media. I have gone on to suggest that we need to analyse afresh the pursuit of media strategies by news sources. Precisely such strategic action was central in the 'Eurocommunism' debate and is also occurring in contemporary debates about the future of Europe.

The clashes of a decade ago marked a moment of change in Western European politics, although it is easier to recognize that now than it was then. Illusions that a 'Eurocommunist' *terza via* between capitalist democracy and state socialism was about to be born in Western Europe could hardly survive the rapidly fragmenting impact of national politics in France, Italy and Spain. The result was that by the beginning of the 1980s, as party political alliance patterns began to shift, we next began to hear talk of a 'Euro-Left' that might embrace those non-ruling Communists most distant from Moscow (notably the Italians) and social democrats and socialists elsewhere (in particular, in West Germany and France). Armen Antonian (1987: ch. 13) has argued that 'Eurocommunism' should be interpreted as a return to the pre-World War I socialist movement and as an attempt to retrieve the lost Marxist socialist heritage. If anything, the 'Euro-Left' initiative was an even more explicit move to surmount the divisive legacy of the October Revolution.

Today, the national particularism of the Left still seems more impressive than its coherence at a European level – a 'Europe' which has now broadened out to include much of the old East. Nevertheless, although the 'Euro-Left' slogan and its predecessor 'Eurocommunism' have enjoyed limited success both in mobilizing political forces and in articulating the specifics of a new social order, they did prefigure a profound change whose actual moment of realization none could have predicted with any accuracy: namely, the end of the historic split between the Second and the Third Internationals. Ten years on, with the implosion of the Soviet bloc, the basis for any such continued division in Europe has indeed disappeared. But if a Europe-wide democratic socialism is to be created it will have to forge a complex new political identity in conditions of great uncertainty. Some of the attendant complexities are explored later, in Part III.

Notes

1 Moreover, our analysis of the label's patrimony has been independently confirmed by Augusto del Noce (1978: 7–8). Del Noce observes that when he used the term 'Eurocommunism' in an article in *Il Tempo* (15 November 1975) he thought he was coining a neologism. He subsequently discovered that the term had already been used by Frane Barbieri in *Il Giornale Nuovo* (26 June 1975). They differed, however, in their objectives. Del Noce, a philosopher, wanted to coin a concept as part of a philosophical investigation of the Italian Communist Party's strategy. Barbieri, a journalist, simply wanted to designate a rather fluid state of affairs. But, as Chapter 7 shows, intentions do not invariably secure outcomes in a dynamic intellectual field.

References

Antonian, A. (1987) *Towards a Theory of Eurocommunism: The Relationship of Eurocommunism to Eurosocialism*. New York: Greenwood Press.

Bourdieu, P. (1990) *In Other Words: Essays Towards a Reflexive Sociology*. Cambridge: Polity Press.

Curran, J. (1989) 'Culturalist Perspectives of News Organizations: A Reappraisal and a Case Study', in M. Ferguson (ed.), *Public Communication: The New Imperatives. Future Directions for Media Research*. London: Sage. pp. 114–34.

Curran, J. (1990) 'The New Revisionism in Mass Communication Research', *European Journal of Communication*, 5 (2–3), June: 135–64.

George, A. (1991 forthcoming) 'The Discipline of Terrorology', in A. George (ed.), *Western State Terrorism*. Cambridge: Polity Press.

Hall, S., Critcher, C., Jefferson, T., Clarke, J. and Roberts, B. (1978) *Policing the Crisis: Mugging, the State, and Law and Order*. London: Macmillan.

Herman, E. and O'Sullivan G. (1989) *The 'Terrorism' Industry: The Experts and Institutions That Shape our View of Terror*. New York: Pantheon.

Hocking, J. (1988) 'Counterterrorism as Counterinsurgency: The British Experience', *Social Justice*, 15 (1), Spring: 83–97.

del Noce, A. (1978) *Futuro Prossimo? Ipotesi, Giudizi, Discussioni sull'Eurocommunismo*. Bologna: Capelli Editore.

McNair, B. (1988) *Images of the Enemy: Reporting the New Cold War*. London: Routledge.

Miliband, R. and Liebman, M. (1984) 'Reflections on Anti-Communism', in R. Miliband, J. Saville and M. Liebman (eds), *Socialist Register 1984: The Uses of Anti-Communism*. London: Merlin Press. pp. 1–22.

Rupnik, J. (1988) 'Totalitarianism Revisited', in J. Keane (ed.), *Civil Society and the State: New European Perspectives*. London: Verso. pp. 263–89.

Said, E. (1981) *Covering Islam: How the Media and the Experts Determine How We See the Rest of the World*. London: Routledge & Kegan Paul.

Schlesinger, P. (1989a) 'Rethinking the Sociology of Journalism: Source Strategies and the Limits of Media Centrism', in M. Ferguson (ed.), *Public Communication*. London: Sage. pp. 61–83.

Schlesinger, P. (1989b) 'From Production to Propaganda?' *Media, Culture and Society*, 11 (3), July: 283–306.

Schlesinger, P. and Lumley, B. (1985) 'Two Debates on Political Violence and the Mass Media: The Organization of Intellectual Fields in Britain and Italy', in T.A. van Dijk (ed.), *Discourse and Communication: New Approaches to the Analysis of Mass Media Discourse and Communication*. Berlin and New York: De Gruyter. pp. 324–49.

Schlesinger, P., Murdock, G. and Elliott, P. (1983) *Televising 'Terrorism': Political Violence in Popular Culture*. London: Comedia.

Schmid, A. (1984) *Political Terrorism: A Research Guide to Concepts, Theories, Data Bases and Literature*. Amsterdam: North-Holland; New Brunswick, NJ: Transaction Books.

Schudson, M (1989) 'The Sociology of News Production', *Media, Culture and Society*, (3), July: 263–82.

4

On the Shape and Scope of Counter-Insurgency Thought

'Counter-insurgency' thinkers in the West are among the hired prize-fighters of the bourgeois state, to take liberties with a well-known remark. Their business: the prevention of revolution. Their vision of the world is Manichaean: here the Free World; there Communist Totalitarianism. The nets of the counter-insurgent are cast wide indeed. For where there is subversion, insurgency is likely to follow hard upon it. And from little insurgencies do revolutions grow.

Counter-insurgency thinkers may be regarded as intellectuals working within or for the repressive apparatus of the state. Their function is to produce ideas of a strategic and tactical kind for the use of that apparatus in winning counter-revolutionary wars. Such ideas, translated into repressive techniques, are meant to be serviceable in assisting the security of the established order. However, it is not only the practical implications of counter-insurgency thought which are of sociological interest. Such thinking is also a significant form of ideology. A key feature of any counter-insurgency campaign is propaganda and 'psychological operations'. As the Americans put it in Vietnam: WHAM . . . Win Hearts and Minds.

This chapter sets out to analyse the ideological features of some contemporary British counter-insurgency writing. Given the recent growth of sociological interest in the state it is quite astonishing that this area of research should have been almost entirely neglected by sociologists in this country. Outside academic sociology itself, however, there has clearly been growing interest, particularly in Britain. Counter-insurgency and the related issue of 'political terrorism' have been discussed by historians (for example, Iviansky, 1977; Laqueur, 1977a and b) and political scientists (for example, Wilkinson, 1974). The most insightful recent work has been produced by Marxist investigative journalists (Ackroyd et al., 1977; Bunyan, 1977a). In the USA, sociological interest in this field is a long-established one, and some substantial work has been produced there which greatly enhances our understanding of the integral role played by counter-insurgency in the American imperium and in the domestic class structure (Copans, 1975; CRCJ, 1975; Leggett, 1973).

Counter-insurgency is no innocent or neutral technical concept. Rather it carries its own ideological baggage with it. Such an approach to the world is a central element in the *Weltanschauung* of what Barnet has labelled the 'national-security managers', who, from their 'vantage-point in the national-security bureaucracy' of the USA see 'revolution in the under-developed world as a problem in the management of violence' (1972: 35). Consequently, as Eqbal Ahmad has observed, counter-insurgency as a practice

> involves a multi-faceted assault against organized revolutions. This euphemism is neither a product of accident nor of ignorance. It serves to conceal the reality of a foreign policy dedicated to combating revolutions abroad and helps to relegate revolutionaries to the status of outlaws. The reduction of a revolution to mere insurgency also constitutes an *a priori* denial of its legitimacy. In this article counter-insurgency and counter-revolution are, therefore, used interchangeably. (Ahmad, 1973: 325)

I follow Ahmad's usage here. A consideration of counter-insurgency thinking goes well beyond the area of foreign policy. It is currently highly relevant for an analysis of the *domestic* exercise of state power in numerous Western European states faced with 'terrorism' (Britain's Irish problem being just a case in point) and has been of notable importance in internal policing in the USA since the eruption of the 'new politics' of the 1960s.

Counter-insurgency, social science and imperialism

Counter-insurgency thought is a fairly modern invention. Of course, there is a sense in which it could be seen as being as old as the need for repression itself. But in the sense in which it is considered here it is very much the product of Western colonial and imperial expansion and the consequent relations of dominance imposed on the Third World. It is of some interest to note that the term 'pacification' was coined in the late eighteenth century by the British, who then had some little local difficulties in India (Fairbairn, 1974: 46). The earliest codified counter-insurgency principles were later evolved – also in India – during the nineteenth century when a succession of 'small wars' broke out. The kind of knowledge developed by the army was 'political as well as military since the British were concerned to view pacification as a means of permanently consolidating power' (Fairbairn, 1974: 52). A further opportunity to develop counter-insurgency techniques came during the Boer War, when much was learned about concentration camps and cordoning systems. In the case of the USA, 'pacification' of the indigenous Amerindians was a necessary concomitant of internal colonization. And in Britain the problems resulting from a similar approach to its 'oldest colony', Ireland, are still with us.

Interestingly, recent critical historical reappraisals of the rise of anthropology have illuminated, *inter alia*, moments in the history of counter-insurgency thinking.

Setting the scene, Talal Asad (1973: 16) has observed that anthropology is

> rooted in an unequal power encounter between the West and the Third World which goes back to the emergence of bourgeois Europe, an encounter in which

colonialism is merely one historical moment. It is this encounter that gives the West access to cultural and historical information about the societies it has progressively dominated.

It would be thoroughly mistaken to see the production of anthropological knowledge as simply constructed for the use of colonialist domination. The picture is complex and contradictory and merits the exhaustive discussion it has received elsewhere. However, by and large, anthropologists 'did not treat the colonial situation in a scholarly fashion. Few studied settlers and administrators, for example, and this robbed their work of a vital dimension of reality' (Kuper, 1975: 147). Until the nationalist revolutions after World War II, it was possible for anthropologists to assume uncritically the legitimacy and stability of the imperialist social order which underpinned their object of study.

The thoughts of early counter-insurgents differed inasmuch as they *were* self-consciously designed to uphold the conquests of imperialism. What they did share with anthropologists of pre-war vintage was a set of assumptions about the legitimacy of the imperialist order. It is no historical accident, therefore, that *some* anthropologists came to perform a dual role, quite expressly using their skills to gain intelligence for the war efforts of metropolitan powers. Naturally, such actions raise ethical problems. Of central importance is the duplicity involved in gaining access to, and information about, a people ostensibly for the 'science of man' – while in actuality binding it to the uses of a power faced with an insurgency. It is of interest to consider one or two such instances, before confronting more contemporary material. *Plus ça change* . . .

W.F. Wertheim (1974) tells of the Islamist and anthropologist C. Snouk Hurgronje's activities on behalf of the Dutch colonial administration in Indonesia. The Dutch were faced with an insurrectionary war in Atchin in the 1890s. Hurgronje used his access to the Atchinese to discover the leaders of the revolt and to recommend repressive tactics to the authorities.

A more familiar example, perhaps, comes from British colonial history and concerns the part played by various social scientists aiding the Kenyan administration to deal with the Mau Mau insurrection. Work conducted included research by the eminent prehistorian Louis Leakey into the Mau Mau oath of allegiance in order to devise ways, in accordance with traditional Kikuyu ritual, to break the hold of the oath. Leakey's express goal was to defeat the Mau Mau. Later on, several researchers from the East African Institute for Social Research were hired to investigate ways of changing the system of land tenure. The political goal was to create a stable middle peasantry unwilling to support the Mau Mau because it had something to lose (Buijtenhuijs, 1975).

Such enterprises are truly small beer by comparison with the research currently engaged in by social scientists working in US counter-insurgency programmes. The classic, most infamous, instance is Project Camelot. The project was devised by the US Defense Department's Special Operations

Research Office (SORO), and 'fronted' through the American University of Washington. The pretensions of the project were grand indeed – a complete science of counter-revolution for the use of the American military. 'Document No. 1' made the purposes plain enough:

> Project Camelot is a study whose objective is to determine the feasibility of developing a general systems model which would make it possible to predict and influence politically significant aspects of social change in the developing world. Somewhat more specifically, its objectives are: *First* to devise procedures for assessing the potential for internal war within national societies; *second* to identify, with increased degrees of confidence, those actions which a government might take to relieve conditions which are assessed as giving rise to a potential for internal war; and *finally*, to assess the feasibility of prescribing the characteristics of a system for obtaining and using the essential information for doing the two above things. (cited in Horowitz, 1974: 47–8)

At one and a half million dollars a year, for three to four years, success would have been cheap at the price. Leaving aside for the moment the questionable methodological assumptions, and the validity of Camelot's theory of counter-revolution, we might note that the revelations about the proposals sparked off an ethical debate concerning the rights and wrongs of 'strategic social science'.

The abandonment of Camelot did not end the story. It was, after all, a project designed to garner sociological knowledge for the purposes of state intelligence which was actuated by the success of the Cuban revolution. Since the problem of 'red subversion' in Latin America continues to exist, so does counter-insurgency research. Camelot was followed by the setting up of think-tanks, this time funded 'privately' under the auspices of CRESS (the Center for Research in Social Systems). Many projects are currently being funded by the US military-industrial complex, taking in such diverse themes as population control, the psychological mechanisms of allegiance to guerrilla groups, research into attitude changes, and the creation and fostering of élites sympathetic to capitalist forms of ownership. In addition, there have been attempts to 'recover' the lessons of British and French operations (notably in Malaya and Algeria) with a view to applying them in the future.

Such thinking is not restricted to colonial and imperialist domination alone. It is of just as much significance in ensuring the maintainance of those domestic class structures which provide the social basis for imperialism itself. Indeed, as Leggett (1973: 322) has pointed out, there is an inescapable 'interlock' between domestic power relations in the USA and the uses of counter-insurgency both at home and abroad.

The Cold War and counter-insurgency

In the contemporary world, all insurgencies, according to most Western military thinkers, are ultimately tied up with 'world communism' in one or other of its hydra-headed manifestations. The logic of present counter-insurgency thought is shaped by the history and development of the Cold War; and whether it is crude or sophisticated, it faces the limits posed by a Cold War perspective.[1] This proposition may be concretely illustrated by reference to the most celebrated post-war French doctrine, and also to contemporary British thinking.

La guerre révolutionnaire

The French doctrine of *la guerre révolutionnaire* was forged from the experience of revolutionary war in Indo-China and applied in the context of the national liberation struggle in Algeria. The group of French military officers who constituted the doctrine's theorists had different tendencies in their thinking. None the less, the broad outline of their vision may be taken as an ideal type for an examination of the shape and scope of Western Cold War perceptions of revolution. Current British thinking, as we shall see, has much in common with it.

For the French military thinkers of the 1950s revolutionary war in general was seen as part of a 'holy war' being waged on the West:

> Dominated by a resourceful ideology, one powerful enough to suppress and master its internal contradictions, the Communist nations are understood as a single entity which is threatening to storm the ramparts of the West. Traditional measures will in this instance be unavailing. *La guerre révolutionnaire* demands an antithesis that will in many respects resemble rather than differ from it, a *guerre contre-révolutionnaire*. It can only be found in the intensive study and critique of revolutionary tactics, and in the fastidious preparation of proper counter-measures. (Kelly, 1970: 424)

Revolutionary action must therefore be stood on its head. Or perhaps more exactly, a mirror image of its methods must be assembled to combat it. Such action is performed in the context of a set of clearly formulated assumptions about the international world order, and the role of the revolutionary war in it. In his analysis of the *guerre révolutionnaire* theorists, Ambler (1966: 309–10) has comprehensively summarized their assumptions:

> First, since the early 1950s a nuclear stalemate between East and West has rendered nuclear war most unlikely. In fact, the most probable form of war which the West will be forced to fight (indeed which it is already fighting) is subversive, revolutionary war. Second, the universal revolutionary war now in progress is unlike conventional war in that its primary object is not defeat of the enemy but physical and moral conquest of the population. Third, that same revolutionary war is being conducted by international communism, and may be characterized as *permanent* and *universal*. It uses anti-colonial nationalism as a tactic to overwhelm the West by surrounding and weakening it. The battle for Algeria, like that for Indo-China before it, is part of World War III; its outcome may well be decisive in the struggle between communism and Western civilization. Fourth, in order to defend itself, the West must do the following: it must adapt to its own purposes some of the techniques of the enemy, especially in regard to propaganda, indoctrination and organization; and it must perfect a Western ideology with which and for which to fight.

There are a number of points which need to be added to this before turning to a consideration of present British thinking.

1 'World communism' is presented as a monolithic structure, even though when the *guerre révolutionnaire* school were writing the Sino-Soviet split was in progress or had taken place.

2 National liberation struggles are not seen as generated by factors internal to imperialist domination, but rather as the products of manipulation. A more sophisticated variant of this thesis acknowledges that nationalists are not necessarily *conscious* Communists, or alternatively, that they are not aware of subterranean Communist manipulation.

3 Methods and techniques are a central obsession of the school. The various exponents of the art of counter-insurgency, Col Trinquier, Commandant Hogart and Col Lacheroy, to name but the most prominent, were exceedingly concerned to find a new method of response. A key concept was that of *action psychologique*: the *guerre révolutionnaire* school believed that revolutionary wars were conducted by skilful manipulators of the masses.[2] Thus it was a question of waging an adept propaganda campaign and imbuing the contended-for population with Western ideology. This 'injection' of the right modes of thought was to be supplemented by an extension of military control of the population and the imposition of a repressive apparatus on it to *pre-empt* subversion.

Current British counter-insurgency thought

The British state's 'problem of order'

In counter-insurgency thought it is the 'problem of order' which is addressed, from the standpoint of threatened power-holders. The theoretical assumptions implicit in such an approach have been made quite clear by Harry Eckstein (1964) in his discussion of 'internal war'. By this, he means action *against* the state, demonstrating thereby his conservative orientation. From this point of view, the sociology of revolutionary warfare is essentially the sociology of crises for state power. Looked at through Eckstein's functionalist spectacles, insurgency is disequilibrating, 'involving serious disruption of settled institutional patterns' (1964: 12). Above all, this orientation concerns itself with the maintenance and reproduction of the existing social order. Such an approach tends to take the legitimacy of the state for granted, and to be interested in the causation of revolutions as an administrative problem, rather than as one of sociological theory. As will be seen, this perspective recurs in the writing examined below.

The recent spate of writing on counter-insurgency and 'terrorism' in Britain is not surprising given the present substantial urban guerrilla war in Northern Ireland, one which has at times threatened the social order on the mainland itself. It would be intriguing, if space permitted, to explore some of the parallels between Franco-Algerian and Anglo-Irish relations. At all events, both have been stimulants to military thinking, and a corpus of British writings akin to those of the *guerre révolutionnaire* theorists is evidently building up.

It is not Ireland alone which has provoked counter-insurgency thought amongst British military intellectuals. The 'new politics' of the 1960s raised questions about the maintenance of 'law and order' on the streets. An enhanced security consciousness has also been brought about by the spate of hijackings and political kidnappings undertaken by various political groups, and the often related development of 'transnational terrorism'. Of central importance in the calculations of counter-insurgents has been Britain's present economic crisis, and the extensive industrial and political conflict this has produced. It is important to relate this form of conflict and its possible containment to the way in which the British state has been dealing with the situation in Northern Ireland.

The British Society for Social Responsibility in Science has documented the growth of repressive technology – for example, water cannon, CS gas, rubber bullets and sensory deprivation techniques – suggesting that 'Ireland's greatest value to the British Army may well prove to be that it provided a laboratory for the development of techniques soon to be needed at home' (BSSRS, 1974: p.1; cf. Ackroyd et al., 1977). It is clear that the British state is making preparations for 'internal defence' and it seems probable that the possibility of a showdown with the trade union movement has acted as a spur to these developments. It should not be forgotten that major strikes in the 1970s have been the occasion for declaring states of emergency. The 1970s have also been a period when plans for an 'alternative' structure of emergency government to that of liberal democracy have been refurbished, and when exceptional legal powers have been granted by Parliament.

These plans are embodied in the army manual *Land Operations Volume III: Counter-Revolutionary Operations*, which details the structure of a crisis 'working triumvirate' of the police, army and the civilian government in the event of a severe threat to national security (Bunyan, 1977b). A number of recent Home Office circulars also detail plans for emergency control, considerable emphasis being placed on information policy. Under this regime official news would be disseminated by a War Time Broadcasting Service (WTBS), run principally by members of the BBC's staff and others from the Central Office of Information (Bunyan, 1977a and 1977b; Kelly, 1976).

It has been suggested that such developments are moves towards a 'strong state'. Thus, for instance, Minnerup (1976) has analysed the emergence of such a state in Western Germany (from whence the term derives) as only in part a response to terrorism. Among the features of this strong state are the extension of police powers, the notorious *Berufsverbot* (or 'extremists decree') prescribing political tests for employment in the state sector, and restrictions of the legal rights of political defendants at trials. The longer-term significance of such changes, Minnerup argues, is that they furnish instruments of repression before they are actually needed.

On this point his analysis converges with that of Bunyan and Ackroyd, et al., who see the development of the strong state as to a large extent an anticipation of sharpening industrial and political strife as the West's economic crisis continues. With such a machinery of repression to hand, industrial militancy could as a last resort be dealt with by techniques employed in the repression of terrorism. Naturally, this analysis is conjectural. It does, however, seem to make sense of many piecemeal developments.

Some British counter-insurgents

This section indicates in a very preliminary way some of the sources of military intellectual production in contemporary Britain (cf. Ackroyd et al., 1977: ch. 11, for further details). A full picture of the institutional substructure of British counter-insurgency thinking would require a chapter in its own right; relatively little is still known about its funding, personnel, the relationships between the various institutions concerned, links between counter-insurgents and various sectors of the state, and the uses of the media of communication.[3]

Any reader of literature in this field is bound to be struck by the number of items produced under the auspices of the Institute for the Study of Conflict (ISC). This body gained a certain notoriety in late 1976 due to revelations in the *Guardian* (20 and 21 December) of apparent links between the ISC's director, Brian Crozier, and CIA personnel. According to Peter Chippindale and Martin Walker, authors of the reports, Mr Crozier's news service, Forum World Features (FWF), was funded by the CIA via an intermediary 'front' company in the USA. The ISC was an outgrowth of FWF. When FWF ceased to exist in 1974 it was replaced by another company, Rossiter Publications, which continued to receive funds from the same source. Mr Crozier denied these allegations (*Guardian*, 31 December 1976). Mr Crozier is author of numerous pamphlets on counter-insurgency, the editor of a book entitled *We Will Bury You: Studies on Left-Wing Subversion Today*, and the author of several books, notably his *A Theory of Conflict*, which is discussed below.

A close associate of Mr Crozier is Robert Moss, who edits the *Economist*'s confidential subscribers-only 'Foreign Report', and who writes for that newspaper on guerrilla wars. He was, for a time, the *Economist*'s correspondent in Chile during the Allende period, and made a name for himself as a devout opponent of Popular Unity's attempt to achieve a transition to socialism. His book *Chile's Marxist Experiment* was, according to the *Guardian*, published in a series indirectly funded by the CIA, the 'World Realities' series. Mr Moss is a member of the council of the Institute for the Study of Conflict, and together with Mr Crozier a member of the (far-Right) National Association for Freedom (NAFF). Mr Moss worked for Forum World Features and has written pamphlets for both the ISC and the International Institute for Strategic Studies (IISS).

Another NAFF activist is Sir Robert Thompson, who also wrote a book for FWF. He is perhaps the best-known internationally of the British counter-insurgency writers, and is noted for his role as an advisor to the American war effort in Vietnam. Sir Robert is the author of *Defeating Communist Insurgency*. His general approach seems to have been influential on current thinking, but he appears to have little to say about contemporary Britain.

A further prominent figure is Major-General Richard Clutterbuck, who holds a doctorate in social science from London University, and is a lecturer in politics at Exeter University. He is a military intellectual in a university setting, and has written extensively on counter-insurgency. His book *Protest and the Urban Guerrilla* is considered below. Dr Clutterbuck is engaged at present in some research on terrorism and the mass media.[4]

Major-General Frank Kitson is probably the best known of recent counter-insurgency writers, and a figure in the Left's demonology. He too is a military intellectual, but this time one who writes from within the army. His book *Low Intensity Operations*, considered below, caused something of a *frisson* when it came out in 1971. Kitson has been taken most seriously, and with good reason, for he is clearly out to evangelize, believing that considerable change is necessary in military training. Others writing in the field include Anthony Burton, author of *Urban Terrorism*; he has a military and journalistic background, and has written for the IISS. Geoffrey Fairbairn, an historian with a military background, is another writer on counter-insurgency who is a member of the Institute for the Study of Conflict. He has written *Revolutionary Guerrilla Warfare*, which is one of the less crude products of the ISC school. Fairbairn's base is primarily an academic one. So is that of Paul Wilkinson, lecturer in politics at Cardiff University.[5] He has written a book entitled *Political Terrorism* which purports to be a theoretical essay in political science, but which is much more an undeclared counter-insurgency text. A full critique of this is presented later on. Wilkinson also has a connection with the ISC, having written a pamphlet for them entitled *Terrorism vs Liberal Democracy*.

As may be seen, interest in this topic lies very much on the liberal to far Right of the political spectrum. It would seem to be growing. Such a rise in interest is a reflection of the changing political situation in contemporary Britain, some elements of which were sketched out above. Intensive counter-insurgency thought is, at any time, a response within the state, and by those who seek to influence it, to a perceived threat of revolution. Such a perception has evidently grown of late.

The elements of contemporary British counter-insurgency thought

What basically unites recent British writing is the 'scenario' it paints. It might best be characterized as a form of right-wing catastrophism.

The Russians are coming

British counter-insurgency writers take it as axiomatic that ultimately all forms of protest are linked to a usually Soviet (sometimes Chinese) Communist Plot to Subvert the West. Their view reminds one strongly of the one inculcated into Philip Agee when he first joined the CIA: 'The central theory is that communist attempts to set up dictatorships around the world are really manifestations of Soviet expansion which in turn is determined by the need to maintain CPSU power at home' (1975: 34–5). Within such a general framework recent developments in Western politics are interpreted as shifts towards Soviet-style regimes. Thus Robert Moss in *The Collapse of Democracy* instances events in Portugal and Chile as ultimately linked to Soviet plans for world domination. Moss concurs with Brian Crozier that, with the growth of Eurocommunism, 'the battlefields are located in our territory' (Moss, 1975: 19). Crozier depicts Eurocommunism as a 'more sophisticated approach to the problems of revolution' and the 'outcome of deep reflection in Moscow upon the extraordinary events of 1968'; as such it is part of the process of ripening the West for take-over (1974: 114–15). This perspective is closely akin to that of Sir Robert Thompson, whose expertise lies in South-East Asia. Thompson states: 'Just as within a country a communist insurgency cannot be dealt with in isolation, so, in a world wide context, it is not an isolated event, but an integral part of the continuing communist underground aggression by means of subversion and terror' (Thompson, 1972: 156). Kitson (1971: 19) perceives wars of national liberation as forms of subversion advancing the interests of the USSR, Cuba and China, and popular fronts as simply camouflage for the local CP.

   Political change in the West, therefore, is seen as an extension of the Cold War. In *that* zero-sum game the West is portrayed as the likely loser. There are two positions in the 'world revolution/Communist take-over' thesis, which are closely akin to those taken by theorists of the *guerre révolutionnaire* school. The crude version holds that the Russians/Chinese/ Cubans are simply manipulators of unwary dupes. The other, more sophisticated variant is that while there may be genuine nationalist insurgencies, these are always prone to perversion by the local branch of the Kremlin (Clutterbuck, 1973: 146).

   Thompson inclines to the crude school and provides us with a typology of those involved in insurgencies. There is no genuine basis for revolutionary war, he argues, as is clear from the social composition of the insurgent movement. The 'naturals' (Communists deep down) swell their ranks by drawing in the 'converted', and things really get off the ground when the 'deceived' (the congenitally simple) provide a mass following (1972: 35–6). Kitson operates with a similar motivational model, considering that the 'hard core' mobilize the 'politically conscious idealists' for protest; and when confrontations with security forces occur, the 'hard core' capitalize to establish mass sympathy (1971: 84–5). Conspiracy theories run through all of the writings considered here.

Subversion in Britain today

As we know, the price of liberty is eternal vigilance. An axiom which frequently crops up in counter-insurgency writing is that the best insurgency is no insurgency at all. And the way to achieve this desirable state of affairs is to nip subversion in the bud. The counter-insurgents do not thereby put themselves out of business. Far from it. Once you decide to look out for subversion you have a permanent meal-ticket. It requires a formidable bureaucracy to scan the passing scene for signs of rot. There are always subversives. (One should perhaps look to the Grand Inquisitor or to the Jew-Detector in Max Frisch's *Andorra* for the appropriate models.) Signs of subversion may be found in many contexts. Consider the definition advanced by Kitson of subversion as 'all measures short of the use of armed force taken by one section of a country to overthrow those governing the country at the time, or to force them to do things which they do not want to do' (1971: 3). Such 'non-violent subversion' includes activities such as political and economic pressure, strikes, protest marches, propaganda, small-scale violence. With the exception of 'small-scale violence', these activities look like the exercise of rights supposedly guaranteed the citizens of liberal democracies. Such a list provides a chilling insight into the counter-insurgent's view of liberal democracy. The very functioning of 'normal' political life is seen as subversive. That the above pursuits, lawful in the terms prescribed by liberal-democratic legality, should be singled out underlines an essential point: that civil and political rights are at the centre of the terrain in which social conflicts take place, and that they are not static 'achievements', but rather the objects of continual struggle. In the counter-insurgent's scenario legitimate and legal dissent is recategorized as subversion. Hence, no political activity can be above suspicion, for there are always mind-benders waiting to pounce.

Students and academics

In Clutterbuck's vision the cause of 'protest' is to be laid at the door of a militant minority able to dupe the rest. He gives a 'statistical' breakdown of the student population, which contains: 1–3 per cent 'activists'; 10–30 per cent 'protesters'; 60–80 per cent 'mainstream'; 10–20 per cent 'hearties'; less than 1 per cent 'fascists' (1973: 189). His book is almost entirely silent about the organized Right. At all events he does not give a detailed run-down on such organizations as the National Front and nascent British vigilantism. Rather he concentrates on the affiliations of Left radicals, providing potted material on the CP, SLL, IWC, Solidarity, IS, IMG,

CPGB (ML) and suspect journals such as *New Left Review*. Even Amnesty International and the *Sunday Times* are taken to task for their unhelpful attitude to the Army in Northern Ireland. This is really an exercise in political rhetoric, which identifies all forms of left-wing thought and action (excepting the Labour Party moderates) as especially worthy of suspicion. 'Protest' and the 'urban guerrilla' are linked in terms of guilt by association and not theoretically.

Crozier too sees the Left as the prime threat to social stability, arguing that the 'ideological extreme Right' are 'few and relatively unimportant' (1974: 107). It is important to be alert to the formation of clandestine revolutionary groups: 'The universities are breeding grounds for such movements. If students or faculty members become elusive or secretive in their movements or travel round to excess to other universities, it may well be they are engaged in incipient revolutionary activities' (1974: 144).

Strikes

There is impressive unanimity concerning industrial action and its dangers. Consider Kitson's much quoted scenario for the later 1970s:

> If a genuine and serious grievance arose, such as might result from a significant drop in the standard of living, all those who now dissipate their protest over a wide variety of causes might concentrate their efforts and produce a situation which was beyond the capacity of the police to handle. Should this happen the army would be required to restore the position rapidly. (1971: 27–8)

Robert Moss is somewhat more direct in his approach, observing that

> Britain need not be governed in fear of strikes with adequate preparations – accumulation of stocks of coal and oil, organization of private road transport, contingency planning for the use of resources and civilian volunteers – and with an intelligent political education campaign, a determined government can survive even a general strike. (1975: 117)

Mr Moss has learned the lessons of Chile, about which he has written so extensively. For Dr Clutterbuck strikes are one of his 'two particular flashpoints' (student activity being the other). It is important, he argues, for the 'strike weapon' not to be 'misused for other than industrial purposes'. He concedes the possibility of a 'right-wing backlash' resulting in a worrying spate of strike-breaking. One favoured solution is the labour legislation of the 1960s and 1970s (1973: 250–6).

The media and psychological warfare

Whether a particular exercise of force is legitimate or not is a central theme in any discussion of counter-insurgency. Van Doorn has noted how modern armies engaged in counter-revolution – and by extension those supporting them ideologically – 'fall back on the legal form of legitimacy by denying the legality of their opponents and emphasizing the need to maintain law and order. Referring to their opponents as "subversive elements", "terrorists", "extremists", and "bandits" is part of this general trend' (1975: 103). Such characterizations will be more than familiar to those who have followed the evolution of the current conflict in Northern Ireland. It is more important to recognize that such concepts are ideological constructs. In everyday and mass-media discourses they tend to be handled without a critical awareness of the ways in which they pre-manufacture a version of reality favouring those in power. Harries-Jenkins has argued that in a liberal-democratic regime the use of armed force in the maintenance of law and order provokes a crisis of legitimacy for the military and the state more generally (1976: 48–51). This means that the management of information and the organization of propaganda become crucial weapons in the struggle to justify military intervention and to gain public support. It is not surprising, therefore, that all counter-insurgency theorists have something to say, if only in passing, about the role of the media, and it is generally to their detriment. Burton (1975: 9), for instance, notes their importance and considers that to publicize 'urban terrorism' is to risk an imitation effect. In fact, most of the writers considered seem to be paid-up subscribers to the long-discredited stimulus–response theory of media 'effects': namely, that the content of a communication is injected into a passive recipient who has no choice about how to interpret what he or she is told.

Given such a view, they are understandably worried when 'the television coverage of revolutionary wars – that of situations such as Vietnam and Ulster – is invariably one-sided and detrimental to the official side in the conflict' (Crozier, 1974: 30). For Crozier, it is clear that subversive elements are at work when themes are presented in the media which bring 'a regime into disrepute, causing a loss of confidence on the part of the ruling establishment, institutions, and government' and provoking a 'breakdown of law and order' (Crozier, 1974: 202). Kitson is on the same ground when he argues the need for 'the machinery for exploiting success in the minds of the people' (1971: 78). Fairbairn takes a more sophisticated line, arguing that fellow-travelling has taken something of a hold in the West, and that there are lots of gullible people around who fit in with the objectives of 'totalitarian psychological warfare' and fall for such misleading concepts as 'national liberation front' without realizing that such notions mask the ambitions of power-hungry élites (1974: 286, 290).

With this background it is easy to understand current anxieties in the British state about the effectiveness of the security forces' propaganda war in Northern Ireland. While counter-insurgency theorists seem generally to argue that uncensored media work against the interests of the state, recent research in Britain would tend to deny this view. It has been shown, for example, that the British Army has had a positive portrayal in the media and that the state has been successful in systematically discrediting the Provisional IRA (Elliott, 1976). It has also been argued that, contrary to the myths, the British state has exercised considerable and generally successful indirect control over the BBC (Schlesinger, 1978). Chibnall (1977) has shown how in the past decade a number of themes have converged in British media coverage of 'law and order', particularly through a gradual conflation of the labels of 'criminal violence' and 'political violence'. These two media categories have in turn been subsumed under the broader media concept of 'the violent society'. Thus bank robberies, vandalism, anarchist and IRA bombings, and industrial conflict have all eventually come to be presented in terms of the same catch-all category of 'violence'. Given counter-insurgents' perception of industrial militancy as a threat to the established order, the depiction of strikes, picketing, and so forth, as forms of violence not fully distinct from, say, 'terrorism' or 'mugging' has important ideological consequences. In particular it tends to delegitimize trade union activity and its goals.

Given Crozier's significant role in this field, it is worth concluding this section by considering his advice on getting the right views across:

> All governments should have a department, or even several departments, specifically charged with authoritative but unattributable information. It should be the function of such departments to correct misleading or subversive allegations – not by distorting the truth, but by giving trusted journalists access to supporting evidence, under seal of confidence, and to trust them to write their own stories unaided. It is not a question of censoring the news, but of making sure that one-sided versions of events that serve no other purposes than those of totalist groups and their foreign supporters do not go unanswered. (1974: 206–7)

This type of policy bears precious little relationship to the classical liberal ideology of the freedom of the press. Its cynical approach to news management is in utter contradiction to Crozier's profession of concern for safeguarding democracy. It implies an incorporation of the media into the information policy of the state which preserves democratic forms but converts their substance – hardly a strong position from which to attack 'totalists'. That is not to say that we should have any illusions about present-day news management practices in Britain. Indeed, police and military sources currently make use of the techniques Crozier describes, and have done so historically, as for example during the 1919–21 IRA campaign (Chibnall, 1977: ch. 6). It is perhaps no accident that Crozier's approach bears such a striking resemblance to the 'grey propaganda' line of the CIA according to which information 'is ostensibly attributed to people or organizations who do not acknowledge the US government as the source of their material and who produce the material as if it were their own' (Agee, 1975: 70).

Responses to subversion and insurgency

Counter-insurgency thinkers conventionally divide insurgencies into a number of phases. Subversion unchecked develops into isolated acts of terrorism. Terrorism becomes guerrilla war. And finally, guerrilla war becomes full-scale conventional war. At each stage the legitimacy of the incumbent government is under assault. Space does not permit a full discussion of this issue or of the 'graduated responses' the state is advised to make. However, it is possible to give some brief indications of the conventional wisdom to be found.

All the experts agree that if you can nip subversion in the bud then you will have no problems later. In order to do this an effective intelligence system is needed. Moss calls for 'a permament anti-terrorist force' and 'centralized coordination of anti-terrorist planning' (1975: 235). He is echoed by Crozier, who calls for 'Departments of Unconventional War' bringing together experts from security, special branch, intelligence, psychological warfare, interrogation, special operations, bomb disposal, trained anti-guerrilla troops and also linguists and anthropologists (1974: 207). Kitson, who must be understood as an evangelist, calls for a profound change in army thinking, and the creation of a 'community of experts'. The underlying assumption present in current work is that the state needs to anticipate threats, as the 1970s will be characterized by 'civil disorder accompanied by sabotage and terrorism, especially in urban areas': in such a situation the 'tactical handling of information by operational comman-ders' is of the foremost importance (Kitson, 1971: 199). Such views express a particular view of military professionalism which tends to contradict liberal-democratic ideology. The creation of specialist cadres for improved social control is directly connected with the vision of a complete alternative structure of government outlined in the army *Land Operations* manual and the Home Office circulars.

There is wide agreement that the onset of an insurgency – the use of armed force by a section of the people against the government' (Kitson, 1971: 3) – very likely entails the suspension or modification of normal legal practices. However, such changes have to be handled cautiously, as they are tied up with the legitimacy of the incumbents, and this has already been questioned. In the event of martial law being declared in some areas it is important to 'plan for peace, that is to prepare for the handing back to the civilian authority of areas and functions which have temporarily become the concern of the military' (Burton, 1975: 214). Kitson shrewdly argues that it is both 'morally right' and 'expedient' for an impartial legal system to be retained, but this must be married with tough anti-guerrilla legislation (1971: 69). This line echoes Thompson's 'second principle' of counter-insurgency: 'The government must function in accordance with the law'. But the legal system is now on an emergency footing, with simplified laws of evidence and procedure, deportation laws, collective fines, imprisonment for supporting insurgents and detention for suspects (1972: 53–4).

Interestingly, Crozier and Moss part company with the rest by their explicit advocacy of an 'authoritarian solution'. Both argue with commend-able candour that 'an authoritarian solution is preferable to a totalitarian solution' (Moss, 1975: 278). Authoritarianism is identified with Franco's Spain, a regime where 'instead of ramming politics and ideology down people's throats, it confers upon them a benefit not to be despised – the freedom to opt out' (Crozier, 1974: 200). This is much to be preferred to the totalitarianism of Eastern Europe, or seemingly socialism of whatever variety in Western Europe.

When one considers the directly analogous ideology of the *guerre révolutionnaire* school, it becomes clear that, ultimately, liberal democracy must go by the board. This is *implicit* in Kitson's writing (as a serving officer he is presumably not permitted public heresies) where he argues the need for 'counter-organization' – 'a method by which the government can build up its control of the population and frustrate the enemy's attempts at doing so' (1971: 79). He has persisted in this view in a subsequent book (Kitson: 1977: chs 23, 24).

Revolution has no objective social basis

This theme is an important one, and the questions it raises concerning the causation of revolutions go well beyond the scope of this chapter. The position taken by British counter-insurgency thinkers is implicit in what has so far been said. Their heavy reliance on manipulative/conspiracy theory for explaining the origins of an insurgency makes small groups of politically motivated men the key *explanans*, rather than objective conditions. This view is dominant in the writings reviewed and, as we shall see, particularly open to attack in critiques of counter-insurgency thought. Essentially, the writers examined here stress the intervention of *consciousness* and *ideology* in a very Leninist way. True, there is grinding poverty in the Third World, or an economic crisis in the capitalist West. But it takes some trouble-maker to stir things up. The organizers of subversion *select* their cause in order to develop support (Kitson, 1971: 29; Thompson, 1972: 21). A particularly blunt statement of this view is to be found in Crozier (1974: 14):

> the social environment in itself is not the cause of the rebellion, even if it is its essential background. A rebellion begins when somebody feels strongly enough about it to do something: in other words to rebel. What goes on in the mind of the potential rebel leader is more important than what surrounds him.

Fairbairn, in similar vein, has repudiated 'the spurious argument that revolutionary wars erupt spontaneously out of conditions grown socially and economically intolerable': this view is simply a 'propaganda weapon in the hands of sympathizers with revolutionary warfare' (1974: 71–2). This view is also (not surprisingly) to be found among American counter-insurgents, such as Eckstein (1970), who argues for the primacy of the *perception* of social conditions, and is concerned to establish that there is no firm correlation between objective factors and 'internal war'. In a nutshell, it seems as though the approach considered here is both voluntaristic and idealist.

From counter-insurgency to political sociology

Most of the work discussed above does not present itself as 'academic'. Certainly, it is dressed up with footnotes and, in some instances, manifests considerable erudition. However, its propagandist and ideological purposes are not likely to be in doubt. Paul Wilkinson's *Political Terrorism* (1974) is in a different category. The book's importance lies less in its intellectual content than in the fact that Wilkinson's academic standing boosts the credence of 'terrorism studies'. The next few pages should therefore be read as a case study in revealing how counter-insurgency doctrine may be presented as political sociology.

A shifting object of study

Wilkinson begins (1974: 11) by arguing that the main concern of his text is with 'political terror: that is to say the coercive intimidation by revolutionary movements, regimes, or individuals for political motives'. In fact Wilkinson ends up looking at something rather different. Towards the end of the book, just before launching into an assault on 'terrorist' threats to liberal democracies, he draws the lines less generously. The study *now* attempts to contribute to 'a theory of revolutionary terrorism' (p. 129). Significantly, the idea of terror produced by regimes has entirely faded from the picture. This is no accident in terms of the logic of the book's development, which ends as a piece of tactical advice to the rulers of the liberal-democratic capitalist state. What remains, then, as an object of study are small groups of politically motivated men *out of power*: the exercise of state power has ceased to be a question.

Defining 'political terrorism'

A linchpin in Wilkinson's definition is the idea that political terror must have an 'indiscriminate nature' (p. 13). In his condemnation of indiscriminate murder he is widely supported – and who could disagree? (cf. Finer, 1976; Rapoport, 1971). Further, he sees all terrorist action as 'implicitly amoral and antinomian' (p. 17). This is rather different. To suggest that there can *never* be a moral basis for, say, selective terror against vicious oppressors is far from incontrovertible. Moreover, not *all* terrorism is, in fact, indiscriminate. Assuming the IRA were 'terrorists' in 1919–20 (rather than the military wing of a popular anti-colonialist movement), they were, in fact, highly selective in their targets, eliminating British agents and intelligence officers, rather than, as in the current campaign, setting off bombs in public places. To cite this instance raises terminological issues, of course. To define someone as a terrorist is to undermine his legitimacy. For this reason, if for no other, 'guerrilla', 'freedom fighter' and 'commando' vie strongly for acceptance in the market-place of labels. Wilkinson does consider this point, and offers a caveat: 'moral and evaluative considerations are integrally involved. The student of terrorism, therefore, has to be on his guard against polemical uses of the term' (p. 21). The student of 'terrorism', it seems to me, has already made up his mind.

Wilkinson's definition cannot escape polemical consequences. He is aligned with the common-sense definition of terrorism current today which presents it essentially as action taken against the state, rather than action taken by the state (Sobel, 1975). Consonant with this is his concern to 'identify what possible prophylactic political, social, or economic measures may be taken to prevent it . . . [and] what effective anti-terrorist actions of a short-term nature should be taken, particularly by constitutional democratic governments which are already subject to terrorist attack' (p. 22). These are the classic concerns of the counter-insurgency thinker. Instead of asking 'Why has this happened?' we are on the displaced territory of 'What can we do about it?'

Wilkinson's typology

Wilkinson claims to have made a typological advance over a book such as E.V. Walter's *Terror and Resistance* (1969), and argues: 'It is necessary to construct a more flexible typology which is not tied to the ruler–ruled dichotomy and which stems from motives other than revolution and repression' (p. 35). Accordingly, he distinguishes the following.

First, 'revolutionary terrorism', where 'many movements and factions have resorted to systematic tactics of terroristic violence with the objective of bringing about political revolution' (p. 36). The prototype here is the Terror during the French Revolution. It is worth noting however, that this period was one of revolutionary action organized by the state (Hobsbawm, 1973). The relevance of this observation will be clear shortly.

The next category (and here Wilkinson claims to innovate) is 'sub-revolutionary terrorism', which is 'employed for political motives *other than* revolution or governmental repression' (p. 38) and is to be found where there are cultures of violence, feuds and assassinations, etc. Wilkinson considers this type of activity to have 'marginal political effects outside highly traditional autocracies' (p. 40). Whether, say sectarian murder in Northern Ireland, which is undoubtedly 'sub-revolutionary', is so marginal in its effects is doubtful.

Just as Walter is only interested in state terror, so is Wilkinson essentially uninterested in his third category: 'repressive terror'. This is defined as 'the systematic use of terroristic acts of violence for the purpose of suppressing, putting down, quelling or restraining certain groups, individuals, or forms of behaviour . . . It may be mainly directed at insurgents or suspected insurgents' (p. 40). That this is not a 'clean' category is obvious. The *revolutionary* Jacobins employed *repressive* terror against their enemies.

Wilkinson ignores the relevance of his last type – repressive terror – for an analysis of the liberal-democratic state. His entire approach is based on the assumption that where the forms of liberal democracy exist, repression necessarily does not. For him repression is identified purely and simply with a military mobilization in defence of the established order – shades of the night-watchman conception of the state. In such instances, says Wilkinson, 'If the government is provoked into introducing emergency powers, suspending habeas corpus, or invoking martial law, it confronts the paradox of suspending democracy to save it' (p. 109). But this seeming paradox melts away if we conceive of the liberal-democratic state somewhat differently. It should be related to the class relations which it acts to maintain and reproduce. Developments within the state towards overt repression are not simply expressions of concern to safeguard a threatened democracy, but also, more fundamentally, action taken in defence of the structure of underlying capitalist relations.

An analysis of the role of overt repression needs, therefore, to be more dynamic and processual. While the repressive apparatus of the liberal-democratic state is most *visible* at moments of crisis, that does not mean it has suddenly sprung into existence. Every liberal state can be seen as in a process of tooling up for repression as it meets successive threats to its monopoly of violence and to its fundamental social relations. It is not therefore the *liberal* state which defends itself through tough measures, thereby, in effect, abolishing itself. Rather, it has become a repressive one. It is also important to note that a counter-insurgency capacity and a 'strong state' do not necessarily simply fade away when an immediate danger has passed. The central problem with Wilkinson's analysis is that it is based on the opposition of two static types. In actuality his repressive type (p. 40) must be placed in a continuum with his constitutional type (p. 109).

Applying an unsound typology

To be more precise I shall focus on one example in his sketchy repertoire. From evidence such as the British Society for Social Responsibility in Science's study *The New Technology of Repression* and John McGuffin's disturbing account of *The Guineapigs* (1974) in detention centres, it is clear that within the British state machine's operations in Northern Ireland what Wilkinson calls 'the systematic use of terroristic acts of violence' has been part and parcel of administrative practice in combating the IRA. In his preface, McGuffin (1974: 9) describes how fourteen 'men were selected as unwilling and unwitting subjects upon whom army psychologists, psychiatrists and "counter-insurgency strategists" could experiment in that particular field known as "SD" – Sensory Deprivation'.

Now, is this evidence – not, incidentally, produced by Wilkinson when he discusses Northern Ireland and the IRA – not exceedingly relevant for a discussion of what he terms a liberal democracy? While the British mainland may make claim to this form of regime, there is little ground for extending this characterization to Northern Ireland, where a state machine has made discrimination against and repression of a large minority into a routine practice (De Paor, 1971; Downing, 1977). By Wilkinson's own criteria, and not mine, any reading of recent history in Northern Ireland should set that statelet into the repressive category; for 'No repressive state appears to be able to dispense with a secret police *apparat* whose members are specially trained in the methods of murder, torture, forced confessions, denunciation, subversion, etc.' (p. 42).

It is often contended that Britain used murder gangs in Ireland in the past, to say nothing of what is asserted today. Wilkinson specifically mentions as repressive 'torturing and intimidating detainees to extract information' (p. 42) – the very subject of McGuffin's book. And yet he continues to classify British rule in Northern Ireland as that of a liberal democracy:

> In so far as IRA violence has been directed against the British government since 1970 in order to force a British withdrawal from Ulster and the destruction of the Unionist regime it must be described as a campaign against a liberal democracy. But it must be admitted that, ever since the establishment of the Unionist regime in Stormont in 1922, the Northern Catholic population has suffered from political, social and economic discrimination. Moreover the Special Powers Acts introduced in Ulster in 1922 gave the government sweeping powers to suppress any unwelcome forms of political opposition. (p. 116)

This is an oddly incoherent set of statements. On the one hand, the IRA must be described as against liberal democracy and, on the other hand, it mounts a campaign against a regime which is described as lacking both social justice and liberality, surely the defining ideas of liberal democracy itself. Wilkinson has failed to analyse the *relationship* between Northern Ireland and the rest of the United Kingdom, which stems from the Government of Ireland Act 1920 and the Ireland Act 1949. It is a double-think to divorce the regime in the Province from that on the mainland. It is surely disingenuous for someone writing in 1974, after a lengthy period of Direct Rule (a phrase, incidentally, straight from the handbooks of colonialism), to attempt to talk of *two* separate political systems. And it is naïve for a political scientist not to observe the causal link between the indiscriminate violence presently, and unjustifiably, being inflicted on innocent civilians in Britain, and the British state's conduct of Irish policy. Wilkinson's handling of this concrete case generally discredits his theoretical approach to the problem of terrorism in liberal democracies.

Sociologist or counter-insurgent?

What Wilkinson's approach to the concept of liberal democracy leaves out is the theoretical possibility of considerable repression within discrete *sectors* of a society governed by such a regime. Where are we to draw the line marking off the liberal from the repressive state? How large does this sector have to be? What are the implications for the legitimacy of liberal-democratic politics? These are the unasked questions. *A theory of 'terrorism' in liberal democracies may, at the same time, in certain circumstances, need also to be a theory of sectoral repression.*

It is at this point that we necessarily enter counter-insurgency territory. Wilkinson here performs a function, and argues in a style, which is indistinguishable from the Thompsons, Clutterbucks and Kitsons. Thus he argues for governments to combine reform with strong security measures as part of a 'two wars strategy' (p. 138). This was a technique employed by Magsaysay in the Philippines, where it enjoyed success (Taber, 1972: 120–3). Governments, argues Wilkinson, must strike a balance between repression and reform, and not be 'too soft with terrorists' (p. 139). Further, Wilkinson advocates special powers acts proscribing the membership of certain organizations and the banning of marches. He shows a political realism shared by Brigadier Thompson in advocating that 'impartial procedures of appeal and judicial review' be linked with special powers legislation. But he seems to be contradicting himself when he says: '*No democratic* government worth the name would deserve continuing public support if it went over to military rule for any length of time' (p. 141, emphasis added).

This extraordinary statement is most revealing. For counter-insurgents the administrative goal of defeating insurgencies overcomes the ostensible end: making democracy safe. Thus, for public consumption, what is important is to maintain democratic *forms*. Wilkinson is in fact working with the concept of a militarized 'democracy', and it is the logic of counter-insurgency thought which leads him there.

Critiques of counter-insurgency

Counter-insurgency thought and practice have been the objects of sporadic criticism on various grounds. In conclusion, let us consider the recurrent questions.

Ethics and politics

Obviously, to engage in counter-insurgency research implies taking an ethical stance. Anti-revolutionaries make the maintenance of order and the demands of the state their first priority. If guerrillas swim like fish in the sea of the people, as Mao puts it, counter-insurgents think up ways of catching the fish. In doing so they necessarily endorse the legitimacy of incumbent regimes (whether in an imperialist context, or in a domestic one), often justifying this on the grounds of averting something worse. Lucian Pye has characterized the role of such a strategic social science in the Third World as one of 'accumulating insights on the art of controlling rebels who would destroy the prospects of democratic development and establish the rule of tyrants' (1964: 179). This is a more attractive sales pitch than arguing for active support for imperialist relations of domination.

It is an open question whether social scientists *ought* to lend themselves to this kind of operation. Project Camelot definitely posed the question of whether to adopt the problems of the state as one's own, and to work within paradigms not of one's own making. Subsequent revelations concerning the role of sociological advice on 'action programmes' in Thailand (Copans, 1975), and the Pentagon Papers' disclosure of social scientists' involvement in the formation of US policy in Vietnam, have only served to underline the fact that ethical choices remain on the agenda. Ethical choices in the area are indissolubly linked to political commitments, and the position which these entail on the desirability of violent social change in particular societies at particular times.

Fallacies of counter-insurgency

Most attention has focused on the question 'Does counter-revolution work?' Obviously, sometimes it does, sometimes not. To ask such a question opens up a Pandora's box of theoretical problems concerning the causation of revolution. Does mounting an effective anti-revolutionary campaign necessarily presuppose an adequate theory of revolution? It seems doubtful. What is in question, though, is the long-term effect of such campaigns. W.F. Wertheim has noted a whole range of measures pursued in the interest of averting revolutions, and distinguishes three major forms of response taken by the state: reform, diversionary propaganda and repression. His conclusion is that 'all known attempts to forestall revolutions are sooner or later abortive' (1974: 293). This is perhaps an article of faith rather than historical fact.

Critics of counter-insurgency have tended to share the position taken by Wertheim. One 'fallacy' which Robert Taber has identified is

> the view that revolution is the (usually deformed) offspring of a process of artificial insemination, and that the guerrilla nucleus (the fertilizing agent so to speak) is made up of outsiders, conspirators, political zombies – in other words, actual or spiritual aliens – who somehow stand separate from their social environment while manipulating it to obscure and sinister ends. (1972: 19)

Undoubtedly, such an approach does characterize those considered in this chapter. Conspiracy theories rarely, if ever, do justice to the complexity of social reality. Of course, it is true that a mechanistic and rather monistic theory of this kind *may* sometimes do the requisite work of explanation and assist the successful exercise of repression. However, counter-insurgency theorists do tend to have a somewhat metaphysical commitment to this line, and it is anyway no doubt good propaganda to maintain it. To talk of alien creeds is to legitimize homespun common sense – which may well be a poor substitute.

Another 'fallacy' identified by Taber is the obsession with 'methods': 'The methods fallacy . . . is . . . the old-fashioned notion that guerrilla warfare is largely a matter of tactics and techniques, to be adopted by almost anyone who may have need of them, in almost any irregular warfare situation' (1972: 20). Without doubt, all the theorists considered here do have a strong commitment to the view that if the right techniques are employed subversion and insurgency can be repressed. If winning hearts and minds doesn't work their owners can in the last resort be subjected to some form of military rule without the dressing of civilian legitimacy. Obsession with methods may produce an awareness of the role of ideology. The *guerre révolutionnaire* school is a case in point: for them the manipulation of consciousness was a centrally important technique. But an obsession with the manufacture of a counter-revolutionary ideology may be self-defeating as it seems likely to exclude full consideration of those objective factors which, counter-insurgents attest, play so minor a role in revolution.

The way ahead

The analysis of counter-insurgency both as practice and as ideology is of particular importance when considering power in the contemporary state. The growth of counter-insurgency is particularly interesting in the case of liberal-democratic regimes because of the contradictory pull between democratic forms and militarized practices, one which eventually creates a fundamental crisis of legitimacy. Hence, developments in the 'internal defence' of Britain and some other Western European states make the study of counter-insurgency of urgent relevance. In particular, attempts to forestall 'Eurocommunist' advances and the response to continued economic crisis may well make the strong state a much more common form of regime.

A theory of 'political terrorism' in liberal democracy is likely to be misleading if it excludes a theory of state power. It must also consider the possibility that sectoral repression exists despite the existence of democratic forms. In fact, we cannot, as counter-insurgents do, simply take the state for granted and ask administrative questions about social control. We must make the state an essential part of the *explanation* of the origins and development of an insurgency. This has been done recently to some extent in the work of Kohl and Litt (1974) on Latin American guerrilla movements. I have sought to show that the dominant way of thinking about insurgencies in liberal democracies is misleading because it ignores awkward questions about the nature of the liberal-democratic state.

Postscript

Counter-insurgency thought is organically related to the interests of power-holders and a species of service research, akin to that in other areas of state policy. In its discourse, 'insurgency', 'terrorism', 'subversion' are the symptoms of a disease. This chapter has been a study of what C. Wright Mills called 'social pathologists', and the intellectual productions of those examined here contain the fairly cohesive domain assumptions of a professional ideology. Nothing stands still. And I hope that readers will not feel misled when I inform them that 'counter-insurgency' ceased to exist some time ago. Kitson notes how the US Army has now

> stopped referring to 'counter' insurgency and 'counter' subversion, and redesignated the business as 'internal defence and development'. That part of 'internal defence and development' provided by the armed forces to maintain, restore, or establish a climate of order is known as 'stability operations', a term designed to emphasize the fact that the purpose of destroying the insurgents is to provide the stability which the country requires so that it can progress and develop. (1971: 52–3)

All those applying for posts in this area of social pathology take note.

Acknowledgements

I am grateful to the following for helpful criticisms of this chapter: Philip Elliott, Robbie Guttmann, Robert Peck, Adam Roberts, Roger MacNally and Nira Yuval-Davis. I should also like to thank those who so constructively commented on the paper at the 1977 BSA conference, and at a subsequent presentation to the CSE Day School on Law and the State in May 1977. Any sins of omission are mine entirely.

Notes

1 The general role of counter-insurgency thought in Western capitalist states needs to be examined in relation to *other* ideological currents. Why should a crass World Communist Conspiracy theory still be so vigorously propagated at a time of so-called *détente*? An explanation might well begin with the ideological division of labour. Ready-to-hand, stylized explanations are serviceable for mass consumption, and culturally supported by a wealth of symbolism delegitimizing the revolutionary Left. Simple theories are also functional in sustaining military morale. But élites need to know better: cf. *Problems of Communism* and *Foreign Affairs* for well-informed views. The question of variants of Cold War ideology is explored in Chapters 5 and 6 below.
2 Cf. Roberts (1977) for evidence of South African attempts to apply this thinking.
3 Fairbairns (1974) has documented some of the links between the armed forces and the higher education sector, focusing on 'defence lectureships' and research funded by the UK Ministry of Defence, the US Department of Defense and NATO at sixty-five universities and colleges in Britain; she has also pointed out the PR role of military education committees.
4 This was subsequently published as *The Media and Political Violence* (London and Basingstoke: Macmillan, 1981, 2nd edn 1983).
5 Cf. Postscript 1990 for more details.

References

Ackroyd, C., Margolis, K., Rosenhead, R. and Shallice, T. (1977) *The Technology of Political Control*. Harmondsworth: Penguin.
Agee, P. (1975) *Inside the Company: CIA Diary*. Harmondsworth: Penguin.
Ahmad, E. (1973) 'The Theory and Fallacies of Counter-Insurgency' in J. Leggett (ed.), *Taking State Power*. New York: Harper & Row.

Ambler, J.S. (1966), *The French Army in Politics*. Columbus: Ohio State University Press.

Asad, T. (ed.) (1973) *Anthropology and the Colonial Encounter*. London: Ithaca Press.

Barnet, R.J. (1972), *Intervention and Revolution*. St Albans: Paladin.

BSSRS (British Society for Social Responsibility in Science) (1974) *The New Technology of Repression: Lessons from Ireland*. BSSRS Paper 2.

Buijtenhuijs, R. (1975) 'Comment vaincre les Mau Mau: quelques observations sur la recherche contre-insurrectionnelle en Kenya pendant l'état d'urgence', in Copans (1975); reprinted from *Sociologische Gids*, Sept–Dec. 1972.

Burton, A. (1975), *Urban Terrorism*. London: Leo Cooper.

Bunyan, T. (1977a) *The History and Practice of the Political Police in Britain*. London: Quartet Books.

Bunyan, T. (1977b) *Time Out*, 363, 4–10 March.

Chibnall, S. (1977) *Law-and-Order News*. London: Tavistock.

Copans, J. (1975) (ed.) *Anthropologie et Impérialisme*. Paris: Maspéro.

CRCJ (Center for Research into Criminal Justice) (1975) *The Iron Fist and the Velvet Glove: An Analysis of the US Police*. Berkeley, Calif.

Crozier, B. (1974) *A Theory of Conflict*. London: Hamish Hamilton.

Clutterbuck, R. (1973) *Protest and the Urban Guerrilla*. London: Cassell.

De Paor, L. (1971) *Divided Ulster*. Harmondsworth: Penguin.

Downing, J. (1977) 'Northern Ireland: Beyond History and Religion', in *Thames Papers in Social Analysis*. Series 1: Northern Ireland. London: Thames Polytechnic.

Eckstein, H. (ed.) (1964) *Internal War: Problems and Approaches*. Glencoe, Ill.: Free Press.

Eckstein, H. (ed.) (1970), 'On the Etiology of Internal War', in G.A. Kelly and C.W. Brown Jnr (eds), *Struggles in the State*. New York: Wiley.

Elliott, P. (1976). *Reporting Ulster*. Centre for Mass Communication Research, Leicester University.

Fairbairn, G. (1974) *Revolutionary Guerrilla Warfare: The Countryside Version*. Harmondsworth: Penguin.

Fairbairns, Z. (1974) *Study War No More*. London: CND.

Finer, S.E. (1976) 'On Terrorism', *New Society*, 22 January.

Harries-Jenkins, G. (1976) 'Legitimacy and the Problem of Order', in G. Harries-Jenkins and J. van Doorn (eds), *The Military and the Problem of Legitimacy*. Beverly Hills, Calif., and London: Sage.

Hobsbawm, E. (1973) *The Age of Revolution*. London: Sphere.

Horowitz, I.L. (ed.) (1974) *The Rise and Fall of Project Camelot*. Cambridge, Mass: MIT Press.

Ivansky, Z. (1977) 'Individual Terror: Concept and Typology', *Journal of Contemporary History*, 12.

Kelly, G.A. (1970) 'The French Doctrine of la Guerre Révolutionnaire', in G.A. Kelly and C.W. Brown Jnr, *Struggles in the State: Sources and Patterns and World Revolution*. New York: Wiley.

Kelly, P. (1976) 'Home Office Prepares for War', *The Leveller*, December.

Kitson, F. (1971) *Low-Intensity Operations*. London: Faber.

Kitson, F. (1977) *Bunch of Five*. London: Faber.

Kohl, J. and Litt, J. (1974) *Urban Guerrilla Warfare in Latin America*. Cambridge, Mass: MIT Press.

Kuper, A. (1975) *Anthropologists and Anthropology*. Harmondsworth: Penguin.

Laqueur, W. (1977a) *Guerrilla: A Historical and Critical Study*. London: Weidenfeld & Nicolson.

Laqueur, W. (1977b) 'Interpretations of Terrorism: Fact, Fiction and Political Science', *Journal of Contemporary History*, 12.

Leggett, J.C. (1973) *Taking State Power*. New York: Harper & Row.

McGuffin, J. (1974) *The Guineapigs*. Harmondsworth: Penguin.

Minnerup, G. (1976) 'West Germany since the War', *New Left Review*, 99.

Moss, R. (1975) *The Collapse of Democracy*. London: Temple Smith.

Pye, L. (1964) 'The Roots of Insurgency and the Commencement of Rebellions', in Eckstein (ed.) (1964).

Rapoport, D.C. (1971) *Assassination and Terrorism*. Toronto: CBC Learning Systems.

Roberts, A. (1977) 'South Africa Resorts to Psywar', *New Society*, 21 April.

Schlesinger, P. (1978) *Putting 'Reality' Together: BBC News*. London: Constable.

Sobel, L.A. (1975) *Political Terrorism*. New York: Facts on File.

Taber, R. (1972) *The War of the Flea*. St Albans: Paladin.

Thompson, Sir R. (1972) *Defeating Communist Insurgency*. London: Chatto & Windus.

Van Doorn, J. (1975) *The Soldier and Social Change*. Beverley Hills, Calif., and London: Sage.

Wertheim, W.F. (1974) *Evolution and Revolution*. Harmondsworth: Penguin.

Wertheim, W.F. (1975) 'La recherche contre-insurrectionnelle à l'aube du XXe siècle', in Copans (1975); reprinted from *Sociologische Gids*, Sept–Dec. 1972.

Wilkinson, P. (1974) *Political Terrorism*. London: Macmillan.

Postscript 1990

If anything, British terrorism studies have institutionalized themselves further, with one significant recent development being the formation of the Research Foundation for the Study of Terrorism in 1989. The chairman of the Foundation's trustees, and director of the Research Institute for the Study of Terrorism and Conflict which it supports, is Professor Paul Wilkinson, now of St Andrew's University, and formerly at Aberdeen, who has become the leading British academic and media commentator, and an important international policy adviser in the field. His early work has been considered at some length above. His more recent writing, which retains the same assumptions, has been criticized elsewhere along very similar lines to my own (cf. George, 1991, forthcoming; Herman and O'Sullivan, 1989: 176–83). Such criticism has but a marginal impact upon the 'terrorological' edifice. But without it important arguments just pass by on the nod, and this has a wider public significance, because terrorism studies expertise is frequently called upon, and seemingly never questioned.

References to postscript

George, A. (1991, forthcoming) 'The Discipline of Terrorology', in A. George (ed.), *Western State-Sponsored Terrorism*. Cambridge: Polity Press.

Herman, E. and O'Sullivan, G. (1989) *The 'Terrorism' Industry: The Experts and Institutions That Shape our View of Terror*. New York: Pantheon.

5

Some Aspects of Communism as a Cultural Category

with Philip Elliott

This is an exploratory essay and not a definitive analysis. It begins with an illustrative discussion of some of the dominant images of communism in Western culture, proceeds to a brief account of the way these images have been grounded in theory and then relates the limited range of interpretations revealed to our current work on ideological production.

Communism provides a critical case through which to investigate the ramifications of this production system. It has served liberal capitalist societies as a polar opposite in terms of which to define themselves. This position has most recently been challenged by the development of 'Eurocommunism'. Communist parties, which claim to be working within the framework of bourgeois legality, to be following their own roads to socialism independent from Soviet models and guidance, to respect and advance the integral rights of the citizens of the liberal democracies, have fudged the clarity of the contrast. In the chapter which follows we have detailed some of the ideological repair work which this has inspired. 'Eurocommunism' has been assimilated into classic Cold War models inspired by the theory of totalitarianism by developing a number of critical tests to show the continuities between the new doctrine and the old. Currently the most important of these tests is the continuance of democratic centralism in the party organizations. Politicians, foreign policy specialists and élite newspapers have all lighted on this as the critical flaw which allows 'Eurocommunism' to be bracketed once again with communism proper.

Our contention is that a survey of ideological interpretations of communism itself helps to reveal what Bourdieu has called the 'master patterns' of our culture:

> Culture is not merely a common code or even a common catalogue of answers to recurring problems; it is a common set of previously assimilated master patterns from which, by an 'art on invention' similar to that involved in the writing of music, an infinite number of individual patterns directly applicable to specific situations are generated. (Bourdieu, 1971: 192)

Much of our account of the treatment of communism will be devoted to cataloguing items in the 'common code'. More often than not the 'art of invention' turns out to be a simple case of repetition. But because communism is clearly outside the boundaries of the legitimate in capitalist society, its treatment reveals much about the way those boundaries are maintained. More particularly the various counterpoints between communism and rationality which are to be found worked out in the theory of totalitarianism and implicit in popular accounts justify our claim that the subject touches on a master pattern of the culture.

In this chapter we argue that an analysis of the ideological mediation of interpretations of communism discloses four major themes. These four themes are closely akin to those which predominate in wartime propaganda against an enemy. First, those identified as *different*, as outside society, are always a potential enemy. The more *threatening* the behaviour of the outsider seems, the more fully is the identification of the (internal) enemy realized. But the continuing presence and support of outsiders has to be accounted for. Within the given society's terms, such support as they may find is *irrational*. However, there are occasions on which the *similarity* of outsiders to ourselves may be stressed as a way of countering the positive claims of enemy ideology.

Taken together, these four themes provide a complete circle of arguments against communism (and enemies more generally). But to talk of 'circles' is to overemphasize the coherence and self-sufficiency of these patterns of meaning. The pressure for intellectual consistency is less than the pressure to keep the ideological armoury well stocked. Thus, though we are dealing with the results of various types of intellectual labour, this labour was not undertaken simply because intellectual problems arose. On the contrary, the intellectual problems arose out of a fundamental political conflict the terms of which provided the motor for intellectual production. The political conflict has also been critical in the allocation of means for the production and distribution of the ideology at all levels so that it can be found extensively disseminated in many different forms while alternative views languish in various cultural ghettos.

Images of communism

In many ways the most important feature of the coverage of communism and Communist countries in the Western media is not what is said but how much is not said.

The idea of *difference* thrives on the lack of any coverage which might contradict it and allows a relatively limited range of stereotypes full play in such coverage as there is. Whole areas of news routinely covered for Western countries are hardly touched in news from Communist countries. The standard explanation for this is that it is impossible to report from such countries because of restrictions placed on Western journalists by authorities who do not accept Western news values. The public heart-searching which has accompanied occasional stories or programmes about 'ordinary life' behind the Iron or Bamboo Curtains, however, suggest that there is more to it than that. Thus, for example, 'China Week' on BBC 2 in 1978 concluded with a discussion programme in which a group of Western commentators on China were specifically concerned to counter any impression given in previous documentaries that ordinary, smiling Chinese were ordinary, smiling people.

Inattention, coupled with bursts of stereotypical coverage, is also to be found in the way communism is treated in Britain.

In the biographical files on British Communist leaders to be found in a BBC press cuttings collection donated to Leicester University Library in 1977, clippings from the Communist newspaper the *Morning Star* predominated by a factor of roughly two to one. The few clippings from the non-Communist press were mostly letters to the editor written by the subject of the file. West European Communist leaders, though rather more important in the context of their own countries' political systems, had not been subject to any more extensive archiving. Only the Italian party secretary warranted his own file, started in 1974. (The BBC stopped filing into the collection at the end of 1975.)

These clippings provide a useful indication both of general press coverage and of what an important media organization thought important to preserve from that coverage for the use of its own journalists and programme makers. It provides a convenient way of tapping the general media culture within which production takes place (Elliott, 1972) and provides one systematically surveyed source of data for the illustrations used in this chapter.

Others are the news magazines *Time* and *Newsweek*, which we have studied for the past three years since 'Eurocommunism' became a topic on the international agenda. They provide a similar entrée to the general media culture at an international level as they are widely used by journalists and broadcasters around the world as a guide to style, presentation and interpretation as well as an information resource. *Time* and *Newsweek* regularly divide their coverage of world affairs into Europe, America and the Rest of the World. Russian stories appear only occasionally in the European section. Apart from accounts of the military threat facing the West, of which more below, stories on Russia, East Europe and other Communist countries deal mainly with three types of differences, in standards of personal and political freedom, in economic well-being and in style of life. As Mrs Thatcher pointed out in her second 'Iron Lady' speech in July 1976, 'their way of life is not our way of life'.

Currently, personal and political freedom takes the form of coverage of President Carter's campaign for human rights. Only the title and level of attention are new, however. Reports of trials and other evidence of dissent have been a continuing pre-occupation of the British press. Trials of dissidents in Russia provide contemporary evidence of lack of freedom as well as continuity with earlier periods of trial and terror in the Soviet Union under Stalin. Now, as before, Communist governments can be seen as demanding and achieving conformity of word and deed from their citizenry in ways which would be unthinkable in the West. Strikingly the predominant visual image of ordinary people in Communist countries is as part of collectivities, marching military or athletic displays or the Chinese variant, singing and chanting at school or work. The presumption that individual lives and emotions are natural, and will flourish come what may, has provided novelists with a recurrent theme to make the point that such systems are not only different but flawed (Ruhle, 1969).

Communism is also flawed as an economic system, hopelessly bureaucratic and inefficient by contrast with the market economies of the West. Rationing, shortages and black markets provide another familiar theme of life in Communist countries. Occasionally used to provide evidence of the militarism of Communist governments in diverting resources away from meeting people's desires, such stories mostly reinforce the view that capitalism is the natural and necessary way to produce goods. If a Communist country does succeed in producing consumer goods it may be because it has cheap production costs or some other unfair economic advantage, but more likely it is because it has reintroduced quasi-capitalist markets and incentives. Quasi-capitalism has most commonly been discovered in marginal Communist countries such as Yugoslavia; but, according to the Western media, recurrent attempts have been made to introduce it in most Eastern bloc countries. These include Russia and most recently Hungary, according to *Time* (13 March 1978). In that issue, improvements in the Hungarian economy were contrasted with an unreconstructed case with a picture of a queue captioned 'Communism in practice: lining up to buy sausages in Poland'. Poland also provided the venue for one of *Time*'s East European economy stories in 1977 which reported that the economy's failure to produce new cars had led to a flourishing car repair and second-hand car dealing trade, based on quasi-capitalist retailing.

Alert to signs of quasi-capitalist techniques in the economic field, Western media have also been reassured to find evidence that Western consumer styles have their attractions no matter what the regime. The contracts won by the Pepsi Cola company to have their product manufactured in Russia probably achieved the most attention in recent years. According to *Time*, however, the latest 'concession to consumer tastes unprecedented for a communist nation' was in Hungary, where Levis were to be manufactured under licence: 'Blue jeans have long been regarded by the Communist regimes of Eastern Europe as a symbol of capitalist decadence and on occasion officially denounced in the media' (*Time*, 12 June 1978). The new move showed the regime bowing to consumer pressure as exerted through high prices on the black market. However, 60 per cent of Hungarian jean production was to be sold back to Levi Strauss, who would benefit from the low-cost production. The lure of consumerism, Western music, entertainment and fashion is a convenient counterpoint to the standard account of life under communism as drab, ordered and regimented.

Another contrast which has come into vogue recently is that between consumerism and puritanism. Incoming communist regimes in such countries as Cuba, Vietnam and Mozambique have come to be regarded as excessively moral, the new puritans of our age. While the immediate contrast with the decadence and corruption of the previous regimes reflected some credit on the new leadership, moral puritanism transfers the ideas of control already established in the political and economic fields. It also develops a long-standing feature of Communist countries in Western eyes, the lack of fun and attractions as shown by the absence of beautiful women, handsome men or more simply of any people who appear to be enjoying themselves.

The notion that people living in Communist states do not spontaneously express joy in public has been a theme played upon at least since the onset of the Cold War. The US novelist Ayn Rand, a noted anti-Communist, gave voice to the 'socialism is sorrowful' thesis when testifying in 1944 to the House UnAmerican Activities Committee. Commenting on a recent American film, *Song of Russia*, she held that it must be pro-Russian propaganda since it showed Russians smiling. Representative John McDowell questioned her about this:

McDowell: Doesn't anybody smile in Russia anymore?
Rand: Well, if you ask me literally, pretty much no.
McDowell: They don't smile?
Rand: Not quite that way no. If they do, it is privately and accidentally. Certainly,
 it is not social. They don't smile in approval of their system.

(Hellman, 1977: 2)

It is worth noting that though the image of unsmiling moral rectitude has become well established, it contrasts sharply with an earlier view of communism as a subversive threat to Western morality. The Russian Revolution, like the French before it, seemed to have implications for the overthrow of the moral as well as the political order. Fear of subversion lives on in the demonology of the Right. In 1970 the Dowager Lady Birdwood warned, on the evidence of a film magazine published by the Italian Communist Party, that the Communists were trying to foment the permissive society and undermine Western morality.

The older view also lives on as nostalgia. The *Sunday Times*, the same newspaper which carried Lady Birdwood's warning, reported a year later on a European conference of Communists held in London. An Irish delegate, Betty Sinclair, was quoted as remembering that when she joined the party in the 1930s 'Mother was terribly worried. In her mind communism was free love and everything. Sometimes I was wishing it was true.' Like their predecessors after 1789, church leaders united with political leaders after 1917 in making much of the threat to established morality. Religious leaders generally remain convinced and often outspoken anti-Communists but they are not given prominence in the vanguard of the popular anti-Communist crusade. This is to be expected, given the persistent and repeated analogy between communism and religion and the confusion this evidences over what should be regarded as the morality of modern society.

The *threat* posed by communism has two related dimensions, internal subversion and external force. The two are related by communism's international connection with Russia and by the tendency to look for foreign connections in any case of internal violence, as has been pointed out in the previous chapter (Schlesinger, 1978). Counter-espionage and spy cases provide one of the main types of subversion to receive wide attention in factual and fictional media. There have also been periodic red scares in British politics and industrial relations. The last two have occurred immediately before and after parliamentary elections in 1974 and 1966. International red scares began almost immediately after the revolution in 1917. Nevertheless as Lippmann and Mertz (1920) made clear in their study of the *New York Times'* coverage of Russia after the revolution, 'red peril' was only one of a number of contemporary newspaper themes. Until the armistice was signed it was largely eclipsed by the 'German peril', that Germany would manage to capture or coerce Russian support for its war effort. The red peril came into prominence only after the allies had no further need of Russian assistance and had intervened against the Soviet government. Both the historic and contemporary cases highlight the role of the political authorities in sanctioning the scare.

Current accounts of the external threat concentrate on Russia's military might, achieved by her ability to direct her economy and suppress consumerism, and her aggressive foreign policy, as evidenced most recently in Africa. *Time* and *Newsweek* both give such foreign policy issues considerable attention and regularly assess the balance of power between East and West. Such assessments give prominence to apprehensive accounts by NATO spokesmen of the growth of Russian military might on land and sea and in the air.

If the external threat is currently embodied in military force, the internal threat is almost invariably encapsulated in the single, ubiquitous metaphor of 'reds under the bed'. According to Partridge (1977) the phrase came out of the McCarthy period in America but its precise origins are obscure. Repeated use, however, has made it the almost inevitable accompaniment of any report involving Communists. The red scare prior to the general election of February 1974 provided a representative selection of straight uses as well as a number of permutations. The three terms in the phrase can all be transformed so that the reds are not under but in, that they are under various other features of modern life, depending on the particular pun suitable to the topic of the report, or that it is not reds but some other group providing the threat. In 1974 two notable puns were 'reds under the coalbeds' with reference to the miners' dispute and 'reds under the crib row' with reference to a religious education syllabus introduced in Birmingham which included a forty-page section on communism. A Cummings cartoon in the *Daily Express* had the trade union leadership in a bed together, wearing hammer-and-sickle lapel badges (foreign threat) and warning each other, 'Things are serious! TEDS UNDER THE BED threatening our movement' (original capitals). This replacement of reds with a politician (Edward – 'Ted' – Heath) threatening them is relatively unusual compared to left-wing attempts to transpose the figure so that the threat to society comes from the Right. Such attempts achieve little prominence but provide a useful illustration of the general bias of the culture in which left-wing meanings can only be insinuated by reorganizing right-wing figures.

The most poignant permutation during this period, however, came from the *News of the World* of 24 February: 'Vote for the Red who's left my bed!' announced the headline to a story that 'even though the Red has gone from her bed a heartbroken wife is hard at work canvassing for her communist husband in the election . . . because "I love them both, my husband and the Communist Party"'.

So far as headline writers are concerned, reds and beds are conveniently short words which alliterate and allow a variety of permutations. Repeated use has made their meaning crystal clear and yet a number of complex allusions are involved. It must be a particularly insidious and all-pervasive threat if it can reach people in such a sheltered, private place as bed. Bed is connected with two main activities. 'Reds under the bed' is both a reminder to be watchful, on one's guard at all times, and a warning against seduction. Seduction is a common metaphor to explain how people, particularly intellectuals, come to be Communist supporters. The red threat reaches people where they should be most secure and so are weak and defenceless. Its morality is that of the eavesdropper and seducer.

Irrationality is frequently invoked to explain how and why people come to hold and support ideas which are both alien and threatening. This set of meanings brings us to some of the closest parallels between the interpretation of communism and propaganda in war, a parallel which is particularly evident in contemporary counter-insurgency thought, much of which is, of course, explicitly anti-Communist. More than conventional warfare between separate states, the wars of liberation of the past three decades have been contests for the support of the population. The forces of the imperial power have been in close contact with the native population. There have been various attempts in the different wars to distinguish between belligerent and non-belligerent natives, the enemy and the innocent, in other words to establish an account of *difference*. However, as Bourdieu has pointed out in his study of the Algerians, on the ground such distinctions break down in common colonial attitudes and administrative treatment of the native population:

> On the one hand, certain Europeans claimed that the war of liberation was being carried on by a handful of conscienceless killers directed by cynical ringleaders who sought to stir up against France, by ruse and terror, populations that had really remained faithful to her, but, on the other hand, the behaviour of these same people appeared to be based, consciously or unconsciously, on their real feelings that all 'Arabs' were in league with one another and were supporters of the National Liberation Front. (Bourdieu, 1962: 153–4)

Bourdieu's argument is that that such conflicts are systemic, the product of a widening gap between a dominant and dominated society, held together only by force. The various imperial ideologies, however, have pictured such struggles as the result of anti-colonial conspiracies.

Conspiracy theories come in all shapes and sizes but are particularly characteristic of cases like those under discussion in which there are problems identifying the enemy physically and isolating his doctrines morally. In 1955 the *Daily Sketch* warned its readers: 'A communist must be smoked out usually. He doesn't have to declare himself, usually. That's what's so frightening.' In his analysis of dictatorship, Franz Neumann (1964) identified the conspiracy theory of history as one of the popular supports of state power, involving racialist or nationalist doctrines to show the conspirators as threatening and different. The threat posed by the conspiracy has been made credible and sinister by being linked to a power source outside the nation-state. Neumann's examples of important conspiracy theories include the Jesuit, the Jewish, the Masonic, the Capitalist and the Communist.

Again, the Algerian War provides a good example of the way such theories are ideologically self-generating, regardless of evidence, a process in which military personnel and institutions were centrally involved. In his comprehensive discussion of the French military doctrine, *la guerre révolutionnaire*, Ambler notes that 'For those Indochina veterans who viewed the Algerian rebels as simply the "Viets" displaced from tropical rice paddies to the North African bled, it seemed that the similarity between FLN and communist tactics was proof enough that the rebellion was under the direction of Moscow' (Ambler, 1966: 311). There were certain inconvenient facts, however, such as the early condemnation of the FLN by the French Communist Party and the FLN's concern to keep its distance from the Algerian Communist Party. Recognition of these by more sophisticated ideologues meant that they gave the simple equation a more generalized twist so that 'revolutionary war was, by definition, a communist phenomenon' (ibid: 313).

The same equation, in its simple or generalized version, has been repeated by military and political authorities and disseminated by mass media in all countries which have countered insurgency in their overseas fields of influence. British politicians of the Right have interpreted the Northern Ireland troubles in such terms and the interpretation has occasionally been given wider credence. In October 1971 the British press considered the second congress of the Irish Communist Party as evidence of Communist trouble-making. The *Times* was sceptical, but the *Sunday Telegraph* anounced that 'attempts by Russians to foment the Northern Irish troubles as well as to exploit them for propaganda purposes abroad are widely regarded as a significant factor in the crisis'. Subsequent *Daily Telegraph* reports suggested that the factor was significant for Brian Faulkner, the beleaguered Prime Minister of the Province, in his attempts to secure support locally and from the British government and people.

On another occasion in 1973, the *Daily Mail*, in an editorial titled 'Whose Red Hand', raised the spectre of communism in a way which neatly showed how conspiracies, once recognized, have to be explained. Before the troubles, the *Mail* pointed out, there had been no Communists in Ulster. In the current local elections more than one hundred Communist candidates were standing: 'There was never a more dramatic illustration of how communism feeds upon chaos and breakdown.' Flaws in the system let in communism in much the same way that unsanitary conditions breed vermin and disease.

When John Gollan became General Secretary of the British Communist Party, the British press recognized with relief that the new secretary embodied the connection between communism and poverty in appearance as well as family origins. The *Evening Standard* underlined the contrast between the outgoing secretary, Harry Pollitt, who 'looks like a lot of people's idea of a farmer or small businessman', and Gollan, who 'looks like a lot of people's idea of a communist. He has that lean and hungry look. He appears indeed almost emaciated' (14 May 1956). For *The Economist*, the contrast had sinister implications for all concerned:

> It is probable that the comrades are about to discover that the old easy-going ways of roly-poly, earthy Harry Pollitt have ended . . . The gaunt, intense figure of Mr Gollan will be watching them all the time. It is possible that after inflicting considerable damage on the British people he may destroy the British Communist Party.

Acceptance that society is flawed is much less common than the other ways of accounting for communist conspiracies. For the sake of consistency the four modes of explanation may be summarized as the four f's – flaws which let the infection in, force and fooling which put the general population at risk, and fanaticism which is the only way of accounting for the conspirators themselves.

Force is hinted at in *The Economist*'s reference to Gollan, like Big Brother, watching the comrades. It is embodied in the use of the term 'terror' to include both control by totalitarian state and acts of violence by revolutionaries against state power. Two similarities have allowed this equation of such apparently disparate phenomena. Both violate the individual's rights and person. So they are unnatural. Both gain effectiveness from unpredictability. So, in a sense, they are irrational. Arthur Koestler's title *Darkness at Noon* links the unnatural to the irrational with wonderful economy.

The terror equation, applied to the Communist state and liberation movements, is read as evidence that they are part of the same international conspiracy. In the colonial wars, allegations of terror have had more mundane propaganda purposes in accusations of atrocity – unnatural horror and explanations of how the enemy gains support to carry on the fight, by force, Coercion by terror is a recurrent explanation of how a minority of conspirators are able to turn themselves into a majority of the population. It is to be found in cases as diverse as the Dutch in Indonesia in the 1940s and the British in Northern Ireland thirty years later:

> In the Dutch military ideology the only major distinction seemed to be the line drawn between the Indonesian population – victims of terror – and the enemy, i.e. the terrorists, who were first and foremost the enemies of their own people. The military mission was officially conducted in terms of 'Justice and Security' or 'Law and Order'. (Van Doorn, 1971: 82)

In the Dutch case the revolutionary (Communist) terror could even be linked to the experience of past totalitarian (fascist) terror as a consequence of the Japanese occupation. Van Doorn quotes the commander-in-chief's order of the day for 17 December 1948: 'Remember that you are bearers of justice and security, to a population that has long been subjected to terror and oppression' (ibid: 83).

Much of the 'art of invention' involved in interpreting communism depends upon drawing parallels and making associations between contrasting phenomena. Such arguments from *similarity* upset the basis on which positive and negative distinctions are drawn and so allow the enemy's ideology to be tackled on its own ground, and deflated by ridicule. A case discussed further below is the parallel between communism, militantly atheistic, and religion. Other examples include the attention given to the survival of class, wealth and status differentials in Communist countries and ironic assertions that, for all their progressive, revolutionary protestations, Communists are fundamentally conservative.

The risk that people would be *fooled* by positive attractions has long been accepted as inevitable when dealing with communism. Lippmann and Mertz (1920) quote an editorial from the *New York Times* of 28 December 1918, arguing the case for allied intervention against Soviet Russia. The *Times* considered the argument that soldiers of the advancing force might be contaminated by the Bolshevik argument and concluded:

> The Allies can fight Bolshevism now, before its teeth have grown, and run the risk of having the cruder minds among their soldiers debauched by the argument that ignorance should rule knowledge, or they can wait until Bolshevism has spread that argument through the cruder minds not only of their armies but of their whole populations, and then fight it with their morale thus impaired. It ought to be a choise easy to make. (cited in Lippman and Mertz, 1920: 18)

The *Times'* worry about 'cruder minds' smacks of the protective élitism which has informed many other accounts of those most likely to be taken in by communism, and is characteristic of the counter-insurgency doctrine discussed in Chapter 4.

But, as well as the poor, uneducated and simple-minded, continued anger has been expressed that the well-educated too are easily fooled. The *Daily Sketch* feature of 18 June 1955, quoted above and titled 'The Enemy Within' warned against a Young Communist 'attempt to poison the impressionable minds of young teenagers', with accounts of the way in which prominent Communist intellectuals such as Palme Dutt and James Klugmann had been recruited. Klugmann, the suave Cambridge graduate, was won for 'the cause' because the communists kidded him that anti-fascism and communism were identical. Palme Dutt, the Anglo-Indian High Priest of this godless religion, switched from being a pacifist to a communist when he was a brilliant Oxford undergraduate and an impressionable one.

The *fanaticism* of the hard core of conspirators has already been illustrated tangentially above. To liken Palme Dutt to a high priest, for example, is to link him to some ancient discredited religion which forced or inspired unquestioning obedience rather than to any contemporary faith. The analogy between communism and religion is one that can be found at all levels in Western culture. At a popular level, the attack from a rationalist perspective provides another 'explanation' of Communist support. Thus, for example, *Time* captioned a picture of Santiago Carrillo speaking in the Spanish elections as 'Carrillo preaching to the party faithful'. The audience listening to the General Secretary of the Spanish Communist Party were not voters to be convinced in terms of the liberal model, but believers who had already made the necessary 'leap of faith'. The analogy is so ubiquitous that it is easy to miss, hidden in apparently common-sense usages of words such as 'doctrine', 'schism', 'creed' and 'belief'. The ambiguities of this analogy, and the confusions involved in many of the ways in which it is popularly used, expose some of the basic assumptions of liberal capitalism and bring us to some of the major and continuing problems of social analysis.

The claim that the revolution embodies a new faith is at least as old as the French Revolution. Among commentators on that event there were some who made the claim positively to celebrate reason and others who used it negatively to denigrate the new movement as requiring faith in a shabbier god than the old. Burke, who was one of the latter, held that the true religion was necessary for the leaders of men to inspire awe at the trust they had received from 'the one great Master, Author and Founder of society'. The revolution, by contrast, was religion perverted. This allowed Burke to make the connection between fanaticism and violence: 'The Cardinal of Lorraine (instigator of the St Bartholomew's day massacre) was the murderer of the sixteenth century, you (the teachers of the Palais Royal) have the glory of being the murderers in the eighteenth; and this is the only difference between you' (Burke, 1910: 139). Burke went on to draw the general moral that history would 'teach a civilized posterity to abhor the misdeeds of both these barbarous ages . . . It will teach posterity not to make war upon either religion or philosophy, for the abuse which the hypocrites of both have made of two of the most valuable blessings conferred upon us' (ibid: 140).

A contrasting identity between communism and religion as moral crusades has been apparent to others. A post-revolutionary *New York Times* headline quoted by Lippmann and Mertz draws the parallel to applaud Bolshevik opposition to Germany, the common enemy. Even church leaders, normally staunch opponents of the anti-Christ, can be found making a virtue of the comparison. Thus, for example, Geoffrey Fisher, when Archbishop of Canterbury, declared: 'There are only two kinds of people in the modern world who know what they are after. One, quite frankly, is the communist. The other, equally frankly, is the convinced Christian . . . The rest of the world are amiable non-entities.' Belief and commitment have an attraction in a secular, sceptical age as a sure way of giving life meaning. *The God That Failed*, the wistful title of Richard Crossman's post-war collection of recantations by ex-Communists, captures this spirit. In its turn, the phrase has captured the imagination of British sub-editors.

But the scepticism of the age ensures that for the most part the communism–religion analogy is intended to pour contempt on both phenomena. This contempt has been given a peculiarly Protestant twist in Anglo-Saxon culture by recognizing the parallels to be drawn between international communism and the Catholic Church. As George Orwell put it in *The Road to Wigan Pier*: 'The Communist and the Catholic are not saying the same thing, in a sense they are even saying opposite things and each would gladly boil the other in oil if circumstances permitted; but from the point of view of an outsider they are very much alike.' This 'clerical thesis' applied to international communism has recently been transformed into the 'reformation thesis' of Eurocommunism. As may be seen from the detailed discussion in Chapter 6, the possible value of this interpretation in Western culture was quite apparent to Eurocommunist leaders like Santiago Carrillo. After the publication of his book in which the new doctrine was firmly enshrined in the title, Carrillo was only too happy to play Luther to Brezhnev's Pope for the entertainment of the Western press. On the occasion of his tour of the United States, the media transformed Luther into St Paul, the missionary of the new church. Enrico Berlinguer, the Italian Communist Party secretary, on the other hand, tends to double the role of heretic with that of papal leader, issuing encyclicals to his followers or in one case reported in the American news magazines to the rival claimant of that office, the Pope.

Anti-Catholicism is exploitable for Communist leaders because the church, and its organization and doctrines, was one of the first and most important targets to come under fire as society changed under the impact of science, rationalism and industrialism. The complex, intricate processes involved in these developments took several centuries to work themselves through and provided a continuing subject for analysis and theorizing. A legacy of the classic sociologists, however, is to collapse these into a single major contrast between traditional and modern society (Kumar, 1978). This was recognized and labelled in different ways by different authors. Consistently, however, they put religion, as traditionally understood, on the historic side of the divide. Some, such as Saint-Simon, Comte and Durkheim, conceived, in their different ways, that a new society might generate religion in a new form. Communism, itself a child of the Industrial Revolution, became a candidate for such a role. The analogy taken up in popular culture, however, was not the one with the idealism of a new religion so much as the one with the bureaucracy of a new church, complete with the paraphernalia of prophets, sacred texts and interminable exegesis.

Theories behind the images

The range and variety of imagery discussed in the previous section belie its fundamental consistency and the element of circularity already mentioned. The explicit and theorized working out of the consistency and coherence of the model is a separate function within the ideological production system carried out mainly by social and political philosophers. Much of the effort to develop coherence and consistency has gone into the elaboration of the theory of totalitarianism in the post-war period, a theory which depended on associating the old enemy, Hitler's Germany, with the new, Stalin's Russia. This provides us with an important example of a theory which has been heavily criticized in academic, political science circles but which survives virtually unscathed among popularizing élites and in popular accounts. This is not surprising, since, as David Lane has pointed out, 'In the Western world, "totalitarianism" is by far the most pervasive and politically important interpretation of the USSR and other states modelled on her.' As such it has functioned as 'a meta-theory, that is, a set of orienting statements to society. Its role, especially during the Cold War, has often been as a kind of "counter ideology" to Soviet Marxism' (Lane, 1976: 44). Barber (1969) has noted the profusion of actual definitions of a totalitarian system; for the purposes of economy we will cite the one by Friedrich (1969) which has been a focus of debate in political science. Friedrich enumerates the following characteristics: a totalist ideology; a single party, ideologically committed, and usually led by one man; a fully developed secret police; and monopolistic control over mass communications, weapons and all organizations, especially economic ones (Friedrich, 1969: 126). Various writers, such as Barber (1969), Curtis (1969) and Lane (1976) have effectively rejected the applicability of this definition to Soviet-style systems. It has been rejected at this academic level both for its factual inaccuracy and for its concomitant essentialism. But this academic rejection has been self-contained. It has had little effect on the use of the concept in journalism. The disavowal of totalitarian theory in academic political science is founded on a close evaluation of current developments among state socialist regimes. One may speculate that its continued viability at the popular level is based upon the general lack of knowledge of such societies and particularly of post-Stalinist developments which follows from the lack of media attention noted above. Nevertheless it is important to note that some academics have not abandoned totalitarianism, in particular those who have most access to other influential élites. Raymond Aron found a use for it in his recent critique of 'Eurocommunism', as has

Jean-François Revel in writing of the 'totalitarian temptation' currently facing the West. Two critics of totalitarian theory, Spiro and Barber, have presented a coherent and convincing account of how the concept has 'helped the United States to re-rationalize a complex and unpredictable world in simplistic terms of good and evil' (Spiro and Barber, 1970: 7). They argue that 'totalitarianism' has had several distinctive but related uses. First, if World War II was against totalitarian states, the stripping away of totalitarian structures in the case of Japan, Italy and Germany and their conversion to democracy make sense of the USA's post-war alliance policy. Second, the 'logic of totalitarianism' – in particular, alleged Soviet expansionism according to the 'domino theory' – is used to explain the threatening behaviour of the Communist bloc. Behind this lurks the world conspiracy theory so beloved of counter-insurgency theorists. Third, in the struggle between democracy and totalitarianism there is no neutral ground in the Third World, and to stop countries becoming totalitarian (that is, Communist), American intervention is justified. As we have seen, these are the forms of interpretation which do the work at a popular level.

Two of the outstanding theorizers of critiques of Marxism, who are, at the same time protagonists of liberalism, are Karl Popper and Raymond Aron. They share a considerable ability to write with clarity and verve. Their work is therefore enjoyable to read and, more importantly, accessible not just to limited academic publics, but also to the whole range of the intelligentsia. Aron has been a press commentator of renown for many years, as well as an academic polymath of astonishing range. Popper has been credited with the achievement of making it now irrational to accept Marxist assumptions as a basis for theorizing. His political philosophy has enjoyed added weight from his standing as one of the most celebrated contemporary philosophers of science. Popper's most elaborated critique of Marxism is contained in his two-volume *Open Society and its Enemies*. The book was completed in 1943 and published with the help of H.A. Hayek, who is a major critic of Marxism in his own right, as well as a currently influential figure in right-wing economic theory. Popper's *Open Society* was written in the 'expectation that Marxism would become a major problem' (Popper, 1974: viii) in the post-war world. For Popper, the open society is identified with a number of characteristics, some of which are connected with his views on scientific progress. Today's open society is 'an interventionist democracy' which upholds rationality in the specific empiricist sense of 'critical reason'. It has put capitalism and the worst of economic exploitation behind it, and applies methods of 'piecemeal social engineering'. This is the age of the post-capitalist technocracy – not Popper's phrase, but undoubtedly a conception he shares with Aron. In its critique of Marxism, therefore, *The Open Society* is at the same time an affirmation of the new modes of organization of Western capitalism, but on an essentially abstract and philosophical plane. That is not to say, however, that its ideological import is unclear.

What Popper tries to show is that a planned transition to socialism is *logically* impossible, and that reformism is *logically* more defensible than revolution. Political activity, like science, should proceed by conjectures and refutations, and the apotheosis of such pragmatism is the theory and practice of liberal democracy. Popper's goal is to provide a scientifically endorsed philosophy to legitimize present-day capitalism.

Popper's Manichaean world-view is reflected in the binary structure of his thought. Utopians, unlike liberal pragmatists, start with a blueprint for the perfect society. Revolution is therefore to be one great experiment, but it may well be a total failure. You cannot logically determine the 'ideal state' before taking practical measures to bring it about. But Utopians refuse to recognize their irrationality in trying to plan society and necessarily resort to violence. The system of concepts operating here is crystallized in Popper's essay 'Utopia and Violence' (Popper, 1976: ch. 18), written in 1948, when the Cold War was well established. The polarities are these:

reason/violence
true rationalism/false rationalism
argumentation/violence
intermediate aims/ultimate ends
social reform/inadmissible Utopian blueprints
rational attitude/emotional attitude

Aron has been much more directly involved in political debate in France than Popper has in Britain. Much of his work covers the same ground as has been outlined here already, especially his separation of the 'pluralist-constitutional' states of the West from the totalitarian ones of the East. Like Popper, he has been concerned with stressing the irrationality of Marxism, and has emphasized even more strongly Marxism's supposed prophetic characteristics. The continuity in Aron's analysis is evident from *The Opium of the Intellectuals* (Aron, 1955), where he castigates the seduced *gauchistes* just before the Krushchev 'revelations', right up to *My Plea for our Decadent Europe*, where the creeping *sinistrisme* of a new generation is attacked.

In *The Opium of the Intellectuals*, Aron's basic purpose is to demonstrate the similarities between Marxism and religion, and to argue that Marxism is a surrogate for religion. He claims to have been a coiner of the term 'secular religion' to analyse this phenomenon and argues that the Communist Party 'approximates to a church which is the trustee and guardian of the message of salvation' (1955: 268). Aron develops the religious parallels at length, suggesting that the Communist Party has taken on the claims of Catholicism in its imposition of orthodoxy. Because of this (turning Marx on his head), Marxist ideology deserves to be called an opium of the people. In this book, Aron advances an argument for the end of ideology – in the sense of an abandonment of dogma – as a desirable goal. The imagery of organized religion reappears in his later polemic against the 'Eurocommunists'. There he warns Frenchmen that they are in danger from a party 'linked to the ideocratic community, whose metropolis is Moscow'. He continues: 'to judge from the statements of the most "advanced" protestants among Eurocommunists, they are still halfway between loyalism to the Rome of yesterday and their announced reformation' (Aron, 1977: 47).

From this sketch what emerges very clearly is the way in which rationality is identified with the practice of liberal democracies in the West. Thus the positions taken have a positive legitimating role, affirming the economic and political foundations of capitalism, and appropriating the concept of freedom and identifying it with the 'open society'. The slogan 'the end of ideology' asserted the same connection. The classic formulation is to be found in the work of Daniel Bell, who argued that 'ideology, which was once the road to action, has come to a dead end' (Bell, 1962: 393), a confident assertion of liberal consensualism riding high on the back of 'affluence'. Ideology is identified with passion and emotion, and these have no place in the contemporary order. Marxism itself need hardly be taken seriously:

> Few serious minds believe any longer that one can set down 'blueprints' and through 'social engineering' bring about a new utopia of social harmony . . . In the Western world . . . there is today a rough consensus among intellectuals on political issues: the acceptance of the welfare state; the desirability of decentralized power; a system of mixed economy and political pluralism. In that sense, too, the ideological age has ended. (Bell, 1962: 403)

Seymour Martin Lipset expressed the same sentiments more succinctly, and with a complacency ironic to the contemporary eye, when he said: 'the fundamental political problems of the industrial revolution have been solved' (Lipset, 1960: 406). This takes us directly into the world of reasonableness and common sense, the world of post-industrial techno-cracy. Rationality is embodied in the Western system, but lamentably absent elsewhere. Thus: 'Ideology and passion may no longer be necessary to sustain the class struggle within stable and affluent democracies, but they are clearly needed in the international effort to develop free political and economic institutions in the rest of the world' (Lipset, 1960: 417).

Edward Shils theorized the view that a liberal society could only tolerate constitutional opposition. The diminution of ideological politics showed itself in a 'civility' which is 'compatible with other attachments to class, to religion, to profession, but it regulates them out of respect for the common good' (Shils, 1972: 60). Ideological politics was not merely emotional but a positive manifestation of a pathological state: 'Every society has its outcasts, its wretched, and its damned, who cannot fit the routine requirements of social life at any level of authority and achievement' (Shils, 1972: 53). Following Aron, he went on to argue that ideological politics was but a contemporary instance of millennarianism, and that one should note the paranoid tendencies of many such religious leaders.

The end-of-ideology theorists, whether conservative or liberal, joined, therefore, in celebrating consensual, 'civil', pluralistic capitalist democracy as the embodiment of rationality, and in posing the proposition that ideological thought, the prime instance of which was Marxism, was the result of an intellectual disorder in the shape of a quasi-religious – and unrealizable – vision.

Conclusion

In recent years 'creating reality' has begun to vie with 'mirroring society' as the slogan to summarize the role of the media. Mirroring was a favourite among broadcasters and journalists. It meant, among other things, that they did not carry sole responsibility for the nature of their output. Students of the media have adopted 'creation' from phenomenological sociology, and it has played a part in reviving the idea that the media are, after all, powerful.

Our argument in this chapter is that while it improves on 'mirroring', 'creation' gives a misleading account of the role of the media. Once more, it tends to put them under the spotlight, at the centre of the stage. 'Creation' is to be preferred in so far as it denies that the media are purely passive reflectors of the world. It laid the foundation for the critique of impartiality, objectivity and the other ground rules supposedly explaining media practice by drawing on the critique of positivism in social science. But while talk of 'creation' reasserts the active conception of the media, it none the less is liable to credit them – and the much-studied news media especially – with too much power to define reality.

Others have also been at pains to show that the media do not act in isolation; that their themes are supplied, taken up and repeated by other agents of what Stan Cohen, following Lemert, calls the 'societal control culture'. The consonance between many media accounts and the definitions produced by other agents of social control, 'primary definers' in Stuart Hall's phrase, has provided one way of showing the integration of the media into the general culture, and thus to counter the temptation to treat them as the sole constructors of reality. In this chapter we too have been concerned with the limits on media creativity, exploring ways in which the constructions of journalism are related to, and derived from, broader constructions in the dominant culture. We have identified some of the continuities which exist between popular media accounts of Communist parties and leaders and socio-political theorizing about communism at an intellectual level.

The types of theme identified here can be found in a wide range of cultural products. Our analysis could be extended from journalism and social theory to fictional representations, again at élite and at mass levels.

The relationships between these various cultural levels and specialized functions have been inadequately theorized in most discussions. Heavy reliance is still placed on a version of mass society theory which assumes that there is a process of diffusion downwards. Hirsch, for instance, in a recent paper, distinguished two media sectors: first producer, small audience, élite media, which he sees as the centres of cultural creation. The mass media are seen as the distributors: 'Quite simply, the role of producer organizations and media is to create new cultural forms, ideas, patterns and products, whereas distributor media select from these to present standardized and watered-down versions to the mass public' (Hirsch, 1978: 3).

There are grounds for questioning both the openness of the system and the direction of flow envisaged in such a model. We have hinted at some of the mechanisms which give the dominant account currency in different forms throughout the system. Alternative views certainly exist but tend to be systematically isolated, available only to specific publics at particular points. In the next chapter, by examining the debate on 'Eurocommunism', we provide a complementary sociological account of the production of ideology by different groups, Marxist and 'bourgeois', élite and popular, variously organized and supported and oriented towards distinctive audiences, addressed through specific types of media.

In our analysis of the origins of the term we show the struggle to appropriate the term by Western Communist parties. The term itself (although this is little known) was coined on the Right. It became unstable when it acquired positive rather than purely negative connotations. This successful act of appropriation by the Communists of an originally anti-Communist term is perhaps exceptional. Communists in the West are outsiders, and much attention is given to explaining why. Labels such as 'subversive' and 'irrational' become more fully explicated. Violent deviance, or deviance which can be made to appear violent, may be left to condemn itself as beyond reason.

Communists, however, are themselves concerned to dispute the dominant version of rationality and to proffer an alternative. Much attention has been devoted to showing how, and why, this is itself irrational. In the course of doing this, the theorist-intellectuals and the producers of popular culture have, at least implicitly, had much to say about the type of rationality current in industrialized capitalist society. This has been a major topic in classical sociology, and is still integral to attempts to understand the course of social change. It is, moreover, central to the question of boundary maintenance. For in the theory of totalitarianism 'reason' is the baseline from which criticisms are developed, and reason – in the guise of common sense – is similarly appealed to in popular accounts of communism at a more implicit level. We would argue, therefore, that a discussion of the interpretations of communism available in the dominant culture affords a way into grasping one of its master patterns, and that these interpretations should not be catalogued as a mere set of propaganda techniques. They are much more fundamental.

References

Ambler, J.S. (1966) *The French Army in Politics, 1945–1962*. Columbus: Ohio State University Press.

Aron, R. (1955) *L'Opium des Intellectuels*. Paris: Calmann-Lévy.

Aron, R. (1977) *Plaidoyer pour l'Europe Décadente*. Paris: Robert Laffont.

Barber, B.R. (1969) 'Conceptual Foundations of Totalitarianism', pp. 3–52 in Friedrich et al. (1969),

Bell, D. (1962) *The End of Ideology*. New York: Free Press.

Bourdieu, P. (1962) *The Algerians*. Boston, Mass: Beacon Press.

Bourdieu, P. (1971) 'Systems of Education and Systems of Thought', in M.F.D. Young (ed.), *Knowledge and Control*. London: Collier Macmillan.

Burke, E. (1910) *Reflections on the Revolution in France*. London: Everyman.

Cohen, S. (1973) *Folk Devils and Moral Panics*. St Albans: Paladin.

Crossman, R. (ed.) (1949) *The God That Failed*. New York: Harper.

Curtis, M. (1969) 'Retreat from Totalitarianism', pp. 53–121 in Friedrich et al. (1969).

Elliott, P. (1972) *The Making of a Television Series*. London: Constable.

Freidrich, C.J. (1969) 'The Evolving Theory and Practice of Totalitarian Regimes', pp. 123–64 in Friedrich et al. (1969).

Freidrich, C.J., Curtis, M. and Barber, B.R. (1969) *Totalitarianism in Perspective: Three Views*. London: Pall Mall.

Hellman, L. (1977) *Scoundrel Time*. New York: Bantam.

Hirsch, P. (1978) 'Institutional Functions of Elite and Mass Media', paper presented to the International Sociological Association's World Congress, Uppsala, Sweden.

Kumar, K. (1978) *Prophecy and Progress*. Harmondsworth: Penguin.

Lane, D. (1976) *The Socialist Industrial State*. London: Allen & Unwin.

Lippman, W. and Mertz, C. (1920) 'A Test of the News', *New Republic*, 4 August.

Lipset, S.M. (1960) *Political Man*. London: Heinemann.

Neumann, F. (1964) 'Anxiety and Politics', in *The Democratic and Authoritarian State*. New York: Free Press.

Partridge, E. (1977) *A Dictionary of Catch Phrases*. London: Routledge & Kegan Paul.

Popper, K. (1974) *The Open Society and its Enemies*, Vol. 2. London: Routledge & Kegan Paul.

Popper, K. (1976) *Conjectures and Refutations*. London: Routledge & Kegan Paul.

Revel, J.-F. (1978) 'The Myths of Eurocommunism', *Foreign Affairs*, January: 295–305.

Ruhle, J. (1969) *Literature and Revolution: A Critical Study of the Writer and Communism in the Twentieth Century*. London: Pall Mall.

Schlesinger, P. (1978) 'On the Shape and Scope of Counter-Insurgency Thought', pp. 98–127 in G. Littlejohn, B. Smart, J. Wakeford and N. Yuval-Davis (eds), *Power and the State*. London: Croom Helm.

Shils, E. (1972) 'Ideology and Civility', in *The Intellectuals and the Power*. Chicago: University of Chicago Press.

Spiro, H.J. and Barber, B.R. (1970) 'Counter-Ideological Uses of "Totalitarianism"', *Politics and Society*, November: 7–21.

Van Doorn, J. (1971) *Armed Forces and Society: Sociological Essays*. The Hague: Mouton.

6

The Rise and Fall of a Political Slogan: The Case of 'Eurocommunism'

with Philip Elliott

The term 'Eurocommunism' is an ideological construct. Our object in this chapter is to chart its origins, development and elaborations in current ideological struggles. It is no small irony that a concept coined by anti-Communists should have largely set the terms of reference for Marxist and non-Marxist theorists alike. This irony is twofold: first, the adoption of the term by Communists; and second, the tendency for the term to 'take off', to run away from the purely anti-Communist meaning intended by its creators. This latter development has produced its own fair share of ideological repair work. The sociological significance of such developments lies in the way in which it illustrates how the ideological initiative may be taken by crucial élites, how they may, to a certain extent, lose it and then once more regain it.

'Eurocommunism' provides a useful case to investigate the division of labour which exists between different ideological élites. There is a distinction to be drawn between those who report events and provide information for political and economic élites, those who analyse such information and assess its implications for policy and those who interpret events directly or indirectly for popular consumption. We shall have occasion below to elaborate these distinctions and suggest in a preliminary way how they relate to different institutional positions, different types of journal and different communication media. In our view there is no simple process of dissemination or popularization working downwards through these strata. The construct of 'Eurocommunism' itself has only achieved limited distribution in English-language media. Accounts of related phenomena in truly popular media in Britain have largely been managed in pre-Eurocommunist, that is Cold War, terms. Our analysis of the system through which knowledge and meaning is produced and distributed leads us to expect that this will continue to be the case.

Ideological élites in the West – here consisting of politicians, journalists and academics – generally build up a considerable investment in established patterns of thought. Occasionally, particularly in moments of crisis, they have to engage in ideological retooling. So far as communism is concerned, such a process of retooling has been necessitated by the change in international relations from Cold War to *détente* and by the emergence, particularly since 1956, and latterly 1968, of a number of significant developments in major Western European Communist parties. These developments have had to be located and interpreted, and have posed problems for the dominant, static, ideological framework, which is based on assumptions of Communist totalitarianism and the unquestioned writ of Soviet orthodoxy in the international Communist movement. Western political élites have faced the problem of explaining the gap between the traditional Cold War view of communism and the current professions of, in particular, the Italian, French and Spanish Communist parties (the PCI, PCF and PCE). This problem was forced on to the agenda as these parties approached political power in their respective countries. Our contention is that the coining of the term 'Eurocommunism' and the development of the subsequent debate have reflected the need to make major ideological adjustments at a time of *détente*. This has given rise to a number of differing non-Marxist views, which are explored below.

We should say, at the outset, that we do not take the view that a 'Eurocommunist' phenomenon as such exists. That there are convergent analyses and programmes amongst some Western Communist parties cannot be doubted. That these have been produced by similar structural developments in capitalism's present crisis, that they have been actuated by a rejection of Stalinism and the Soviet model as the sole road to socialism, and that they reflect a new appraisal of the prospects of revolution in Western Europe, can also not be doubted. But such considerations do not, in our view, add up to a homogeneous phenomenon – as is implied by the term 'Eurocommunism'. Nor does that somewhat *ad hoc* set of links between major Western Communist parties and some socialists as yet constitute a coherent movement about to change the face of Europe. Potentially, of course, it might herald a *rapprochement* between elements of the Third and Second Internationals. But in our view, an assessment of the political prospects in Western Europe needs to pay more attention to *national* realities, rather than to overemphasize convergence.

The origins of the term

It is hardly surprising with a term which has had such considerable ideological reverberations that there are three separate claims to have coined it.[1]

Alfons Dalma, an Austrian journalist of Croatian origins, based in Rome, and contributor to a right-wing book entitled *Euro-Kommunismus*, asserts that the Catholic philosopher Augusto del Noce first thought up the label (Dalma et al., 1977). Given the greater strength and the more detailed support for the other two claims, our conclusion is that del Noce is not the most significant of the originators.

The second claimant is Arrigo Levi, editor of the liberal Turin newspaper *La Stampa*, and columnist on Italy for *Newsweek*. In December 1976 in *Newsweek*, Levi speculated on whether he himself was the originator of the term in an earlier *Newsweek* column in December 1975. In that first column he had set out in a remarkably prescient passage why 'Eurocommunism' was on the world agenda:

> The evolution of 'Eurocommunism' – which has also been called 'white communism' or 'neo-communism' – may become a decisive factor for European history and East–West relations. It challenges the traditional political balances in the West but it also threatens the rigidity of Soviet power in the East. In the end, who will be more affected? To some extent this is a consequence of détente, a diplomatic strategy of movement that demands much greater inventiveness than the old 'trench warfare' of the Cold War. (*Newsweek*, 15 December 1975)

The passage was buried in a discussion of developments among the European Communist parties associated with another postponement of the pan-European conference. The lack of prominence and the range of alternatives offered suggested that the choice of a single ideological figure had yet to be made and the choice was moving from one which alerted Italians to a new danger in their midst to one which had wider potential on the international scene.[2]

However, the most precise and best-documented claim has been made on behalf of Frane Barbieri, a Croatian who was formerly editor-in-chief of the Belgrade weekly *Nin*, and who in 1974 joined the editorial staff of the anti-Communist Milanese daily *Il Giornale Nuovo*. This newspaper was expressly set up in that year in order to combat the growing strength of the Italian Left by a number of prominent journalists from *Il Corriere della Sera* who dissented from the *Corriere*'s leftish line. According to one of *Il Giornale Nuovo*'s editors, Enzo Bettiza (who is also a Liberal senator for Milan), the term was first used by Frane Barbieri 'writing an editorial on "Brezhnev's expectations"' (*Giornale Nuovo*, 26 June 1975). He continues: 'It was not exactly intended to be a pro-communist formulation; and indeed one leading Spanish Marxist (Ramón Tamames) classified it in the Western vocabulary next to Winston Churchill's "Iron Curtain", and Walter Lippmann's "Cold War". *Is it then, our word or their word?*' (Bettiza, 1978: 21–3, emphasis added). This question is a crucial one. It makes central and explicit the issue of how ideological constructs are to be controlled. Bettiza's observations were made in *Encounter*, to which he is a regular contributor, and which, as will be seen, has figured importantly in the ideological activity focused on 'Eurocommunism'.

The 'archaeology' of the term is revealed in greater detail in an interview with Barbieri conducted by Dr Manfred Steinkühler, a West German diplomat (Steinkühler, 1977a). This interview presents Barbieri's assumptions and intentions when he coined the neologism 'Eurocommunism'. He says that he was particularly influenced by the formulations of two of the leaders of the Spanish Communist Party, Santiago Carrillo and Manuel Azcárate, concerning a 'genuine European alternative' to Soviet-style socialism in the context of developed Western capitalist societies. Barbieri makes the point that in originating the term 'Eurocommunism' he was specifically intending a contrast with Arrigo Levi's 'neo-communism' which he felt went 'too far'. In an elaborate account, which deserves to be fully quoted, he explains his intentions further:

> I decided to use the expression 'Eurocommunism' because I considered it to be geographically precise, but considered it ideologically imprecise. By contrast, the expression 'Neo-communism' is a much more defined, self-contained concept. 'Eurocommunism' is an ideologically fluid, imprecise phenomenon, which I would not completely deny has a new ideological component. However, I would not acknowledge it to be a self-contained ideology. This does not mean that 'Eurocommunism' has no social basis whatsoever. It does, but of an instrumental manner, in so far as it makes use of existing social arrangements. Precisely because of this, since it is not clear what 'Eurocommunism' actually is, I ask myself whether an EEC ruled by the Eurocommunists would remain an EEC in the same way it was created. Today, the European Community is bringing West European traditions to fulfilment. The Eurocommunists say that they want to remain independent from both the USA and the USSR. If you were to follow the Spanish Manifesto-Programme you could infer that their intention was also a step-by-step Europeanization of the Soviet system. But that is an illusion. A Eurocommunist Europe would definitely mean the Sovietization of Europe. (Steinkühler, 1977b: 348–9)

For Barbieri, the Eurocommunists have a developed conception of the stages to the seizure of power, but none of how they should actually exercise it; they lack a fully developed critique of the Soviet system; they have not specified how democracy is to be guaranteed; and finally, unlike the Yugoslav Communists, they are *dirigiste* and state-centred rather than decentralist. In sum, Barbieri formulated his conception in the framework of a set of theoretical assumptions about recent developments in Western communism, presenting them in a newspaper which is part of the anti-Communist crusade of the Italian Right.

In its origins, therefore, the concept of 'Eurocommunism' was intended to indicate opposition to and scepticism about current trends in some of the major Western Communist parties. But in the next stage of the elaboration of 'Eurocommunism' what was involved was less outright opposition than containment.

Containment theorists

In an article written in January 1976, first published in *Foreign Policy* in spring, and then republished in another élite journal *Across the Board* in July, with a title now including the term itself – 'Eurocommunism: The Italian Experience So Far' – Arrigo Levi outlined three positions on the subject (Levi, 1977a and 1977b). It was rejected by the Right on the essentialist ground that all communism was the same under the skin. It was rejected by some on the Left on the opposite ground that all revisionism was a form of social democracy. But in between there were those who were prepared to take it seriously, though not without necessary caution. Levi outlined two reasons for adopting this third view: one, internal to Italy, that the PCI had shown considerable restraint in avoiding moves which would split the Christian Democrats and make parliamentary government in Italy impossible; the second, the foreign policy point that there were good reasons for taking the PCI's protestations of independence from Moscow seriously. In the *Newsweek* column in which he had first used the term, Levi had gone some way towards accounting for the difference between sceptical opposition as against cautious acceptance by citing its geographical basis, pointing to opposition in Britain and America as against more open discussion in Italy and France.

This distinction between open-minded Europeans and closed-minded Anglo-Saxons has its attractions, but it is impossible to sustain. For one, there were numerous American advocates of containment, and for another several prominent Europeans among the professional anti-Communist backlash (of which more below). American advocates of containment apparently included the American Secretary of State, Cyrus Vance, at least a section of the State Department and US diplomatic service and most of the contributors to influential American foreign policy journals in 1976 and 1977. Articles on Europe in *Foreign Policy* were almost exclusively of this type, including papers by Levi (1977a), two American political scientists, Peter Lange (1976) and Robert Lieber (1977), and an ex-US ambassador turned academic, Laurence Silberman (1977). Similarly, *Foreign Affairs* published papers taking a containment position by Guido Carli (1976), ex-governor of the Bank of Italy and currently chairman of the Italian Association of Manufacturers (Confindustria), Peter Nichols (1976), Italian correspondent of the (London) *Times*, Charles Gati (1977), another academic, James O. Goldsborough (1977), chief European correspondent of the *International Herald Tribune* and *Newsweek* correspondent, and Ugo La Malfa (1978), leader of the Italian Republican Party and Prime Minister designate in February 1979. There were also articles by prominent CP spokesmen (Kanapa, 1977; Napolitano, 1978; Segre, 1976), setting out their case in terms calculated to be appealing to Westerners who were influential in business and politics. Interestingly, European communism slipped off the agenda in *Foreign Policy* in 1978, and *Foreign Affairs* published two essentialist, anti-Communist papers in that year (Chirac, 1978; Revel, 1978).

Both these journals are closely linked to élite groups active in American foreign-policy-making. *Foreign Policy*, with a circulation of approximately 18,000, is published by National Affairs Inc. with the support of the Carnegie Endowment for International Peace. Its editorial board includes prominent journalists such as David Halberstam, as well as foreign policy academics and government officials such as Zbigniew Brzezinski and Elliot L. Richardson. *Foreign Affairs*, published by the Council on Foreign Relations, New York, has a much wider circulation of 72,000. It was founded in 1921 and, as Domhoff has pointed out, is an important 'link in the specific mechanisms by which the corporate rich formulate and transfer their wishes into government policy'. Its major sources of finance are 'leading corporations and major foundations', and the CFR has, until recently, had a great measure of success in placing its members in the USA's defence and foreign affairs policy-making apparatuses (Domhoff, 1969: 28–30). Like the Royal Institute for International Affairs (RIIA) in London, and the Society for Foreign Policy in Bonn, the Council on Foreign Relations (CFR) holds off-the-record briefings for its membership by government officials.

The comparable British journal, *The World Today*, associated with the RIIA, also published articles taking a containment position in 1976 and 1977 (Popov, 1976; Stehle, 1977 and 1978; Timmermann, 1977). So did the bi-monthly of the United States Information Service, *Problems of Communism*. The sophistication and wide-ranging nature of the analyses to be found in this journal certainly defeat any crude conspiracy theorists who would expect a government publication simply to be a propaganda mouthpiece. Rather, its commitment to a balanced appraisal of the options supports our theory of ideological retooling. Policy-makers need answers, not disinformation, and such a journal therefore has an important place in the ideological division of labour. This place is occasionally made quite explicit by contributors. Ronald Tiersky (1976), for example, concluded his account of the possibility of 'non-dictatorial socialism' in France if the PCF achieved a share of power with the warning that those anxious 'Atlantic political élites' likely to read *Problems of Communism* needed to be well informed and not take refuge in reductionist analysis.

Needless to say, there are noteworthy differences between the analyses provided by those whom we have labelled containment theorists. Nevertheless the similarities are more striking, as all have investigated current developments in ways which balance the reasons for acceptance against continuing reasons for distrust. All move to the conclusion that either communism can be socially integrated into bourgeois democracies or that at the very least it can be contained. A number of themes and arguments recur which are summarized below.

First, the argument that the inevitable must be accepted if not welcomed. Thus, for example, Lieber set out the basic pragmatic case that 'in the relatively open, free and pluralistic systems of the West it is extremely difficult to *prevent* change,' and so 'American toleration of reformist or even radical European domestic politics including – if and when it is unavoidable – a role for indigenous Communist parties (e.g. Italy) may be a realistic course of action' (Lieber, 1977: 47–8). Similarly Goldsborough (1977) argued that the policy of quarantining the CPs had not worked, and their 'systematic exclusion from government has contributed to the crises of the countries of Latin Europe'.

Secondly, the argument from incorporation contends that if one of the CPs were to approach political power this could only be exercised within the existing constitutional framework. Ronald Tiersky (1976: 46), for example, a political scientist and author of an authoritative study of French communism (1974), stated this case for France and the PCF with great clarity. 'Given a viable Socialist Party, strong opposition parties, a strong bureaucracy and military, and the historical memory of public opinion, it is extremely doubtful that the PCF leadership could manoeuvre with enough skill to make *its* revolution.' Others (such as Lieber, 1977) have emphasized the role of the national and international economic infrastructure with which any Western government has to deal – including one which included Communists.

Thirdly, the containment theorists accept that the CPs in question have genuinely changed their policies and strategy. Tiersky (1976: 46) was convinced that 'Stalinism is becoming a dying ember in French communism.' Kevin Devlin (1977: 19), political analyst for Radio Free Europe, argued that 'Eurocommunism' derives from the convergent interests of the major Western CPs which 'might be described as the tendency . . . to give priority to their own political interests in the course of adaptation to their sociopolitical environments'.

Fourthly, from the standpoint of international relations Eurocommunism appears to pose a challenge to the Soviet Union as the Communist parties distanced themselves from its leadership and advocated positions attractive to dissidents in the East. Neither Devlin (1977) nor Heinz Timmermann (1977), a member of the Bundesinstitut für Ostwissenschaftliche und Internationale Studien, Cologne, who considered this view, were inclined to give it much weight beside the evidence of continuing contact between the 'Eurocommunists' and the Communist Party of the Soviet Union (CPSU) and their general support for Soviet foreign policies. Nevertheless Timmermann stressed that *détente* was a key condition for the survival of the new developments, and that these would be imperilled if, for example, the PCF pulled out of NATO or if Eurocommunist ideas began to destabilize the Eastern bloc. Timmermann noted Soviet attacks on recent developments, particularly on the PCE leader Santiago Carrillo's book, *'Eurocommunism' and the State*, which showed Soviet fears about Eastern Europe's internal stability. His conclusion, however, was that the USSR would not break with the Western CPs, since they were assisting its foreign policy objectives. More likely was an attempt to split the parties, and to 'Finlandize' them.

Fifthly, there is an economic argument for the political value of the Western Communist parties in stabilizing capitalism which is rarely openly stated.[3] However, articles by John Earle, the Rome correspondent of *The Times Business News*, in *The World Today*, and by Guido Carli, of Italy's Confindustria, in *Foreign Affairs*, in 1976, have explicitly made this case. 'Thirty years of Christian Democratic hegemony have resulted in a wasteful, inefficient and irrational economy,' wrote Earle (1976: 218). Carli too argued that the PCI was particularly well placed to restructure the economy fundamentally in ways the dominant political forces could never achieve – to make the bureaucracy more efficient, renew state control of public enterprises, modernize industry and introduce an effective incomes policy. Thus, he concluded, what is needed is 'a broader political consensus. To believe otherwise is to engage in fantasy politics' (1976: 718).

These arguments with the exception of the international relations one, were repeated by the Communist leaders in the articles published by *Foreign Affairs*. Sergio Segre, head of the PCI's foreign section, Jean Kanapa, head of the PCF's foreign affairs section, and Giorgio Napolitano, the PCI's economics spokesman, all addressed US policy-makers in a way calculated to be reassuring. All took a similar line, stressing their parties' commitment to democracy, the break with the Leninist conception of the dictatorship of the proletariat, their independence from Moscow and their acceptance of such Western institutions as NATO and the EEC, their honesty, efficiency and technocratic bias. They called on the USA not to intervene, particularly when in the Italian case the PCI could make a real contribution to the rehabilitation of the Italian economy and had shown it was not intending to disrupt the political scene.

A commentator who straddles the boundary between those whom we have labelled containment theorists and those who take a fundamental, anti-Communist line is Neil McInnes, author of several authoritative studies of Western communism and European correspondent of *Barrons Weekly*, a New York financial magazine produced by Dow Jones. McInnes follows the methodology of many containment theorists in his study of 'Eurocommunism' published in 1976. He evaluates the CPs' claim to have changed, country by country, and topic by topic. But the method leads him to different conclusions. In spite of his financial connections, he gives the economic argument short shrift, claiming that vague policies and good intentions amount to no more than a form of nationalist, economic populism. The central flaw he identifies in the Eurocommunists' case is their continued addiction to democratic centralism as a mode of internal party organization, a mode which 'enables the boss to catapult his cronies into top jobs' and which threatens that the economic and political management of any society in which they come to power will be carried on by a party bureaucracy of the familiar (Eastern) type. McInnes argues that in the final analysis we are dealing with CPs which

> have abandoned the dictatorship of the proletariat, made numerous comprom-
> ises with the social-democrat and bourgeois parties, relaxed their defence of the
> Soviet Union, and defined international authority in the communist movement –
> but they still seek to maintain the discipline, the tactical suppleness, and the
> centralization of the original Leninist party. (1976: 48)

Fundamental anti-Communists

Few fundamental anti-Communists have been prepared to concede as many points as McInnes. Their arguments are constructed using their own distinctive methodology. Instead of discussing changes in the Communist parties point by point and balancing the alternatives for current policy, fundamental anti-Communists set about identifying those characteristics which still link the Eurocommunist parties to their Stalinist past and so enable them to fit this type of communism into the familiar framework of the theory of totalitarianism. Often the argument is an explicit attack on those in the West who have been duped or seduced into accepting Communist protestations at face value. Walter Laqueur, for example, who entered the field early to counter the political and economic attractions of 'Eurocommunism' (in *Commentary* in August 1976), argued that West European or 'Eurocommunism as it is coming to be called' was the equivalent of pre-war fascism. It offered the promises of economic salvation at the price of freedom. Many contemporary American journalists and intellectuals had been seduced in just the same way as their predecessors had at first been seduced by Mussolini. The equation between communism and fascism has been one of the central tenets of totalitarianism theory, the theory which underpins the anti-Communist attack.

Laqueur is typical of the academic polymaths who take a fundamentalist position. He is director of the Institute of Contemporary History in London, has other appointments in the United States and an interest in contemporary history that includes Weimar, the Middle East, terrorism and guerrilla warfare. He is also a contributing editor to *Commentary*[4] and editor of the Sage series of policy papers, the *Washington Papers*, in which McInnes's study of 'Eurocommunism' appeared. A comparable – and more widely known – figure is Raymond Aron, who is accepted as a global thinker of international standing and whose writing on a wide range of subjects is internationalized through translation.

In 1977 two extracts from Aron's latest book castigating those seduced by Marxism appeared in *Encounter*. In 1955 Aron had published a similar attack entitled *The Opium of the Intellectuals*. In 1977 the attack was titled *Plaidoyer pour l'Europe Décadente (My Plea for our Decadent Europe)*. In this book Aron plays the whole hand of anti-Communist arguments dealt by totalitarianism theory. Of primary significance is 'the Weimar syndrome', defined as 'a situation where the electoral structure of a democracy can only offer a choice between two forms of suicide: either by giving power to those who will destroy it, or by violating its own principle of legitimacy' (Aron, 1977: 8). 'Eurocommunists' are not to be trusted because while they 'may be distancing themselves from the Red capital . . . they remain linked to it by a common faith' (ibid: 10). As evidence of this, Aron also pointed to the continuation of democratic centralism:

> They profess essentially the same doctrines as the Soviets, interpreted in the same manner for years: they have not renounced democratic centralism; and their concept of the regime to come is still identical with the Soviet concept, although they maintain that they will avoid its totalitarian implications. Whether the Eurocommunists are concealing their aims or not is less important than the consequences, probable or inevitable, of their methods and their ideas. (ibid: 18)

The same point has been made by Jean-François Revel, author of *La Tentation Totalitaire*, a book in which he castigates the US 'academic and liberal press establishment' for its gullibility in swallowing 'the myth of Eurocommunism'.[5] In 1978 *Foreign Affairs*, which hitherto had appeared to be an organ of that establishment, published an article by Revel in which he argued that the critical test of de-Stalinization was the purely 'technical' issue of democratic centralism – 'all the rest is literature and impressionistic gossip.' 'Eurocommunism can be logical and coherent only if it results in the disappearance of communism' (Revel, 1978: 297, 305).

Encounter's coverage provides a useful illustration of our general thesis that by 1977 the process of ideological retooling associated with 'Eurocommunism' had slipped out of the hands of the anti-Communists into those of the containment theorists. The magazine was engaged in an attempt to regain the initiative by questioning the protestations of the CPs now calling themselves 'Eurocommunist' in a series of articles and interviews. George Urban, described as 'a writer on contemporary history', conducted two major interviews, one with Lucio Lombardo Radice, a member of the central committee of the PCI, and the second with Altiero Spinelli, preceded by an editorial gloss as follows: 'Europeans were appalled. Altiero Spinelli, one of the founding fathers of Common Market Unity and for many years Italy's High Commissioner in Brussels . . . became a leading spokesman for "Eurocommunism"' (Urban, 1978a: 7). Urban's questions emphasize the same grounds for distrusting the PCI and its strategy as Aron had rehearsed earlier. In 1978 these two interviews, together with others Urban had conducted on Radio Free Europe, were collected in book form with an editorial introduction which repeats the essentialist argument:

> The Eurocommunists are attempting to unbutton the Marxist–Leninist–Stalinist straitjacket in reverse order . . . Whether or not these moves have been merely tactical, their political implications are significant. They reveal a geological fault running through the base of the Eurocommunist initiative . . . Eurocommunism is a freak which must either end in Social Democracy or revert to some form of Leninism. In the first case it will cease to be Communist, in the second it will no longer be Euro. (Urban, 1978b: 8)

Essentialists have a penchant for aphorisms of this type. Revel's version has already been quoted above, and Aron has also made his contribution: 'Eurocommunism is like the Euro dollar: it remains Communism even when it is preceded by the word "Euro"' (cited in *Newsweek*, 2 January 1978).

It would be misleading to give the impression that *Encounter*'s treatment of 'Eurocommunism' simply contained one set of views. Leszek Kolakowski, an ex-Marxist Polish philosopher and author of a recent authoritative history of Marxism (1978), accepted the social-democratization thesis as a possibility: 'So far, we lack empirical proofs that a democratic communism is at all possible, and all the existing proofs are to the contrary. Still, we cannot exclude that a new variant of regenerated Social Democracy could ultimately emerge out of the Communist schism' (1977: 19).

The same point was made in an earlier *Encounter* article by Richard Löwenthal, Emeritus Professor of International Relations at Berlin, who argues the explicitly essentialist case that if the necessary changes occurred then 'Eurocommunism' would 'cease to be communism as we have known it'. However, such nods in the direction of *Encounter*'s more leftish readers have been coupled with fundamentalist anti-Communist assumptions. These included, in Kolakowski's case, an insistence that Eastern European states are still totalitarian, that the 'Eurocommunists' may be sincere, but do they realize the incoherence of their ideas? (cf. Aron and Urban); that 'Eurocommunism may emerge, but so far it has not'; (cf. the French anti-Communist authority Annie Kriegel); that Eurocommunists must 'prove that they really distrust and detest despotism' by breaking with the Soviet Union and international communism, and getting rid of the Leninist party (loyalty tests also proposed by Neil McInnes, Raymond Aron, George Urban and David Owen, the former British Foreign Secretary).

Georgetown University has provided a base for a number of other ideological initiatives in addition to those already discussed. The director of the university's International Labor Program, Roy Godson, and Stephen Haseler, known in Britain for his attacks on the alleged growth of Marxist influence in the Labour Party, collaborated there on a book entitled *'Eurocommunism': Implications for East and West* (1978). The authors set out to reject both the view that a new political phenomenon has come into existence and that a new pan-European movement is in the process of formation. The argument is partly strategic: any advances made by the Western Communists will favour the strategic interests of the Soviet Union. It also rests on the persistence of democratic centralism and is grounded in an unreconstructed essentialism:

> while there have indeed been variations in doctrine and in attitudes towards Soviet hegemony of the international Communist movement, such subtle departures from orthodoxy cannot as yet, in our view, lead to their being dignified as a wholly new category, indigenous to Western Europe, unlinked to the Communist past and experience in the Soviet sphere. (1978: 4)

The authors' refusal to give the term credence is a position shared by David Owen and Walter Laqueur. Their affinity with Owen's views is even more marked when they suggest, as he does, that social democrats should try to split the CPs and detach 'reformist' voters.

Apart from being backed by the International Labor Program, the Godson–Haseler book was also funded by the National Strategy Information Center, a body which exists 'to encourage an understanding of strategy and defence issues on the grounds [*sic*] that, in democracies, informed public opinion is necessary to ensure a viable Western defence system' (1978: 125). Haseler's research while at Georgetown was also backed by the Heritage Foundation, which publishes the right-wing *Policy Review*. Haseler is a member of this journal's editorial board.[6] Clearly, therefore, several sources of funding were specifically combined to make available the means for the continuing ideological counter-offensive based at Georgetown. Haseler and Godson were backed up by a panel of six experts on various national communisms who all contributed background papers for the principal authors – a rather uncharacteristic procedure in academic circles. In addition, some seven assistants are credited.

In 1978 another essentialist voice appeared on the scene in the shape of the *Washington Review of Strategic and International Studies*. But while the voice was new, some old faces were associated with it. The *Washington Review* is published at the Center for Strategic and International Studies, Georgetown University, home of the *Washington Papers*. One of the new journal's editors is Walter Laqueur, and its executive editor is Michael Ledeen, who has also contributed to *Commentary* on European issues. Some contributors to the review, like Rosario Romeo, a professor of history at Rome University (interviewed by the ubiquitous George Urban) and Daniel P. Moynihan, US senator and ex-UN ambassador, have been content simply to fit Eurocommunism into the totalitarian equation. Others have provided more specific political scenarios as, for example, Xavier Marchetti, a former aide of President Pompidou, who took the view that a victory of the Left in the March 1978 French parliamentary elections would be dangerous for both the economy and the state's security. His argument was premised upon an internal domino theory: Mitterrand would be the captive of the socialists' left wing, 'who in turn might turn out to be a hostage of the Communists' (1978: 47). Helmut Sonnenfeldt, who had been one of Kissinger's associates in the State Department,[7] provided a broad international perspective in an interview with Michael Ledeen. Should the West encourage Eurocommunism as a force which would destabilize the Soviet bloc? Sonnenfeldt was cautious, suggesting that it had probably had 'effects in Eastern Europe that add to already existing tendencies toward greater diversity'. But

> the ultimate question for us is whether these effects, whatever their possible benefits, are not offset by the very deleterious consequences that these parties, were they in power, would undoubtedly have on our own Western institutions, Western security, and the relationship among Western European nations and between Western European nations and the United States. (1978: 50)

These scenarios were set out in the context of broader discussions. However, the credibility of 'Eurocommunism' was the central focus of David Owen's speech which was reprinted in the April issue of the *Washington Review*. Owen's position is by no means a simple-minded essentialism. Indeed he takes a rather sophisticated line on the historical development of communism, arguing that its 'natural condition' had 'never been one of monolithic unity; and there is no inherent reason why such unity should prevail today, still less under the direction of Moscow' (1978: 7). However, Owen's main interest lay in stressing the need to maintain strong boundaries between social democrats and Communists. Fraternization across the lines was undesirable. Owen's explicit refusal to use the term 'Eurocommunism', and his reason for doing so – 'the battle is for people's minds' – places him on the same ideological ground as that occupied by *Encounter* and *Commentary*. He is remarkably candid:

> It is deliberate that I have not once mentioned the term Eurocommunism. I am deeply sceptical that any such unified phenomenon exists. It is a dangerous term. It confers a coherence and a respectability on an ill-defined, disparate and

as yet unidentifiable phenomenon. It is very interesting that Western communist leaders are now using the term Eurocommunism. They recognize it has an appealing quality. It is a convenient portmanteau term. It tends to make people suspend their critical faculties, avoid analysing the phenomenon seriously, country by country, and instead take refuge in generalities. 'Eurocommunism' is becoming respectable. It is a term which socialists should eschew. We should give it no currency. (1978: 14)

Walter Laqueur, in an editorial statement commending Owen's views, also showed an awareness of the advantages the term had come to have for the Communists: 'There are great differences between the structures and policies of the Italian and French parties . . . and the term Eurocommunism tends to blur their differences. A good case could be made for declaring a moratorium on its use, but unfortunately this is unlikely to be accepted by all parties' (1978: 3). One can understand such anxieties. The term has become part of the conventional political discourse of élite journals and newspapers. In July 1978 an editorial note in *Problems of Communism* referred to 'trends loosely termed "Eurocommunism"'. The *Daily Telegraph*, no friend of communism of any variety, accepts it as a way of referring to the PCI and the PCE. In February 1979, *The Economist*, in an article discussing European Communist attitudes to events in South–East Asia, pointed to the different positions taken by the PCI, PCF and PCE as evidence of 'a split' in the Eurocommunist ranks – an 'occurrence' which only the use of the term has made possible. While the meaning and the merits of the term remain subjects of controversy, its use does tend to give the parties a positive gloss. They have a distinct position whose basic features are clear. They claim a preference for parliamentary over violent means of achieving power, a respect for political and civil rights, a tempering of the more extreme forms of collectivism in economic and social affairs and a tendency to reject Soviet hegemony in inter-party relations. Clearly there are battles still to be fought on the ideological front.

The ideological division of labour

As our reference to the British ex-Foreign Secretary and his attack on Eurocommunism made originally at Cambridge in November 1977 shows, the distinction between containment theorists and fundamental anti-Communists is not merely an account of individual differences. Rather it leads to an analysis of the different roles in ideological production taken by specific groups of ideological agents. Whereas containment theories appeared mainly in international relations journals published by institutes and organizations closely involved in the development of foreign policy, fundamental anti-Communism has been published in more accessible, quasi-commercial journals like *Commentary* and *Encounter*. Both the foundation of the *Policy Review* and that of the *Washington Review* appear to be attempts to counter containment theorists in the foreign policy field.

Commentary and *Encounter*, however, belong much more to the public sphere, with the role of providing interpretations of developments for further dissemination by politicians and journalists addressing a wider public.

In Britain the main political interventions by Harold Wilson, David Owen and, at an earlier stage, Margaret Thatcher have all followed an anti-Communist line. The only exception has been Eric Heffer, whose version of the social-democratization thesis was published in *The Times* (7 November 1977) and the *Guardian* (29 November 1977). Heffer's *Times* article coincided with Wilson's attack on 'the political plague with no boundaries' in the *Guardian* (7 November 1977) and is evidence of a debate within the labour movement. It is a debate, however, in which those advocating containment or acceptance are largely restricted to working through party journals or left-wing publishing houses, while those taking the traditional anti-Communist line may be confident of reaching a wider audience through wider circulation media. Thus Stuart Holland in his preface to Sassoon's collection of PCI speeches published in 1978 (by Spokesman Books of Nottingham, funded by the Bertrand Russell Foundation) commends it as essential reading for 'people with tired minds, little information or both for whom "Eurocommunism" is an infection of the democratic body politic' and for 'more openminded members of the public who want to know before they judge' (Sassoon, 1978: 7).

This illustrates a crucial point about the nature of the Western cultural system, namely the disjunction which exists between the élite and popular levels, between what might be termed administrative and electoral politics. At the élite level there are grounds for arguing that containment theory was in the ascendant in 1976 and 1977. During this time it apparently coincided with US government policy, founded on the foreign policy consideration that it would do 'them' more harm than it would 'us'. 'Eurocommunism' has hardly been popularized, at least in the English-speaking world, beyond the level of the news magazine and quality newspaper. In so far as it has, what has been involved has been less a diffusion of the debate at the élite level and more of a counter-attack from the fundamental anti-Communists. *Time* and *Newsweek*, for example, while they featured Carrillo's book for its anti-Soviet implications, also featured various anti-Communist tracts and exposés published in France and Spain.

An extended review of 'Eurocommunist' developments in *The Economist* (5 November 1977) quoted only Annie Kriegel, André Glucksmann and Kissinger among Western commentators, all of them prominent anti-Communists. Press reporting of political developments in Europe has accepted the term as a journalistic convenience and so given it currency. Reference has already been made to some of the concern this has provoked among anti-Communists. Michael Ledeen, Laqueur's associate, attacked American reporting of Eurocommunism in *Commentary* in 1977. His article clearly illustrates the counter-attack which was being mounted at that time. Ledeen complained that a term coined to expose Berlinguer's propaganda had come to be treated at face value. But such press reporting, of limited interest to financial and political élites, has to be set against the more popular preoccupation with violence as *the story* coming from the 'Eurocommunist' countries, a story which fits very easily into the paradigm of totalitarianism.

Henry Kissinger, the most prominent anti-Communist of all, has provided a point of reference for almost everyone involved in the debate. He has had access to élite circles such as the International Institute for Strategic Studies, London, the American Enterprise Institute for Public Policy Research and the Hoover Institution on War, Revolution and Peace, and to élite media such as the *Atlantic Quarterly* and *Across the Board*. But his chief importance has been as a publicist and symbol of the essentialist anti-Communist position. In January 1978 this achieved full recognition in a television spectacular, originally made by NBC, and seen in the USA by millions of viewers, according to the BBC which broadcast an extended version on BBC 2 on a Sunday night in what is usually the arts programme slot. Coincidentally, the Carter administration took a public stance against PCI participation in the Italian government at virtually the same time.

'Eurocommunism', Kissinger announced, is communism in Europe, a definition which enabled him to start his exposition with film of the Berlin Wall, the limit of what communism had been able to achieve by force in the West. But now, Kissinger warned, it had found a new way of threatening the West. Through elections it was crossing the wall which had held it in. The programme went on to provide a country-by-country survey in which good points about CP developments were cancelled by bad and in which Kissinger continually repeated a series of slogans to drive home his points. These covered the familiar ground that 'Eurocommunism' was no more than a Machiavellian tactic to gain power, that it would act as a Trojan horse in Western defence, that there was no internal democracy in the parties, that Communist economies were always less productive than capitalist ones, that terror and violence worked in the Communists' favour by provoking a demand for order at any price. Throughout it all there were references to what Kissinger was pleased to call his paradox. Why should communism attract support in the West given the contrast between the prosperity to be found there and the bureaucratic backwardness of Communist states in the East? There, Communism had been tried in practice and found wanting.

Our tentative conclusion to the first part of this chapter, therefore, is that, far from the Western media and cultural system allowing a free flow of debate and opinion, there is a division of labour with important consequences for political communication. Ideological élites, on the one hand, may engage when appropriate in what we termed ideological retooling. On the other hand, at a more general level such innovation is unlikely to change the reliance which the dominant culture and its spokesmen place in their original capital investment, in this case in the essentialism of the Cold War.

From bourgeois to Communist analysis

In the rest of the chapter our primary interest is to chart the manner in which the term 'Eurocommunism' was appropriated by the leadership of the appropriate CPs and to suggest why this occurred. A process of theoretical development was already in train to which the label could be assimilated, although not entirely without difficulties.

The evidence suggests that the term 'Eurocommunism' was coined in mid-1975 (Barbieri) or late 1975 (Levi). Fernando Claudín, in his book *Eurocommunism and Socialism*, is surely wrong about the date when he says: 'Towards the end of 1970 a new word hit the front pages of the international press and rapidly passed into political currency: Eurocommunism. *Originating outside the Communist parties to which it referred*, the term originally inspired reservations in the leaderships of these parties' (Claudín, 1978: 7, emphasis added). As we shall see, these reservations were, with reservations, overcome. For the moment, what is of interest is the vagueness of Claudín's remarks. The term 'Eurocommunism' has been embraced most wholeheartedly by Santiago Carrillo of the PCE, although, even in his celebrated text *'Eurocommunism' and the State*, he has felt obliged to retain the quotation marks. Carrillo's remarks concerning the term are illuminating about the way in which its anti-Communist meaning is transformed and rendered positive:

> the term 'Eurocommunism' . . . is very fashionable, *and though it was not coined by the Communists and its scientific value may be doubtful*, it has acquired a meaning among the public and, in general terms, serves to designate one of the current communist trends . . . the policy and theoretical elaboration which justify 'Eurocommunism' describe a tendency in the modern progressive and revolutionary movement that is endeavouring to get to grips with the realities of our continent – though in essence it is valid for all developed capitalist countries – and adapt to them the development of the world revolutionary process characteristic of our time . . . So 'Eurocommunism' forces itself upon us as a reality, *as long as we cannot find a better definition*. (Carrillo, 1977: 8–9, emphases added)

There has been some doubt about when the three CPs in question began to call themselves 'Eurocommunist'. This is understandable, since the process has been an uneven one: there is some basis for arguing it was in 1976, and some for saying it was in 1977. At the time of the East Berlin conference of European CPs in June 1976, Carrillo was definitely reluctant to use the term, the PCF firmly avoided it, and the PCI made only very qualified use of it. The ideological initiative directed against the CPs in question had been well under way for well over half a year, and clearly Berlinguer in his speech at the Berlin conference felt some riposte was necessary in a context which would gain maximum publicity. After asserting that the West must find its own road to socialism, Berlinguer referred to convergences between the PCI, PCF, CPGB and PCE, and observed:

> It is this new type of elaboration and searching that some people have referred to as 'Eurocommunism'. Obviously, we were not the ones to coin this term, but the very fact that it has gained such wide circulation indicates the depth and extent of an aspiration to see solutions of a new type in the transformation of society in the socialist direction take root and advance in the countries of Western Europe. (Berlinguer, 1976: 61)

What is interesting about Berlinguer's handling of the term is the manner in which he appropriated it and gave it a positive meaning: it was linked to the convergent developments already taking place in several Western CPs. Berlinguer's studied vagueness about its origins and his suggestion that its currency expressed *socialist* aspirations must be calculated moves given the evidence of the earlier part of the chapter.

The quotation above from Carrillo shows him engaged in the same process of appropriation, in presenting its first major popularization by a Western CP leader. According to Claudín, Carrillo first began to use the term in a qualified manner in July 1976 in a report to the central committee of the PCE (in terms which exactly echoed Berlinguer's). The decisive public moment came in December 1976 when Carrillo launched the slogan 'the "Eurocommunist" road to power' (Claudín, 1978: 8). Carrillo's full endorsement is independently confirmed from the date in the preface to his book. One can see, therefore, why some commentators have suggested that the Berlin conference saw the formal launching of 'Eurocommunism' by the CPs themselves (for example, Gati, 1977).

The other date given, which we would consider more acceptable, is the March 1977 meeting of the PCI, PCF and PCE in Madrid. This was labelled the 'Eurocommunist summit' in the press. On this occasion Georges Marchais of the PCF gave an extensive gloss on the term, once again pointing out that the CPs themselves had not invented it. According to the *Morning Star*, 17 March 1977, Marchais said:

> while taking into account the differences that exist between our three countries, our socialist democracy will differ from that which at present exists in those countries which have gone over to socialism. If that is what is meant by Eurocommunism, then we agree. But if it was thought, which none of us did, that Eurocommunism envisaged the establishment of a new international centre, then our reply is a categorical No.

The PCF has never been keen on the term, and some of this reluctance emerges in Marchais' qualifications. However, according to Goldsborough, he had become convinced that the term was working to the CPs' advantage rather than to their detriment.

The next major step in 'Eurocommunism's' appropriation by Communists came with the publication of Santiago Carrillo's book. Carrillo's critique of Soviet 'socialism' provoked outraged diatribes from the CPSU through the medium of the journal *New Times* (June 1977). The *New Times'* attack on Carrillo pointed up the unwillingness of the major

Western CPs to identify themselves as 'Eurocommunist', although this is a point which has received little attention. The CPs which defended Carrillo did so individually, by supporting his right to his own views, but without endorsing them – in particular his criticisms of the nature of the Soviet Union. An editorial in *L'Unità* (28 June 1977) endorsed the line taken by the major Western CPs, but was extremely careful in its use of the term 'Eurocommunism', placing it in quotation marks, and using the prefix 'so-called'. Carrillo's book was described as not being 'a finished exposition of a "doctrine" of "Eurocommunism": a doctrine which does not exist, so much so that there is no organizational centre nor any comprehensive codification, although very significant documents have been underwritten by the interested parties on a bilateral basis'. Later, however, the article singled out a key feature of 'what is called Eurocommunism', namely, 'the relationship between the process of development of political democracy and the big social transformations'.

Clearly, some explanation needs to be sought concerning the different attitudes of the PCI, PCE and PCF towards using the term. The PCE, we would argue, had a most pressing need to achieve national recognition at a time when Francoism was finally collapsing, and had to assert its own democratic credentials. This was most easily done by an attack on Soviet shortcomings. It is noticeable that the PCE flourished 'Eurocommunism' in a very distinctive way. It also attracted most of the public attacks on 'Eurocommunism' by the CPSU. Manuel Azcárate (1977), the head of the PCE's international department and the target of a second attack in *New Times*, chose to argue that the Madrid summit 'has imparted a definite form to the term Eurocommunism', and to reaffirm the need to criticize the Soviet bloc – an emphasis notably lacking from the approaches of PCI and PCF. Claudín has also observed that, while for Carrillo going out on a limb is easier, the other CPs are now closer to power, so 'the maintenance of good relations with Moscow is starting to become a matter of state interest for the two parties'.

The PCI has no problem of identity, and hence little need of the term 'Eurocommunist'. It is the largest West European CP, with a well-established and distinctive road and a long history of expounding it. Berlinguer and other major figures such as Napolitano have, on the whole, tended to limit themselves to appropriating the term, without placing very great emphasis on its diffusion. None the less, it is clear that Berlinguer has been careful to retain some title to the term whereas other members of his party have failed to see the advantage in this. For instance, in the 1977 *Unità* festival in Modena, after a senior party historian had argued that 'Eurocommunism' did not exist, Berlinguer specifically took up this point in his concluding speech on 18 September. He stressed the convergences between the Spanish, French and Italian parties, carefully noting that they did not constitute a regional organization, and argued that this might properly be called 'Eurocommunism' (Radice, 1978). On the other hand, some leaders of the PCI, such as Amendola, have especially stressed the

Italian specificity of their policies. In a style reminiscent of Marchais, Amendola says:

> I think that when people speak of 'Eurocommunism' they are wrong, because there is no such thing – there are as many specific strategies as there are Communist parties. We are opposed to the re-establishment of a single world centre for the communist movement in Moscow – and we are not going to establish a single centre of 'Eurocommunism' in Rome or Paris. (Amendola, 1977)

It is also notable that in the interviews Eric Hobsbawm conducted with Giorgio Napolitano (Napolitano/Hobsbawm, 1977), a book widely debated and translated in Western Europe, there is no mention at all of the term 'Eurocommunism' in the first interview (dated October 1975), and that it only enters during Hobsbawm's second interview (which took place just after the Madrid summit). Napolitano gives the term a rather vague definition and is quick to point out that the same analysis extends to CPs outside Europe, such as the Japanese.

The PCF has been more consistent and emphatic in its nationalism, and in its hostility to NATO and the EEC, than the other two parties. Marchais' line at Madrid was anticipated in one of the party journals (*France Nouvelle*, 28 February 1977) by Gérard Streiff of the PCF international department, who acknowledged the 'broad common themes' being developed by the CPs in advanced capitalist states, but was careful to state that '"Eurocommunism" is not part of our political vocabulary. In fact we do not believe that there are any universal or regional "models" of socialism.' More recently, Jean Kanapa of the party's political bureau enumerated 'the characteristics of Eurocommunism' at the Fondation Nationale des Sciences Politiques in Paris during November 1977. Kanapa observed:

> To conclude, the word Eurocommunism is badly chosen. In effect, it designates a reality which concerns not only the communist parties of Europe, nor all the communist parties of Europe. But we haven't the relish for a war of words . . . The expression Eurocommunism – in the way that we use it – has nowadays, for us, acquired a positive, an offensive meaning; it renders the aspiration of those working for socialism *in* liberty. And it is in that way that it is accepted. No doubt this explains why nowadays the term embarrasses those very ones who invented it. (Kanapa, 1976)

Kanapa's remarks show a clear (and somewhat tongue-in-cheek) awareness of the benefits for the Communist parties which derived from the appropriation of the term, while still keeping a certain wary distance from it.

In sum, our argument is that the term 'Eurocommunism' came to be used by the various CPs (with varying emphases) because it was important for them not to permit a major ideological initiative to be successful. In their response they managed to appropriate the term and develop a positive meaning, thus creating difficulties for those who had initially used the term in a hostile sense. What is noticeable is the extremely rapid diffusion of 'Eurocommunist' texts – through translation – into Western Marxist culture. In this respect the PCI and the PCE must be judged especially good publicists.

An interesting question is whether the CPs are likely to use the term 'Eurocommunist' in the future. With the breakdown of the Common Programme in France, and the failure of the Left to form a new majority, only the PCI is left poised on the threshold of power in the immediate future. There has been a definite tendency for the term 'Eurocommunist' to lose currency in the wider non-Marxist discourse. With only one CP posing a threat to capitalism, and that less serious than appeared in 1974–6, the 'Euro' designation has rather less work to do. The outcome may be that it is dropped – at least for the time being – by the ideologists of capitalist democracy. Given the reluctant record of the PCI and PCF, its future within Marxist discourse also looks uncertain. The only new area in which it has been espoused recently is amongst East European dissidents – as for instance in the manifesto of the SED opposition which appeared early in 1978 in *Der Spiegel* (2 and 9 January 1978).

Conclusion

In this chapter we have presented some of the main types of ideological work which have been done on the growth of communism in Western Europe in recent years. We would not claim that the review is complete, but it is sufficiently comprehensive to make a number of concluding points about the way such ideological work is carried on.

The first and most important point is that ideology has been developed in two different cultural systems, networks of meaning in the Geertzian sense. Each of these is underpinned by different sets of ideologists, organizations and communicating media. Each is available to the other. The ideologues working in one tradition take and make use of material produced in the other. But the relationship between the two is not one of interpenetration and overlap founded on shared meanings. Rather there is a boundary between the two which is crossed only in ways analogous to warfare. Information and ideas are used for intelligence on developments within the opposing camp, captured and converted into the terms of the opposing system or used simply as propaganda with which to engage the other side in battle. The extent of the difference between the two systems is brought out very clearly in Maurice Cornforth's *The Open Philosophy and the Open Society*. Writing 'for Marx' against Karl Popper, Cornforth illustrates how differences over particular topics are all part and parcel of a fundamental difference of approach. As is clear from the title, in the course of his book Cornforth attempts to realign some key symbols.

In the case of 'Eurocommunism', the difference between the content of the two systems can be seen in the different attention given to constitutional, political forms as against economic and class relationships.

It was the possibility of Communists achieving political power through electoral means which first put 'Eurocommunism' on the Western agenda. But what for anti-Communists appeared to be a Machiavellian tactic to gain political power for Marxists involved a reanalysis of contemporary developments in economic relationships and the class struggle. Each system of thought has a different account of political power.

This brings us to a second important concluding point, one about 'Eurocommunism' itself as an ideological figure. There is more to the development of a new sign than its content. Of particular significance is the relationship between the new sign and those which have covered the same subject before. Part of our argument has been to show how the ideological initiative in the creation and development of this figure passed from side to side. In the West, communism is necessarily a counter-culture which seeks to exploit what Vološinov has called the 'multi-accentuality' of ideological signs. Multi-accentuality was particularly apparent in the case of 'Euro-communism' because of the way it developed the understanding of communism available in the West. It disturbed the uni-accentual account of communism established in the dominant ideology. Not only was there the suggestion that there might be 'good Communists' who accepted democratic values, but, more fundamentally, it allowed that there might be a different type of communism, different in the crucial respect that it fell outside the boundaries of totalitarianism theory. The conclusion of that theory has been that all democracy's enemies are fundamentally the same.[8]

It is interesting to recall that until recently all forms of socialism, including social democracy, appeared on the other side of the divide. In his celebrated work *Capitalism, Socialism and Democracy*, Joseph Schumpeter discusses the relationships between socialism and democracy in sceptical terms closely akin to those cited earlier. For example, Schumpeter (1970: 238) argues that there is nothing essential to socialism that makes it democratic, and 'the only question is whether and in what sense it *can* be democratic'. While denying that he is accusing the classical German and Austrian social democrats of the Second International of Machiavellianism or insincerity, Schumpeter does lay emphasis on the opportunism he detects:

> They lived in environments that would have strongly resented undemocratic talk and practice . . . In some cases they had every reason to espouse democratic principles that sheltered them and their activity. In other cases most of them were satisfied with the results, political and other, that advance on democratic lines promised to yield . . . Thus in professing allegiance to democracy, they simply did the obvious thing all along. (Schumpeter, 1970: 238–9)

The question of whether all forms of socialism are inherently anti-democratic is still a live issue. It has been taken up recently by many of the ideologues involved in the crusade against Eurocommunism. In 1978 *Commentary* devoted its August issue to a symposium of twenty-six replies to the question of whether there was an 'inescapable connection between capitalism and democracy'? The preamble suggested that many intellectuals now accepted as plausible what they had once rejected as wrong and politically dangerous, that there 'may be something intrinsic to socialism which exposes it ineluctably to the "totalitarian temptation"'. As well as this implicit reference to Revel, *Commentary* referred explicitly to the 'new philosophers' in France and 'Paul Johnson and others' in England as examples of those holding such ideas in Europe. It is safe to assume that among the 'others' in England was Stephen Haseler, who in 1977 had contributed a piece to *Commentary* on 'The Collapse of the Social Democrats' in which he had cited Revel, the *nouveaux philosophes* and Johnson as signs of hope that some had already warned against the slide of social democracy into socialism.

At this point the ideological battle shifts from the theory of totalitarianism's critique of communism to an effort to develop a particular conception of 'social democracy' as the only possible form of democratic socialism and thereby to monopolize ideological space. This brings us back to 'Eurocommunism', for in another spin-off from his book Haseler argued that 'differences of style and intellectual vitality [apart], the British Labour left is a branch of the "Eurocommunist" movement of Western Europe. It certainly has more in common with "Eurocommunism" than with Northern European parties of social democracy' (*The Times*, 27 October 1978). The danger which follows, according to Haseler in this article, is the break-up of the Atlantic alliance and the unity of NATO. But if Haseler, secretary of the Social Democratic Alliance, a ginger group on the Labour Party's right wing, is content with a single condemnatory point on defence policy, Paul Johnson, ex-editor of the *New Statesman* and currently contributor to the *Sunday Telegraph* and the *Evening Standard*, fights the battle on a wider front. In a piece in the *Standard* (5 December 1978) he welcomed the publication of a new volume of right-wing essays, *Confrontation: Will the Open Society Survive until 1989?* (Institute of Economic Research, 1978), which posed the choice between collectivism and individual freedom. Johnson applauded the growth of a new dynamic orthodoxy on the Right. This includes the *nouveaux philosophes*, 'Fritz' Hayek, author of *The Road to Serfdom*, one of the early texts on totalitarianism and favourite reading of Margaret Thatcher and, on America's east coast, *Commentary*. In the gathering gloom of their own predictions, this group of ideologues are not only whistling to keep up their spirits but passing the music round as well.

Returning to the case of 'Eurocommunism', the recognition of a distinctive new type of communism ran counter to the fundamentally essentialist notion that communism is one, indivisible and identifiable as the enemy. The problems this created were particularly apparent the more discussion of 'Eurocommunism' moved out of élite circles into popular consumption. This brings us to our third concluding point, the light the 'Eurocommunist' case throws on the division of labour that exists between ideological élites in the West.

Problems with public opinion already lay behind *détente*. According to Kissinger's own account, ideological adjustments were necessary to reassure Western publics confused by events in Czechoslovakia, Vietnam, Chile and elsewhere. The problem since has been how to achieve this ideological realignment without abandoning confrontation. One initial attraction of 'Eurocommunism' may have been its anti-Soviet potential. Certainly this was what first impressed the Communist ideologues who attacked it as an anti-Soviet construct. But within the context of the West, its value was much more ambiguous, a new form of communism linked to symbols like Dubcek, of the human face, and Allende, of the democratic road, which had already proved troublesome. It meant that in the West anti-Communists were all the time fighting off the back foot, seeking to show that what they had identified as different was in fact similar, that 'Eurocommunists' were not to be trusted.

In summary, we may conclude that 'Eurocommunism' had four values as a figure in the Western system. Its first was to signal an old danger in a new form. Its second, the foreign policy potential, suggested further disorder in the enemy's ranks with the added attraction that it might provoke dissent in Eastern Europe. A third was the economic potential. If PCI participation in Italian government should prove necessary to help capitalism in that country overcome the crisis, then it was as well that it should be clear that it was not just any old communism but something new, distinct and technocratically flavoured.

The fourth advantage developed in use, from the experience of fighting off the ideological back foot. As a compendious term 'Eurocommunism' made possible a form of argument by contra-example. Any 'good' phenomenon in one country could be countered by evidence of 'bad' practice in another with the suggestion, implicit or explicit, that only the 'bad' was real. The technique reached its apotheosis in Kissinger's broadcast, when he included a section on the Portuguese party, a party which may be 'European' but which no one hitherto had had the nerve to suggest was 'Euro'. The foreign policy value lost credibility when the Carter administration changed its assessment in January 1978. The economic value was always better served by isolating the Italians for special treatment. 'Eurocommunism' is unlikely to survive simply as a convenient compendium. That is essentially a method of defence rather than attack and there is no reason to suppose that spokesmen for the dominant culture will make a virtue of a defensive posture.

As for the CPs, our argument is that 'Eurocommunism' has been used more to appropriate an ideological initiative than as a term of Marxist analysis. Just as the term has 'run away' from its original creators, so it has 'run away' from its appropriators in the CP leaderships. In spite of the care they have taken to distance themselves from the concept, such leaders are commonly identified as 'Eurocommunist' in discussions on the Left, where the term has temporarily acquired as much currency as in mainstream political discussion.

Notes

1 These claims are also set out in the definitive book by Wolfgang Leonhard, *Eurokommunismus: Herausforderung für Ost und West* (1978: 9). This account, which became available to us only after the first version of this chapter had been written, bases its assessment largely on the same sources as ours. While Barbieri's claim is taken most seriously, Leonhard does not consider the origins of the term, or its ideological ramifications to be of especial importance, since his main interest is in exploring the practical, political consequences for the Left of the recent developments.

2 In recent history 'white' has been associated generally with royalist, legitimist and conservative causes, such as the monarchists of France, Spain and Russia. 'Neo' appears to be a more neutral prefix, but in an Italian context there is a particular connection, this time with the contemporary usage of 'neo-Fascist' for parties which are reincarnations of a movement once defeated. 'Euro', however, says something about international co-operation, international capitalism, technocracy and development. It is hard to resist the conclusion that all were fundamentally unsatisfactory to serve as an ideological figure to encapsulate opposition to the growth of the Communist parties in the West, since any such specific designation allowed the possibility that communism might take *different forms*. This runs counter to the established anti-Communist position, founded on totalitarianism theory, and popularized through the Cold War, which takes an essentialist view of communism as one and indivisible. Cf. Clifford Geertz's analysis of another unsatisfactory ideological figure: 'slave labour law' as applied to the Taft–Hartley Act (Geertz: 1975).

3 An apparently favourable assessment of the PCI after the June 1976 elections is available from Euroeconomics, a research combine of major Western banks for FF500, providing its contents are not made public.

4 *Commentary*, like *Encounter*, has been active in countering the threat of 'Eurocommunism', as is detailed below.

5 It is not just at the foreign policy élite level that the war is waged. Aron and Revel occupy crucial roles in the important French political weekly *L'Express*. Aron is president of the editorial board and Revel the magazine's director. *L'Express* currently specializes in anti-Communist crusading. See Walter Schwarz, '£200,000 Damages for Editor', *Guardian*, 23 February 1979.

6 The *Policy Review* was founded in 1977, and the very first article to appear in it concerned the 'spectre of Eurocommunism'. Its author, who is also a member of the editorial board, was Robert Moss, a British journalist who edits the *Economist*'s confidential *Foreign Report*. Moss is well known in Britain for his prominent role in the Institute for the Study of Conflict, a body which specializes in counter-insurgency literature (cf. ch. 4).

7 Sonnenfeldt has already given his name to the 'Brezhfeldt doctrine', associated with the previous American administration, that the spheres of influence of the USSR and the USA should remain stable. 'Brezhfeldt doctrine' is *Le Monde*'s term conflating the doctrines of Brezhnev with those of Helmut Sonnenfeldt as expressed at a meeting of American diplomats in London in December 1975.

8 Cf. the title of Annie Kriegel's polemic against 'Eurocommunism', *Un Autre Communisme? Kriegel's* answer is an unhesitating 'Non, çest la même chose!'

References

Amendola, G., interviewed by Weber, H. (1977) 'The Italian Road to Socialism', *New Left Review*, November–December: 39–50.

Aron, R. (1977) *Plaidoyer pour l'Europe Décadente*. Paris: Robert Laffont; extracts translated as 'My Defence of our Decadent Europe', *Encounter*, September–October 1977.

Azcárate, M. (1977) 'Eurocommunism: A Reality, a Hope', *Mundo Obrero*, March; reprinted in *Euro-Red*, 4: 4–5.

Berlinguer, E. (1976) 'For New Roads towards Socialism in Italy and Europe', *The Italian Communists*, 2(3).

Bettiza, E. (1978) 'Great Illusions in the Face of Danger', *Encounter*, January: 21–3.

Carli, G. (1976) 'Italy's Malaise', *Foreign Affairs*, July: 708–18.

Carrillo, S. (1977) *'Eurocommunism' and the State*. London: Lawrence & Wishart.

Chirac, J. (1978) 'France: Illusions, Temptations, Ambitions', *Foreign Affairs*, April: 489–99.

Claudín, F. (1978) *Eurocommunism and Socialism*. London: New Left Books; Spanish original published 1977.

Cornforth, M. (1977) *The Open Philosophy and the Open Society*. London: Lawrence & Wishart, rev. edn.

Dalma, A. Rovan, J., Razumovsky, A., Vermehren, M. and Ramseier, H. (1977) *Euro-Kommunismus*. Zurich: Edition Interfrom.

Devlin, K. (1977) 'The Challenge of Eurocommunism', *Problems of Communism*, XXVI, January–February.

Domhoff, G.W. (1969) 'Who Made American Foreign Policy, 1945–1963?', in D. Horowitz (ed.), *Corporations and the Cold War*. New York: Monthly Review Press.

Earle, J. (1976) 'The Italian Economy: A Diagnosis', *The World Today*, 32(6) June: 214–21.

Gati, C. (1977) 'The "Europeanization" of Communism', *Foreign Affairs*, April: 539–53).

Geertz, C. (1975) 'Ideology as a Cultural System', in *The Interpretation of Cultures*. London: Hutchinson.

Goldsborough, J.O. (1977) 'Eurocommunism after Madrid', *Foreign Affairs*, July: 800–14.

Haseler, S. (1977) 'Europe: The Collapse of the Social Democrats', *Commentary*, 64(6).

Haseler, S. and Godson, R. (1978) *Eurocommunism: Implications for East and West*. London: Macmillan.

Hayek, F. (1944) *The Road to Serfdom*. London: Routledge & Kegan Paul.

Institute of Economic Research (1978) *Confrontation: Will the Open Society Survive until 1989?* Hobart.

Kanapa, J. (1976) 'Les caractéristiques de l'eurocommunisme', *Recherches Internationales à la Lumière du Marxisme*, 3–4: L'Eurocommunisme; published in 1978.

Kanapa, J. (1977) 'A "New Policy" of the French Communists?', *Foreign Affairs*, January: 280–94.

Kissinger, H.A. (1977a) 'Communist Parties in West Europe: Challenge to the West', *Atlantic City Quarterly*, 15 (3), Autumn.

Kissinger, H.A. (1977b) 'Eurocommunism – Kissinger's Warning', *Across the Board*, September: 82–9.

Kolakowski, L. (1977) 'The Euro-Communist Schism', *Encounter*, XLIX (2), August.

Kolakowski, L. (1978) *Main Currents in Marxism*, 3 vols. Oxford: Clarendon Press.

Kriegel, A. (1977) *Un Autre Communisme?* Paris: Hachette.

La Malfa, U. (1978) 'Communism and Democracy in Italy', *Foreign Affairs*, April: 476–88.

Lange, P. (1976) 'What Is to Be Done – about Italian Communism?', *Foreign Policy*, Winter: 224–40.

Laqueur, W. (1976) 'Eurocommunism and its Friends', *Commentary*, 62(2), August: 25–30.

Laqueur, W. (1978) 'The Eurocommunist Debate' (editorial statement), *Washington Review of Strategic and International Studies*, 1(2), April.

Ledeen, M. (1977) 'The "News" about Eurocommunism', *Commentary*, 64 (4), December: 53–8).

Leonhard, W. (1978) *Eurokommunismus: Herausforderung für Ost und West*. Munich: Bertelsmann.

Levi, A. (1977a) 'Eurocommunism: The Italian Experience So Far', *Across the Board*, July.

Levi, A. (1977b) 'Italy's "New" Communism', *Foreign Policy*, Spring: 28–56.

Lieber, R.J. (1977) 'The Pendulum Swings to Europe', *Foreign Policy*, Spring.

Löwenthal, R. (1977) 'Can Communism Offer an Alternative World Order? Some Lessons of 20th Century Politics', *Encounter*, XLVIII (7), April.

McInnes, N. (1975) *The Communist Parties of Western Europe*. London: Oxford University Press.

McInnes, N. (1976) *Eurocommunism*. Washington Papers, No. 37. London: Sage.

Marchetti, X. (1978) 'The French Left and March Elections', *Washington Review of Strategic and International Studies*, 1 (1), January.

Moss, R. (1977) 'The Spectre of Eurocommunism', *Policy Review*, 1 (1), Summer.

Moynihan, D. (1978) 'The American Political Elite: A Conversation with Michael A. Ledeen', *Washington Review of Strategic and International Studies*, 1 (1), January.

Napolitano, G. (1978) 'The Italian Crisis: A Communist Perspective', *Foreign Affairs*, July: 790–9.

Napolitano, G., interviewed by Hobsbawm, E. (1977) *The Italian Road to Socialism*. Nottingham: Journeyman.

Nichols, P. (1976) 'On the Italian Crisis', *Foreign Affairs*, April: 511–26.

Owen, D. (1978) 'Communism, Socialism and Democracy', *Washington Review of Strategic and International Studies*, 1 (2), April.

Popov, M. (1976) '"Eurocommunism" and the Pan-European Conference', *The World Today*, 32 (10), October: 387–92.

Radice, L.L. (1978) 'Un socialismo da inventare', *Critica Marxista*, 4, July–August.

Revel, J.F. (1976) *La Tentation Totalitaire*. Paris: Laffont.

Revel, J.F. (1978) 'The Myths of Eurocommunism', *Foreign Affairs*, January: 295–305.

Romeo, R. (1978) '"Rome 1984?" A Conversation with G. Urban', *Washington Review of Strategic and International Studies*, 1 (1), January.

Sassoon, D. (ed.) (1978) *The Italian Communists Speak for Themselves*. Nottingham: Spokesman.

Schumpeter, J.A. (1970) *Capitalism, Socialism and Democracy*. London: Unwin.

Segre, S. (1976) 'The "Communist Question" in Italy', *Foreign Affairs*, July: 692–707.

Silberman, L. (1977) 'Yugoslavia's "Old" Communism', *Foreign Policy*, Spring.

Sonnenfeldt, H. (1978) 'The Sonnenfeldt Doctrine Revisited: A Conversation with Michael A. Ledeen', *Washington Review of Strategic and International Studies*, 1 (2), April.

Stehle, H. (1977) 'The Italian Experiment and the Communists', *The World Today*, 33 (1), January: 7–16.

Stehle, H. (1978) 'The Italian Communists on the Parliamentary Path to Power', *The World Today*, 34 (5), May: 135–83.

Steinkühler, M. (ed.) (1977a) *Eurokommunismus im Widerspruch: Analyse und Dokumentation*. Cologne: Verlag Wissenschaft und Politik.

Steinkühler, M. (1977b) 'Ursprung und Konzept des Eurokommunismus: Gespräch mit Frane Barbiere', *Deutschland-Archiv*, April.

Tiersky, R. (1974) *French Communism, 1920–1972*. New York: Columbia University Press.

Tiersky, R. (1976) 'French Communism in 1976', *Problems of Communism*, 25 (1), January–February.

Timmermann, H. (1977) 'Eurocommunism: Moscow's Reaction and the Implications for Eastern Europe', *The World Today*, 33 (10), October: 376–85.

Urban, G. (1977) 'Communism with an Italian Face? A Conversation with Lucio Lombardo Radice', *Encounter*, XLVIII (5), May.

Urban, G. (ed.) (1978a) *Eurocommunism: Its Roots and Future in Italy and Elsewhere*. London: Temple Smith.

Urban, G. (1978b) 'Have They Really Changed? A Conversation with Altiero Spinelli. Eurocommunism, Again', *Encounter*, 1 (1), January.

Vološinov, V.N. (1973) *Marxism and the Philosophy of Language*. London: Seminar Press.

Introduction to Part III

People often talked about languages; seven or eight different tongues were spoken in our city alone, everyone understood something of each language. Only the little girls, who came from villages, spoke just Bulgarian and were therefore considered stupid. Each person counted up the languages he knew; it was important to master several, knowing them could save one's life or the lives of other people.

Elias Canetti, *The Tongue Set Free* (1988).

Their identities (assuming they believed they had them) had, at best, grown over their faces like iron masks. He shed his own identity at will, studied it, put it away, put on another one, in which he studied himself again, as watchful as ever, always finding himself guilty in one way or other. His identities were forged not from the iron of a steadfast lifetime but from extremely light, virtually experimental and inter-changeable materials, and they had not become second nature to him; although they were merely hypothetical, like molecular models scientists construct, he would find himself in each of them. Every one was undeniably *I* to him.

Gregor von Rezzori, *Memoirs of an Anti-Semite* (1983)

'The first step in liquidating a people,' said Hubl, 'is to erase its memory. Destroy its books, its culture, its history. Then have somebody write new books, manufacture a new culture, invent a new history. Before long the nation will begin to forget what it is and what it was. The world around it will forget even faster.'

Milan Kundera, *The Book of Laughter and Forgetting* (1983).

Identity is a quest that is always open, while the obsessive defence of one's origins can at times be as much a form of regressive slavery as, in other circumstances, is willing submission to displacement.

Claudio Magris, *Danube* (1989).

These final chapters tackle the question of collective identity. In the coming years, this theme is certain to become increasingly central in the human sciences, and what is published here is merely an incomplete ground-clearing exercise for work to come.

Chapters 7 and 8 were originally published as a single long essay with a sceptical purpose. While working in a 'European' academic institution, I was struck by the disjuncture between the official ideology of the common culture and the persistence of national diversity amongst my colleagues and friends. Flawed Republic of Letters? Certainly. Euro-Tribe of Scholars? Well, maybe . . .

These next chapters begin by interrogating some recent work in communication and cultural studies to see what lies behind the current talk of 'cultural identity', 'audiovisual space', 'the defence of the national culture' and, last but not least, that powerfully emotive construct, 'European identity'. The approach taken here has been analytical and conceptual, the aim being to look at some of the key assumptions that lie behind the formulations used in contemporary policy debate. Has some serious conceptual thought gone into the plethora of labels and slogans that populate cultural discussion? My conclusion is that there is little or none: the currently fashionable discourse offers respectability and brand identification for a variety of contending politico-economic projects in the cultural domain. Probe further and you simply cannot avoid digging into the theoretical subsoil from which the confusions of the surface spring.

The scepticism that permeates this final part relates in the first instance to the widely assumed role of mass communication in the construction of cultural identities. There is an easy and obvious answer: media *must* be important because they are so prevalent. *Must* they be so? And *how* might they be so in different ways in different circumstances? In Chapter 7 this takes us into a discussion of recent media theory and political debate. However, there is little to be discovered there about how to theorize national identity or the role of cultural processes in its construction. Chapter 8 moves on to consider some noteworthy and largely recent contributions to social theory which begin to provide us with leverage on the profound and far-reaching problems entailed in talking about 'national identity', still the key instance of collective identification in the contemporary world.

My scepticism also concerns the project of 'Europeanization', as is made clear in Chapter 9. This chapter has been written on the run; and, apart from adding passing references to work appearing just as this book goes to press, I have largely left it in the shape it finally assumed (after numerous earlier versions) in the late spring of 1990. The circumstances with which it deals are undergoing continual change, and in the time-scales of academic publishing one cannot be up to date, only at best identify some of the pressing dilemmas that lie ahead.

7

On National Identity (I):
Cultural Politics and the Mediologists

Euro-Angst, Euro-Kultur-als-Lösung

'National identity' has become an all-purpose catchword at the centre of contemporary discussions of the relationships between the production and consumption of culture and the constitution of the nation-state or EEC. The contexts in which this concern is expressed are various, as are the assumptions which inform them.

Inside the EEC, the cultural alarm-bells are ringing. A symptomatic carillon comes from the recent European Commission (CEC) Green Paper, *Television without Frontiers:*

> Information is a decisive, perhaps the most decisive, factor in European unification . . . European unification will only be achieved if Europeans want it. Europeans will only want it if there is such a thing as European identity. A European identity will only develop if Europeans are adequately informed. At present, information via the mass media is controlled at national level. (CEC, 1984a: 2)

So, open up the frontiers and let a thousand programmes bloom. My interest in this quotation (clearly an important one, as it appears *twice* in the report, on pp. 2 and 28) is in its rhetoric and assumptions. Unity is the goal, and 'information' (which may be read as an aspect of 'culture', in a broad anthropological sense) is *the* means to achieving it. Unity at a European level is said to be an outcome of an act of will dependent upon a prior condition: a 'European identity'. But this is in turn dependent upon something else: 'information'. Information (culture) is therefore held to act as a homogenizer or articulator of the will: it is a thoroughly idealist and voluntarist perception of the construction of the desired social order, and a rather improbable explanation.

It would be labouring the point to present too many other instances of such (literally) wishful thinking. However, a further quotation reinforces the point and lets us make another. It comes from a pamphlet on *The European Community and Culture:*

> A community of culture in Europe is already an undeniable fact. Beneath the surface diversity of languages, tastes and artistic styles, there is a likeness, a kinship, a European dimension or identity based on a common cultural heritage. The contributions of different individuals, ideas, styles and values have, over the centuries, created our common civilization. (CEC, 1985: 3)

Once again the same counters come into play. A common culture exists; diversity is merely superficial or epiphenomenal. In fact, the common culture *already* confers an identity on Europeans. Clearly, this is a more affirmative version of the story, in which there is a formulaic solution to the trickly problem of actual cultural variation: unity *in* diversity.

But how are we to imagine this European patrimony? 'Unity in diversity' is one formula among many. There has always been an ambiguity about 'Europe' as a category. In this connection, a nicely instructive book is *The European Inheritance*, conceived during the latter stages of World War II as an 'objective' history of European civilization (see Barker et al., 1954). The initiative came from the History Committee of the Books Committee appointed by the Conference of Allied Ministers of Education in February 1943. Intended to be an improving text for young people, the book's remit was to construct a positive version of European history, putting the Nazi episode behind it, and assessing the post-war divisions quite coolly. In the 'Review and Epilogue', the eminent historian Sir Ernest Barker distinguished between a southern conception of Europe going back to the ancient Greeks of 'a sea, with its surrounding shores and their hinterland' and the 'northern or modern' point of view of 'a long horizontal peninsula, stretching from west to east (or from east to west according to one's choice), which is physically an annexe or outcrop of the vast land-mass of Asia' (1954: 296). It is an obvious point, but worth stating, that all formulae about cultural identity are artefacts which presuppose a standpoint concerning a long and complex historical process. The very vagueness of current Euro-formulae is a token of the problems of coping with that history, especially of war and international rivalry. In a phrase which we shall have reason to discuss further below, the Euro-ideologues must create an 'imagined community' out of a geographical space: 'The Great Europe of the geographers – the Europe which stretches from the West coast of Ireland to the Urals, and from the North Cape to the south coast of Sicily – has always been a spatial rather than a mental and historical unit' (Barker et al., 1954: 346).

Returning to the Green Paper we find that the presumed unity is still in the process of making. Television – especially European programmes – is ascribed a major role in 'developing and nurturing awareness of the rich variety of Europe's common cultural and national heritage' and in promoting the recognition of a 'common destiny' (CEC, 1984a: 28). The Commission's document, however, blithely and (if we impose the condition of a consistent Euro-discourse) contradictorily assumes that the 'creation of a powerful European cinema and television production industry' will 'generate jobs and *help Europe to protect its cultural identity* and its hopes of economic expansion in the face of American and Japanese expansion' (CEC, 1984a: 4, emphasis added). Here the identity apparently already exists: there is a supra-national culture to be defended in which 'Europe' is conceived as an already constituted subject or agent (cf. *Towards a European Television Policy*, CEC, 1984b: 8–9). To cap the rhetoric we have a ritual message from a long-departed father of the Community: '"If we were beginning the European Community all over again,", said Jean Monnet, "we should begin with culture"' (cited in CEC, 1984b: 10). A 'sacred' injunction of this kind legitimizes the seeming inversion of the customary emphasis, the shift from the pre-eminence of the economy to that of culture. However, 'culture' is clearly there to serve economic ends. It functions as a discreet synonym for the protection of domestic production capacities and employment.

Before moving on to inspect other, related rhetorics, it is certainly worth making a point about the vision of European history which underpins the official account. The alleged common culture has come about through 'the contributions of different individuals, ideas, styles and values' over the centuries. But an alternative perception would be one that at the very least insisted upon the devastation effected by centuries of war on the Old Continent and of imperialistic expansion on a global scale – are not these the makers of what we have now? The silence is symptomatic: for the common culture may well be held to be an imaginary one based upon a necessary forgetfulness about the awful past. The present Europe of a 'common culture' is a product of, above all else, the depredations of World War II and the transformed world order which ensued. But that is a tactless thing to say and an inadmissible, suppressed premise of contemporary Euro-rhetoric. Another way of putting this is to say that the present project of 'unity in diversity' distorts to such an extent as to involve the rewriting of history and the necessary recodification of social memory. These are important features of the construction of collective identity which will be considered at greater length below.

Images as cultural defence

The problems of the Eurocrats have become the preoccupations of academics and consultants. One exemplary instance is the so-called 'European Cultural Values Project' (which title assumes what it is intended to discover) based at the European Institute for the Media at Manchester University. In his recent study of *Television in Europe*, Anthony Pragnell (1985) takes the problem of 'what can be done to encourage the greater Europeanization of our television services'. This project was undertaken 'at the suggestion of representatives of broadcasting organizations from the smaller countries of Western Europe. *They feel concern at the effect on European culture and values of the showing of television programmes from abroad, most particularly from North America*' (Pragnell, 1985: 1, emphasis added). *Le défi américain*, once again. That is not new, nor is it trivial. However, what is clearly assumed is the existence of a 'European culture' and of 'European values'. Further, it is also assumed that we can intelligibly speak of 'effects' upon a clear-cut 'object'.

I am less concerned with Pragnell's empirical findings than with what is taken to be the problem and its possible solution. He talks of European fears that

> heavy viewing of programmes from other countries (particularly from the United States with its strong culture or variety of cultures) would over time erode the culture, values and proper pride in their own traditions of the countries of Europe. The fear is also that an undue use of US material would have a similar effect on that common sense of identity in Western Europe as a whole which already exists to a significant extent and which it is the aim of the European institutions to foster. (Pragnell, 1985: 5)

This perception does not strike one as very different in spirit from the cultural imperialism thesis, most prominently espoused over the past couple of decades, in a Marxist framework, by Herbert Schiller and, in a liberal vein, by Anthony Smith (1980). In a recent formulation Schiller has once again argued that contemporary transnational corporations have campaigned successfully 'to break down national broadcasting and telecommunication entities' given their 'near-total access to national information systems. They are well on the way to becoming the dominant force in each national setting, *saturating the cultural space of the nation*.' Because of the 'transnational corporate order's' ability to bypass national authority, *'national cultural protection'* is now futile conceptually (Schiller, 1985: 18, emphases added). 'Cultural space' here functions in the same way as 'European identity'. The key difference in diagnosis lies in Schiller's fatalism about 'cultural defence' and Pragnell's inescapable need to make some sensible suggestions as to how it ought to be achieved.

Pragnell's text quoted above contains numerous significant slippages. It talks of *the* culture of the countries of Europe but also of various traditions. The assumption, certainly implicit, but none the less present, is that these are somehow static objects under assault. But what are the relationships between 'cultures' and 'traditions'? Again – as in the Euro-documentation quoted earlier – it is held that a 'common sense of identity in *Western* Europe' significantly exists. What it is and how we might know it are not considered a problem any more than in the official documentation. 'Europe' and 'Western Europe' are here used interchangeably, but the actual territorial *boundaries* of that area are left quite unspecific. Clearly, they need to be: every accession to 'Community Europe' in some measure *changes* the purported identity.

Pragnell's study has the virtue of attempting clear definitions:

> Culture is to be seen as the amalgam of elements which distinguish communities (of whatever size) one from another. These elements identify, for example, what amuses, saddens and uplifts them; and they govern character formation in the home and what is taught (and how it is taught) in schools and other educational establishments. National values are seen as part of culture and will influence how communities tend to approach (not necessarily with uniform results) moral, ethical and political issues and how they behave. (1985: 8)

As a sensible layman's definition this has much to commend it. Cultures are the shapers of 'national characters', and culture-bearing national entities are seen as producing homogeneous effects upon their citizen-members, and as being collective actors with singular identities. Such a definition takes 'culture' as a finished product and the nation as a stable given. This layman's view, then, is also a perfect instance of a top-down *official* view of what a national culture might be: integral, integrating and integrated. To say that it is 'official' is not to say that it is necessarily élitist – and Pragnell rightly underlines the limitedness of a narrow, high-cultural view.

Pragnell does recognize the cultural contradictions of contemporary nation-states, but brushes them aside:

> There need be no conflict between the idea of national or regional cultures and that of a wider (even if less obvious and developed) European culture. Within nations, there will be variations, sometimes quite marked, among different regional and ethnic groups (and nowadays among age groups). Yet separate group cultures will be tempered and, to varying degrees, unified by a common national culture. Similarly, within Western Europe there are visible elements of common culture, existing already in some fields and emergent in others. (1985: 9)

The national culture model is the supervenient one, on this account, yet it cannot be too impermeable as it needs to absorb elements of the professed European 'common culture' (a descriptively blank space, as in the official literature). Pragnell, researching practically within the Euro-remit, has elaborated very clearly upon the 'unity in diversity' formula. Obviously, though, saying what 'Euro-culture' actually *is* presents an insurmountable obstacle.

The practical thrust of the argument is in line with the Green Paper, namely that of stressing the need to safeguard domestic production. The ground for this, as we have seen, is that imports are potentially harmful, both culturally and industrially. However, Pragnell (1985: 12) wishes to take his distance from theories of 'cultural imperialism' à la Schiller, which he characterizes as implying 'a concerted and coherent policy on the part of the various, and seemingly disparate, production agencies to spread as widely as possible a favourable, but largely inaccurate, image of the American way of life'.

As a rejection of a conspiracy model this is unexceptionable – although, as we shall see, that model is already under assault by a new revisionism. The next move is perhaps more questionable, for, basing himself on some recent research by Elihu Katz and Tamar Liebes (1985) into the complex ways in which programmes such as *Dallas* are 'read', Pragnell (1985: 13) argues in effect *against* the proposition that the importation of culture has strong and clear-cut effects. Obviously, this undermines one of his own fundamental starting-points. This is contradicted once again a little later when it is assumed that a television system functioning as a national public service will act as an integrative force with the common, homogenizing effect of producing 'an informed community . . . conscious of its history, culture and traditions' (1985: 15). This national cultural model is then projected on to the European level, as though a balanced televisual diet à *l'anglaise* could signally contribute to closer union without much more ado.

I have spent some time interrogating Pragnell's assumptions as they offer such a clear-cut case of how a piece of Euro-research works itself out. Clearly, there are many articles of *belief*: that national cultures are largely unproblematic and, given that a European identity already exists (but cannot be described), that adverse cultural effects can with some clarity be identified – an assumption which provides the motor for the whole enterprise. Without presumed cultural damage there would be no cause for cultural defence.

'Audiovisual space' as political metaphor

The rhetoric of cultural defence may employ numerous terminologies. Another distinctive variant derives from the recent debates in Unesco about cultural identity.

At Unesco's 1982 World Conference on Cultural Policies in Mexico City, 'cultural identity' became a keyword both in the General Secretary's summing up and in the reports and declarations pubished after the event. In this context, considerable definitional effort was expended, as the following quotations indicate. In the Final Report, the following was said, *inter alia:*

> Culture belongs to man, to all men. Culture was universal but not one . . . The conference was unanimous in recognizing and reaffirming with conviction and force the equal dignity of all cultures, rejecting any hierarchy in that area . . . It therefore reaffirmed the duty of each to respect all cultures. It could be clearly seen that the affirmation of cultural identity had become a permanent requirement, both for individuals and for groups and nations . . . Cultural identity was the defence of traditions, of history and of the moral, spiritual and ethical values handed down by past generations. (Unesco, 1982: 8)

Obviously, it is too much to expect drafts by committees to have intellectual coherence. However, the confusions and contradictions are important and interesting, particularly given the widespread currency of the central – and the very elastic – concept. The Unesco formulations ride the same steed of 'unity in diversity', but at a different level. All men (and cultures) are equal, so let them respect one another. Clearly, they do not obey this imperative and in the next breath it must therefore be recognized that in the modern world cultures *belong* to various groups, the most important of which are nations – hence the legitimacy of national cultural defence. Thus:

> the importance attached . . . to the promotion of national and local languages . . . Many delegates considered that one could not speak of cultural identity without reaffirming the fundamental concepts of national sovereignty and territorial independence . . . A number of delegates insisted, however, that cultural identity could not be defined solely in terms of national identity . . . As it was not possible to conceive of a cultural identity that had no contact with

others, it could not be seen as a form of introversion, a hermetically sealed entity doomed sooner or later to cave in on itself. (Unesco, 1982: 22–3)

To ride the horse of 'unity in diversity' at the global level is to have an even bumpier trip than within the confines of 'Europe'. Clearly, if language is central to cultural identity, *cultural* identity cannot be equivalent to *national* identity, as various linguistic groups may inhabit a given nation-state or be otherwise linked beyond its confines. A cultural autonomist vision is counterposed to that of the national integrationist in the space of a few sentences, as may be seen. Cultural identities, it is held, are not free-standing, but once that is allowed, the hierarchization of cultures is implicitly admitted if one accepts that cognitive, political and economic power is not uniformly distributed in the world. The problems of domination and inequality cannot be banished by mere words. The ambiguities of the Unesco discourse, then, are these: the pluralizing tendency, which says all cultures are equal, requires the rejection of cultural-identity-as-national-identity, of culture as confined by the nation-state. But the right to distinctiveness, to absolute autonomy, is threatened as soon as 'a dialectic between the internal and the external' (Unesco, 1982: 23) is admitted. Therefore the logic of national cultural defence is uneliminable.

Unesco's preoccupations in the field of culture and that of information flows (as set out in the MacBride Report, 1980) have taken on a particular inflection in the recent research on the possibility of a 'Latin audiovisual space'. In Armand Mattelart's report to the French socialist government (Mattelart et al., 1983, English trans. 1984) the 'unity in diversity' argument becomes transformed into one about cultural defence for a particular range of cultures.

Mattelart and his collaborators, while seeking to establish a 'Latin audiovisual space', observe at the outset that the expression is linguistically ambiguous as 'it covers a geographical area where the status of a "Latin language" varies from official to national to minority and majority language'; moreover, in some countries (notably in Latin America) 'Latinity' was imposed (Mattelart et al., 1984: ix). This might be thought enough to vitiate the project, but no: 'In an age when political, industrial and financial arrangements are being redefined throughout the world, a new "space" can only emerge through the collecting of experiences and the convergence of different historical, cultural and economic heritages' (1984: x). Clearly, this conception of a 'space' filled with a new content yet to be produced functions in much the same way as the aspirations for a 'European identity'. Cultural affinity, ultimately, is held to exist and to be a force sufficiently strong to legitimize the reorganization of geo-cultural boundaries. The project obviously cuts right across the Euro-conception, as it offers a different – indeed opposed – principle of integration.

Again, what interests me about Mattelart's book is less its empirical support (which has become rapidly outdated – a besetting problem of the field) than its conceptual structure and objectives. Ultimately, of course, it is an argument about the reorganization of the world cultural system, with a central focus upon the audiovisual industries. The rhetoric of creating a space plays with the inherent ambiguities of the cultural industries (cf. Mattelart and Piemme, 1982): the 'audiovisual' is both a symbolic arena and an economic one. That ambiguity allows one to make both a cultural and economic argument at one and the same time. The fundamental intention is to reinforce and extend the production bases of those presently disadvantaged in the world audiovisual market. The public appeal, clearly, is to the sentiment that *national* or *Latin* production is essential to the maintenance of particular kinds of identity which would otherwise be threatened.

However, this point is far from unambiguously stated. 'Cultural identity' and national cultural defence, in fact, although clearly at the root of the idea of creating a new 'audiovisual space', are handled as though they were objects of deep suspicion:

> One of the paradoxes of projects linked to the development of new forms of resistance is that they can graft on to their real desire for change the most hackneyed nationalism or even racism. Cultural identity is one of the most notable channels for this ambiguity, and easily slips into a nationalist affirmation of the superiority of one group over others. (Mattelart et al., 1984: 110)

Although 'cultural identity' is nowhere defined, it is negatively characterized by indicating four ways in which it 'serves as a screen to reality': it may result in protectionism without a concomitant production policy; it may be confused 'with the defence of a fixed past'; it may be reduced to 'a national label stuck on what is essentially a transnational copy' resulting in 'picturesque folklore'; finally, its use as 'the standard bearer for an alternative cultural imperialism' is denounced – here, the invention of *Latin* America under Napoleon III is criticized (1984: 17–18). Obviously, 'Latin cultural identity' will not do, so something else has to be found to eliminate the potentially negative connotations: 'Latin audiovisual space'?

In effect a conceptual displacement and substitution occur in which a tainted term, 'cultural identity' is replaced with the grander, uncontaminated one of 'space'. This clearly has the virtue of side-stepping the inherent ambiguities of Unesco's discourse with its central, disabling (deliberate) confusion over the relationship between nationhood and culture. 'Space' is intended to offer an escape-hatch from the problems through its attractive vagueness. However, it cannot do so, as it needs some qualifying adjective. With 'Latinity' (even on the lines of a purged, fraternal variant) we are straight back into the problematic of cultural dominance and defence – *maybe* not amongst 'Latins' themselves, but certainly between them and the rest, particularly the perfidious Anglo-Saxons. All cultures are not equal; 'spaces' are inclusive as well as exclusive and consequently fields of force.

One of the oddities of the exercise, however, is that the new substitution-concept of 'space' is nowhere reflected upon. But then to do that would be to give the game away. For such an attempt one has to look elsewhere to the work of the geographer Torsten Hägerstrand, who in a thought-provoking way (and, so far as one can tell, quite independently of present debates in the cultural field) links a conception of audiovisual space to problems of identity. It is precisely such fundamental questions which receive no systematic development in Mattelart's account, because the very linkage is conceptually denied.

Hägerstrand (1986: 8), taking Sweden as his case, distinguishes two forms of social integration. 'Territorial integration' refers to forms of face-to-face social communication where '*nearness* is the supreme category and therefore thinking, loyalty and acting become highly place-bound'. Evidence of the need for such identification with one's local domicile, he argues, is strong. Counterposed to this is 'functional integration' in the contemporary 'system society', where messages circulate globally. The question Hägerstrand (1986: 13) poses is whether broadcasting can aid the desire to acquire more room for the territorial mode of organization than is presently available. He argues that the message structures of contemporary Swedish society run in two directions; radio and television tend to emphasize the national and international levels, whereas the local press tends to reinforce territorial integration:

> telemedia have an inherent tendency to promote hierarchical and centre-directed links resulting in the withdrawal of people from face-to-face communication. But these limitations do not totally circumscribe the 'possibility space' . . . to most people the locality and region where they live is more than a social space, at least subconsciously. Existence is also bound to a tangible landscape that is a basic resource and an entity to understand and look after. Broadcasting could do a lot to increase the consciousness of space in this aspect also. (Hägerstrand, 1986: 20, 25)

The central point is that according to this view the management of audiovisual space has important consequences for the construction of social identity. Hägerstrand argues for the use of media to reawaken and reinforce a sense of local history, of time and place. It is in this context that he uses the term 'possibility space'. The implication obviously is that the media's 'inherent tendency' to 'nationalize' social space can be consciously counteracted, and that their potentiality for the reinforcement of older-style, territorially based identities is far from exhausted. One point worth noting is that 'audiovisual space' and (socio-cultural) identity do *not* need to be seen as opposed or substitutable terms, but rather can be plausibly used together in such an analytical framework as Hägerstrand's. A further implication is that the concept of space can be handled in a variety of ways. In Mattelart's grand design the principal movement is *outwards* towards the creation of an area of 'Latinity', which, as it cannot yet be defined, remains empty and potentially fillable. In Hägerstrand's case the suggested movement is *inwards* (national space being taken for granted) towards a reinforcement of the local, of the already known. Any further development of thinking about the relationship between social space, the media and forms of cultural identity needs to take both these outwards and inwards movements into account, and that, as will be argued below, requires close attention to the broader processes of the constitution of identities.

The new revisionism

Mattelart's approach marks a retreat from Schiller's: it implies a more pluricentric notion of cultural production than the monocentrist vision offered by the latter. Not all centres are equal, however, and Mattelart seeks an expansion of cultural space for the relatively disadvantaged 'Latins' at the expense of the over-extended Anglo-Saxons. Increasingly, however, we are being offered another image altogether, which implies a total retreat from these global structuralisms and which faces the alternative danger of a collapse into subjectivism. Of increasing prominence is a hermeneutic model of media consumption. A few years ago, Fred Fejes (1981) pointed to a crucial weakness in the media imperialism thesis: namely, that although much can be said in gross terms about the flow of cultural products, techniques and forms of organization, personnel, values and training from centres of cultural power in the North to the South, the *implications* of such cultural flows for those who consume them remain largely obscure. He called for research into the audience to complement and enlarge existing theory.

The supply of new work seems to have been forthcoming and, indeed, some preceded Fejes's intervention. Much of the new revisionism is traceable to the Marxist culturalism of Stuart Hall (cf., for example, Hall, 1977). In some seminal work (much influenced by semiotics) on the 'encoding' and 'decoding' of media discourses in the early 1970s, Hall (1980) opened up a line of enquiry subsequently taken up empirically by David Morley (1980). Morley's work on the audience attempted to relate varying 'decodings' to the social positions of the interpreters. He employed an activist, meaning-constructing conception of the audience, taking his distance from the positivistic effects and 'uses and gratifications' approaches. Morley has subsequently extended his work to take account of the ways in which intra-familial social relations affect the uses and interpretations of television in the home (Morley, 1986). On broadly similar lines this approach has subsequently been taken up and modified by others such as Ien Ang, Peter Dahlgren, Elihu Katz and Tamar Liebes, and Justin Lewis (cf. their chapters in Drummond and Paterson, 1985).

It is worth pausing for a moment to see how this revisionist current has handled the question of cultural imperialism. An apt focus – because it is so much mentioned, and has now been researched in some measure – is the world-beating television series *Dallas*. For Mattelart and his collaborators it figures as 'the perfect hate symbol, the cultural poverty . . . against which one struggles' (1984: 90). Within the revisionist framework its significance is recoded. Katz and Liebes (1985), using viewer discussion groups from various ethnic backgrounds to produce 'ethno-semiological data', have underlined the range of variation of response by people in different cultures. They argue that no single American message is uniformly perceived but that 'the reading of a programme is a process of negotiation between the story on the screen and the culture of the viewers' (1985: 187). Culture, however, shrinks in scope, and appears to be quite outside any relations of power or domination at all.

Ien Ang (1985) also takes up the complexities of audience responses to *Dallas*, basing herself on a voluntary sample of viewers' letters. Her central thesis is that people watch *Dallas* for pleasure and that intellectual exponents of what she calls the 'ideology of mass culture' fail to recognize this. In her view, the high-minded defenders of 'national cultural identities' in Western Europe have focused on the wrong level when they decry American cultural imperialism. They are blind to the multifold engagements of ordinary people with the melodramatic structure of the plot and the characters. Here again, the new revisionist position forces a breach between politico-economic arguments about the production of culture and the ways in which it is consumed and interpreted. However, although the pleasure of the text should not be underestimated, pleasure should not totally displace a concern with power.

This changed orientation has been taken up latterly by Michael Tracey (1985), who has argued for a research programme along more qualitative, ethnographic lines, and for a displacement of the cultural imperialism problematic. We are instead invited to start from the bottom and move upwards: to consider the key datum to be the audience's 'actual experience' of media consumption (1985: 36). He also suggests that it is really the universal responses of 'common humanity' that such research should seek to educe (1985: 41–3). Clearly, this appeal to the essence that lurks within us all goes well beyond Morley's more plausibly differentiated microsociology of tastes.

There is no denying that the new revisionists have a legitimate point in laying emphasis upon the importance of the problem of how cultural products are interpreted. However, their stress upon the micropolitics of the audience may carry with it a subjectivist temptation which is surely to be avoided. That the media imperialism theorists are prone to politico-economic reductionism is fair criticism. However, what they do not lose sight of is the overarching question of how cultural power may be exercised at both the global and the national levels and the ways that these interrelate. While the new revisionists have identified a weak point of the structuralist approach, their micro-level of analysis does not offer an especially good vantage-point for examining how large cultural collectivities constitute their identities.

The need for explicit conceptualization

The foregoing discussion has demonstrated the centrality of such phrases as 'cultural identity', 'national identity' and indeed '*trans*national identity' in current discourse on culture and communication. Despite their prominence, however, it is far from clear what these terms actually mean or, more importantly, that *any* of the writers cited has a coherent view of how such forms of collective identity are constructed.

Underlying the various arguments for cultural defence is one central argument (perhaps more aptly characterized as a widespread *belief*: that the excessive importation of foreign cultural products, in this instance television programmes, can damage or even destroy identities. This view, which is denied by the new revisionism, naturally presupposes that we know a great deal about the effects of cultural consumption. Moreover, the remedy – to consume more of your own, or more of what you think is good for you – is reliant upon exactly the same premise.

Underlying this are unexplored assumptions about cultures and how their borders are constituted, reproduced and modified. Obviously, the debate cannot proceed further unless we begin to conceptualize these processes explicitly. Without such intellectual effort we are unlikely to be able to say anything useful about collective identities and their relation to cultural processes. But in order to do so we shall have to address other literatures. For, in communication research, collective identity functions as a residual category. In other words, we now need to turn around the terms of the conventional argument: *not* to start with communication and its supposed effects on collective identity and culture, but rather to begin by posing the problem of collective identity itself, to ask how it might be analysed and what importance communicative practices might play in its constitution.

Where the experts in communication are silent, there do others speak. The next chapter goes on to examine a number of theoretical positions which relate to the question of collective identity and also to consider some empirical work that bears directly upon the conceptualization of processes of collective identity formation and reproduction.

Acknowledgements

Chapters 7 and 8 were researched and written during my stay as a Jean Monnet Fellow at the European University Institute of Florence during 1985–6. Without the continuous encouragement of Jean Padioleau I doubt whether I would have begun working on the question of collective identity. My thanks too to Bob Jessop, Klaus Gretschmann, Mark Cousins and Martin van Gelderen for written comments, many of which still need to be addressed. I have also benefited much from conversations with Abram de Swaan, Hannes Siegrist, Efraim Nimni and Nira Yuval-Davis.

References

Ang, I. (1985) *Watching 'Dallas': Soap Opera and the Melodramatic Imagination*. London and New York: Methuen.

Barker, Sir E., Clark, Sir G. and Vaucher, Prof. P. (eds) (1954) *The European Inheritance*. Vol. III. Oxford: Clarendon Press.

Commission of the European Communities (1984a) *Television without Frontiers: Green Paper on the Establishment of the Common Market for Broadcasting, Especially by Satellite and Cable* (COM, 84, 300 final). Brussels: CEC.

Commission of the European Communities (1984b) *Towards a European Television Policy*. Brussels: CEC.

Commission of the European Communities (1985) *The European Community and Culture*. Brussels: CEC.

Dahlgren, P. (1985) 'The Modes of Reception: For a Hermeneutics of TV News', in Drummond and Paterson (1985). pp. 235–49.

Drummond, P. and Paterson, R. (eds) (1985) *Television in Transition: Papers from the first International Television Studies Conference*. London: BFI.

Fejes, F. (1981) 'Media Imperialism: An Assessment', *Media, Culture and Society*, 3 (3), July: 281–9.

Hägerstrand, T. (1986) 'Decentralization and Radio Broadcasting: On the "Possibility Space" of a Communication Technology', *European Journal of Communication*, 1 (2), June: 7–26.

Hall, S. (1977) 'Culture, the Media and the "Ideological Effect"', in J. Curran, M. Gurevitch and J. Woollacott (eds), *Mass Communication and Society*. London: Edward Arnold. pp. 315–48.

Hall, S. (1980) 'Encoding/Decoding', in S. Hall, D. Hobson and P. Willis (eds), *Culture, Media, Language*. London: Hutchinson. pp. 128–38.

Katz, E. and Liebes, T. (1985) 'Mutual Aid in the Decoding of *Dallas*: Preliminary Notes from a Cross-Cultural Study', in Drummond and Paterson (1985). pp. 187–98.

Lewis, J. (1985) 'Decoding Television News', in Drummond and Paterson (1985). pp. 205–34.

MacBride, S. (1980) *Many Voices: One World*. London: Kogan Page.

Mattelart, A. and Piemme, J.-M. (1982) 'Cultural Industries: The Origin of an Idea', in Unesco (ed.), *Cultural Industries: A Challenge for the Future of Culture*. Paris: Unesco. pp. 51–61.

Mattelart, A., Delcourt, X. and Mattelart, M. (1983) *La Culture contre la Démocratie: L'Audiovisuelle à l'Heure Transnationale*. Paris: La Découverte; English trans. 1984: *International Image Markets: In Search of an Alternative Perspective*. London: Comedia.

Morley, D. (1980) *The 'Nationwide' Audience*. London: BFI.

Morley, D. (1986) *Family Television: Cultural Power and Domestic Leisure*. London: Comedia.

Pragnell, A. (1985) *Television in Europe: Quality and Values in a Time of Change*. Manchester: European Institute for the Media.

Schiller, H.I. (1985) 'Electronic Information Flows: New Basis for Global Domination?', in Drummond and Paterson (1985). pp. 11–20.

Smith, A. (1980) *The Geopolitics of Information*. London: Faber.

Tracey, M. (1985) 'The Poisoned Chalice? International Television and the Idea of Dominance', *Daedalus*, 114 (4): 17–56.

Unesco (1982) World Conference on Cultural Policies, Mexico City, 26 July–2 August 1982, Final Report. Paris: Unesco.

8

On National Identity (II):
Collective Identity in Social Theory

Collective identity as a problem in social science

The problem of identity has been taken up intermittently in mainstream sociology and political science, although it is difficult to find much in the way of common agreement as to how it should be conceptualized. It is not my intention to review the material comprehensively here, as that has been competently done elsewhere (cf. Sciolla, 1983). Suffice it to say that most writing deals mainly with the relations between the individual and society, and is continuous with the preoccupations of different and earlier conceptual languages with individual 'character' and 'personality' formation.

That is not the level at which the present discussion might best proceed. Some take the view that the category of 'identity' is applicable *only* to individuals rather than to collectivities – a position, for instance, adopted by Berger and Luckmann (1966) in their phenomenological approach to the question. The main burden of the argument against talking of collective identities would appear to be that this involves an inadmissible hypostatization or reification. As Sciolla (1983: 14) points out, this presumes that collective identity be seen as completely external and constraining for the individual, which is a very restrictive conception. She argues instead that:

> There is also the possibility of conceiving collective identity as a result of complex processes, that is as constituted by an autonomous drawing up of boundaries and construction of symbols which nevertheless interacts with the expectations and projections of given individuals and with which it might also come into conflict, in a sort of unstable equilibrium whose outcomes could be either the modification of individual identity (in the limiting case, quitting the group) or the modification of the group's own identity (in the limiting case, the dissolution of its collective identity).

This view has also been espoused by M. Oriol and P. Igonet-Fastinger (1984) in their recent reflections on the category of identity. They too argue that the concept implies theorizing the subjective dimensions of belonging to a group in relation to the objective factors which condition group membership. For them, the very term 'identity' 'becomes the sign of the most pressing invitation to a dialectic: that of always situating "us" in relation to "them", the lived experience in relation to the institutionalized one, the present in relation to history, all of these prescriptions immediately calling forth a reciprocal effort' (1984: 157).

In recent years, the problem of collective identity has been a noteworthy concern of the literatures on ethnicity and social movements. As both Paolo Pistoi (1983: 82) and J.W. LaPierre (1984: 197–8) have pointed out, ethnicity came substantially on to the political agenda in many Western states in the 1960s and 1970s and needed an explanation in its own right. The analysis of the upsurge in ethnic consciousness and action was accompanied by an interest in ethnic identity.

For LaPierre, this has made collective identity a new object and problem for the social sciences. For him, following the pioneering work of Maurice Halbwachs, 'collective identity relates to a collective memory through which the contemporary group recognizes itself through a common past, rememberance, commemoration, interpretation and reinterpretation' (1984: 196). LaPierre distinguishes between defensive and counter-offensive moments in collective identity. There is a paradox, he argues, in that as groups become different they none the less insist that they have remained the same. He also points to the *selectiveness* of memory, whether individual or collective, and assigns a crucial role to the intellectuals in the 'selective interpretation of history' (1984: 203–4).

Pistoi underlines the signal importance of Fredrick Barth's (1969) argument that the *content* of ethnic identity cannot be statically conceived; rather:

> the category of ethnicity is a *form* of social organization, an organizational vehicle which may take on different contents at different times and in various sociocultural systems . . . The critical factor for defining the ethnic group therefore becomes the *social boundary* which defines the group with respect to other groups of the same order, not the cultural reality within those borders. (Pistoi, 1983: 83)

This extremely useful conceptualization of the capacity of ethnic groups to recompose their boundaries and to select out different criteria at different times obviously offers a *dynamic* view of identity. As we shall see, others, in various ways, have addressed the issue in similar terms.

The logic of collective identity

In this section I wish to argue that 'national identity' is best understood as a specific form of collective identity. In order to develop the argument I shall review a range of pertinent literature, in particular drawing upon writings in the field of nationalism. Very little of the material considered is 'purpose-built', which is in itself worthy of note, for it suggests that latterly not much direct thought has been given to the *general* sociological problem of what collective identity is and how it is constituted.

One of the most interesting and sustained attempts to consider that question, however, is to be found in the recent work of Alberto Melucci (1982), and I shall use this as a starting-point.

Melucci's work is centrally concerned with the interpretation of the social movements which flourished particularly in the 1960s and 1970s. The conflicts of those years, he argues (much in the vein of other writers such as Touraine and Pizzorno – see Sciolla, 1983), may be interpreted as struggles for identity. In the context of a critique of significant authors such as Charles Tilly and Mancur Olson on the explanation of collective action, he develops an argument as to how collective identity should be approached. It is this aspect of his work which I propose to evaluate.

According to Melucci, as Western societies move further away from a class-based industrial capitalist model, the concept of identity has become increasingly important for a theory of action which explains the formation and activities of various groups. 'Identity' is conceptualized as 'above all involving the notion of the *permanence* of a subject or of an object through time'. Melucci also points to 'the notion of *unity* which establishes the limits of a subject or object and which allows it to be distinguished from any other'. Finally, he suggests that identity involves 'a relation between two elements which may be *recognized as identical*' (Melucci, 1982: 62, emphases in original).

Such formal criteria may apply to forms of identity both individual and collective, and the first two in particular are redolent of long-standing discussions in the philosophy of mind concerning personal identity. The third criterion is of particular importance for Melucci, who wishes to stress that all identities are constituted within a system of social relations and require the reciprocal recognition of others. Identity, he argues, is not to be considered a 'thing' but rather 'a system of relations and representations'. Furthermore, he proposes, the distinction between individual and collective levels carries no implication for the concept of identity itself; rather, 'what changes is the system of relations to which the actor refers and with respect to which his recognition comes' (1982: 68).

The concept of identity is linked to that of action. Melucci stresses that actors must have a capacity for self-reflection, a perception of belonging and temporal continuity. The maintenance of an agent's identity is seen as a continual process of recomposition rather than as a given, one in which the two constitutive dimensions of self-identification and affirmation of difference are continually locked. An 'identity crisis' in contemporary society is defined as 'the impossibility of maintaining a given configuration in time and in space' (1982: 72). In such a context social movements are seen as coming into their own for they 'offer individuals the collective possibility of affirming themselves as actors and of finding an equilibrium between self-recognition and hetero-recognition' (1982: 72).

After these general considerations, much of Melucci's argument is taken up with the 'new antagonistic movements' of, as he sees it, post-capitalism. This analysis is of tangential interest to present concerns, and I wish to address just a few points.

First, Melucci's focus is above all upon the construction of collective identity at the *sub*-national level: the nation-state as context is taken for granted. I consider this to be a serious weakness as it tends to exclude *'national* identity' as a problem merely on highly contingent grounds deriving from an intra-societal concern. I propose we simply extend Melucci's general approach to that level of analysis.

Secondly, as the approach rejects class-reductionism and the idea that given historical subjects are allocated definite roles, Melucci is able to pose questions as to *why* a given social actor appears on the stage at given moments. To put it differently: identity is seen as a dynamic, *emergent* aspect of collective action. This seems a useful general principle to follow.

Thirdly, considerable stress is laid on the *symbolic* dimension of identity:

> We might define identity as the reflexive capacity for producing consciousness of action (that is, a symbolic representation of it) beyond any specific contents. Identity becomes formal reflexivity, pure symbolic capacity, the recognition of the production of a sense of action within the limits posed at any given moment by the environment and the biological structure. (1982: 88)

Again, given our concerns, the focus upon the cultural level is generally valuable, although no indication is given as to *how* such reflexivity is achieved, or whether specific agents within a collectivity ('the intellectuals') play a particularly important role.

The basic approach to identity, as we have seen, lays stress upon an activistic, meaning-constructing conception; moreover, so it is argued, the principles of analysis of identity remain invariant irrespective of the level at which it is projected. Against these, his own premises, Melucci makes a somewhat questionable move. Contemporary post-industrial societies, he argues, are distinguished in the following way:

> Identity no longer presents itself as 'given' by nature, nor as the simple content of a tradition with which individuals identify. It is no longer only based on belonging to 'normatively regulated associations' (states, parties, organizations). Individuals and groups through their action participate in the formation of identity, which is the result of decisions and projects, rather than conditioning and bonds. (1982: 89)

In effect, what this claims is that the *activism* of contemporary social movements entails a *highly specific* conception of collective identity – one appropriate to them alone. By contrast, more stable identity-conferring entities are seen as inert. This is surely an erroneous contrast within Melucci's own terms and rests upon an assumption that the identity of social movements merits a completely distinctive analysis. However, surely if his general argument as a whole carries force (which I believe it does), the construction of identity within more stable entities ought to be analysed in precisely the same formal terms. This point will be taken up later when the 'invention of tradition' approach is discussed. Suffice it to say that his allusion to traditions takes them at face value, namely as 'traditional', rather than as subject to continuous mutation. Besides, the imputation of static identities to 'states' also unnecessarily limits the capacity of his model to deal with the problem of *national* identity. This odd failure of the imagination is clear from his approach to 'ethnicity'. This is considered overwhelmingly from the point of view of the emergence of new forms of solidarity *within* established nation-states. The central concern is to consider why sub-national groups are impelled to 'rediscover' and use ethnic identity as a politico-economic resource. But that is precisely to miss a very interesting and important question: namely, how collective identity at the broader nation-state level should be analysed. On any reasonable ground that cannot be excluded from the same actionist logic of collective identity, albeit at a more 'remote' level.

Nation as communicative community

One potentially productive line of enquiry into how nations might be characterized is that which focuses upon the role of communication (in the widest sense) as the integrative principle within a determinate group. This approach has a number of distinguished exponents in the history of writing on nationalism. However, it is marked by a blindness reciprocal to that of current communication studies: there the nation-state is under-conceptualized, whereas in the nationalism literature the mass media are usually quite untheorized. We need to move beyond this double impasse. For the most part, the nation is not conceptualized in terms of 'collective identity'; however, there are occasions on which this theme is explicitly addressed. In one of the more recent works in this genre, for instance, W.J.M. Mackenzie (1978) sets out to interrogate the notion of 'collective political identity' in political science. He argues that the term was originally popularized through Lucian Pye's work on political development. Pye, so Mackenzie suggests, picked up the idea of an 'identity crisis' from the work of Erik Erikson in which the focus was the level of *individual* psychic development: 'identity is still . . . the identity which an individual can find through a collectivity; not the metaphor of Pye, that a collectivity can like a person have an identity and crises of identity' (1978: 39). In opposition, Mackenzie argues that the analogy of collective identity cannot properly be built upon that of the individual. Moreover, to argue, as does Pye, that emergent nations are in search of their collective identities is to presume what one purports to demonstrate.

For Mackenzie, the problem of political identity cannot adequately be addressed through conventional political science. Instead of assuming that identities exist we ought to consider under what conditions 'it is possible to realize "common purpose"' (1978: 109). In Mackenzie's view, a concept of collective identity is only acceptable in the context of an extended conception of language:

> The community of communicators, vague though it is, is yet sharper in definition than the community of interest and contiguity in space. The traditional concepts of our modern world, nation, race, religion, class . . . retain their positions of power: but, each can be generalized most effectively in terms of an exchange of, or participation in, symbolic satisfactions. (1978: 165)

On this analysis, then, Mackenzie is engaged in restating the *context* in which the problem of collective (here 'political') identity may be conceptualized. 'Collective identity' and its constitution are a *problem*, not something that may be presumed to exist as a prior condition of political agency. In this emphasis upon the active constitution of political agents Mackenzie converges in part with Melucci's social movement analysis.

Mackenzie is aware of the problem of settling what are the 'natural frontiers' of communicating groups and argues that in principle this can be resolved by generalizing the concept of a 'meeting'. Such encounters should be placed 'under the rubric of social communication, which includes person to person contact by letter and telephone, the linking of specialists by special media, the linking of communities in a selective way by mass media' (1978: 132).

Those interacting in such networks are seen as occupying the same 'social space', and, Mackenzie suggests, those who share a network share an identity. In his terms, 'national identity' is only one of four main types of 'cultural identity' bequeathed by the nineteenth century (the others being race, religion and class).

Underlying this type of argument is the ultimate *indeterminacy* of the boundaries of group identity. If such an approach were to be productively applied to, say, present-day Western Europe, communications (or, in a different idiom, culture) would have to be *institutionally located*. The obvious prime point of reference would be the nation-state and its role in boundary marking and maintenance. That places an empirical constraint upon the question of indeterminacy. For otherwise the argument, whilst re-problematizing how to conceptualize collective identity, does so in a way which makes it impossible to apply analytically. We will reconsider this point when discussing Giddens' work below.

Mackenzie's reference to 'social communication' draws upon the central notion of Karl Deutsch's (1953, 2nd edn 1966) work on nationalism, which offers a conceptual blend of cultural anthropology and communications theory. Deutsch's central thesis is this: 'The essential aspect of the unity of a people . . . is the complementarity or relative efficiency of communication among individuals – something that is in some ways similar to mutual rapport, but on a larger scale' (1966: 188). A nation, then, is held to be a cultural entity with principles of coherence called 'complementarity' and 'relative efficiency'. For Deutsch 'processes of communication are the basis of the coherence of societies, cultures and even of the personalities of individuals' (1966: 87). In fact, nationality is *defined* in terms of such principles: 'What is proposed here, in short, is a functional definition of nationality. Membership in a people consists in wide complementarity of social communication. It consists in the ability to communicate more efficiently, and over a wider range of subjects, with members of one large group than with outsiders' (1966: 97).

This is quite explicitly counterposed to the 'usual definitions of a people in terms of a community of languages, or character, or memories, or past history' (Deutsch, 1966: 79). Complementarity and efficiency in communication are the social cement. However, these principles prove elusive upon interrogation because they offer no criteria of boundedness – precisely the same weakness as in Mackenzie's position. Thus, the concept of complementarity 'might be extended so as to include the actual or probable communicative efficiency of individuals over a range of different social arrangements' (1966: 110). In other words, it is sufficiently indefinite to refer to either a village or a nation. The only limiting condition stated is that at higher levels of complementarity 'peoples are marked off from each other by communicative barriers, by "marked gaps" in the efficiency of communication. Such gaps are relative' (1966: 100). But that merely ducks the problem: how relative is relative? In fact, complementarity and efficiency know no limits *in principle*, so that given the right conditions we might conceivably arrive at the so-called 'global village': one great nation; one widespread language; the end of Babel. At this point the utility of social communication theory as an explanation of nationhood becomes highly questionable.

A further point is that the functionalist conception employed by Deutsch although entailing national *differences* does not deal with the *interaction* between communicative communities (nations) – a matter of central interest for the current debate in communications, as we have seen. It cannot specify *how* the boundaries are maintained: rather, it merely identifies a given people as enjoying complementarity and therefore, *ipso facto*, as a nation. Nevertheless, one of the main advantages is that such an approach is not prey to essentialist conceptions of nationhood. Furthermore, although we need to locate nationally bounded communicative competences in an institutional framework with much greater care, it is important not to dismiss the role of social communication in the construction of national identities. The problem is *how* to locate it, and in what analytical framework, so that its significance in the context of broader processes of collective identity formation may be assessed.

A political roof for culture

Another influential theory in which the cultural dimension of nationhood is of central importance is to be found in the work of Ernest Gellner. This was first formulated in a chapter of *Thought and Change* (1964) and has been elaborated subsequently in *Nations and Nationalism* (1983). Gellner's main objective is to explain the origins of nationalism. Broadly speaking, he argues that the formation of nation-states is the inevitable outcome of processes of centralization set in train by the demands of industrialization, with its concomitant complex division of labour. The impact of industrial forms of production, it is argued, results in the reorganization of earlier (agrarian) forms of social organization. A central demand set up by the emergent social relations is for 'generic training': the ability to be able to do anything, in principle. This, in turn, requires a universal, standardized system of education, using a standardized linguistic medium. This process, Gellner argues, brings about an inevitable 'deep adjustment in the relationship between polity and culture', that is, 'nationalism'. The new formation entails 'the organization of human groups into large, centrally educated, culturally homogeneous groups' (1983: 35) with the consequence that 'Modern man is not loyal to a monarch or a land or a faith, whatever he may say, but to a culture'. By this account 'state and culture *must* now be linked' (1983: 36).

It is worth registering a point of qualification concerning the national education model which Gellner employs. What it basically assumes is that the centralizing, homogenizing tendencies in the system are an outcome of the requirements of industrialization and the division of labour. The account needs to be more nuanced by allowing for conflicts over the creation of national education systems as transmitters of cultural uniformity. As Abram de Swaan (1985) has pointed out, such transformations have tended to be resisted by 'mediating élites' (notably the gentry and clergy) who resented the undermining of their privileged position between state and locality. This is not, however, a decisive objection to the argument, as both Gellner and de Swaan would agree that national education constitutes 'the most significant attempt to break open local communication networks in order to achieve one grand national exchange system' (de Swaan, 1985: 125).

Precisely how Gellner's approach should be interpreted is a matter of some dispute. Anthony Giddens (1985: 214) assimilates it to Deutsch-style communications theory, which seems to me to miss the emphasis upon the role of industrialization at the heart of the theory. For his part, Anthony D. Smith (1973: 72) classifies Gellner's as a language theory of nationalism in which 'Language is the decisive element in any culture, expressing most clearly the collective personality of the group. It follows that nationalism is primarily a linguistic movement and that differences in language will, under certain conditions, produce strife and lead to national secession.' However, as Smith (1973: 74) himself really half concedes, the position is better understood as a cultural theory of the social bonds in industrial society, to which language is central; or, putting it in my terms, as a cultural theory of national identity in which the nature of the culture has definite preconditions in industrial development.

For Gellner, the term 'culture' is to be used in 'an anthropological, not a normative sense' to mean 'the distinctive style of conduct and communication of a given community' (1983: 92). The basic assumption is that the modal form of contemporary society is a nation-state which acts as a 'political roof' (legitimator and defender) of its own *high* culture – meaning literacy in a given language sustained by, in particular, a national education system. For the inhabitants of the modal nation-state the boundaries of their conceptual world are largely limited by the national culture, understood in a sense broader than language alone:

> Culture is no longer merely the adornment, confirmation and legitimation of a social order which was also sustained by harsher and coercive constraints; culture is now the necessary shared medium, the life-blood or perhaps rather the minimal shared atmosphere, within which alone the members of the society can breathe and survive and produce. For a given society, it must be one in which they can *all* breathe and speak and produce; so it must be the *same culture*. Moreover, it must now be a great or high (literate, training-sustained) culture, and can no longer be a diversified, locality-tied, illiterate little culture or tradition. (1983: 37–8)

Let us accept as plausible the argument that the world is tending towards nation-statist mono-cultures, and that the 'limits of the culture' now become the 'national political boundary'. In this formulation, be it noted, 'culture' is actually equivalent to the *official* version of national culture. An important perspective which is left out is that which concerns itself with a view of culture as a site of contestation; in other words, one which *problematizes* 'national culture' and interrogates the strategies and mechanisms whereby it is maintained and its role in securing the dominance of given groups in a society.

A second point concerns the view taken by Gellner of culture as a social product. Given the theory's interest in the transition from the 'agro-literate' polity to the nation-state, via industrialization, the tendency is to view the achievement of a national culture as a largely one-off task. Once integration has taken place and the national language-diffusing education system is in place, the continued reproduction of the cultural boundaries seems secure.

However, I should like to suggest that we need to distinguish between the initial creation of identity-conferring cultures and the problem of their persistence through time. For Gellner, the key agency which ensures virtually automatic reproduction is the national education system, the producer of clerks and diffuser of literacy. However, this view tends to play down the significance of emergent sources of differentiation inside industrial cultures and the new creation of various collective identities which may be in opposition to official, national culture. It is hardly to be disputed that the national culture constitutes an inescapable reference point, but it does not resolve all the problems of collective identity. What it does is to constitute the boundaries for *versions* of national identity.

Gellner does recognize this difficulty for his model of 'one nation, one culture' when he addresses the problem of culturally recognized social difference. It is not the case for all societies everywhere that a universal *appianamento* may be achieved. The failure of some distinctions to erode he calls 'entropy-resistance': 'A classification is entropy-resistant if it is based on an attribute which has a marked tendency *not* to become, even with the passage of time since the initial establishment of an industrial society, evenly dispersed throughout the entire society' (1983: 65). Such entropy-resistant traits (Gellner concentrates at length on a hypothetical 'blue' minority) carry considerable implications for how according to this theory collective identities may be established in given nation-states.

'Blueness', if it functions in a profoundly counter-entropic way, means that a section of the resident population of the state will nevertheless be excluded by the majority from recognized membership of the national community. This makes the internal processes of ideological boundary management a problem of considerable interest.

In one passage Gellner expressly addresses the role of communication in its institutionally specific mass-mediatic sense. (One might consider that this is to give the topic inadequate weight in a theory which lays so much stress on culture and communication.) He rightly takes issue with the view that without the mass media no nationalist ideas would be spread. That notion is obviously silly – akin to the assumption that without coverage of violence there would be no riots, terrorism or wars – and Gellner is correct to dismiss it. However, much more questionable is his formulation of the role of the media in any given national culture today:

> The media do not transmit an idea which happens to have been fed into them. It matters precious little what has been fed into them: it is the media themselves, the pervasiveness and importance of abstract, centralized, one to many communication, which itself automatically engenders the core idea of national-ism quite irrespective of what in particular is being put into the specific messages transmitted. The most important and persistent message is generated by the medium itself, by the role which such media have acquired in modern life. The core message is that the language and style of the transmissions is important . . . what is actually *said* matters little. (1983: 127)

In an echo of McLuhan's phrase, Gellner is arguing that the *media* are the message. That formula is then slightly modified to take account of questions of language and style, and of how such codes invite the audience to understand themselves as members of the moral community. In its general thrust, this argument converges with Benedict Anderson's concep-tion of the nation as an 'imagined community' which will shortly be discussed. However, 'language and style' are not so easily separated from the content of communications as Gellner would have us suppose.

Let us pursue this argument to its logical conclusion. Imagine a National Broadcasting Corporation which imports 50 per cent of its programmes from abroad, with a resultant mix of US soap operas, British costume dramas and worthy travelogues, Brazilian telenovelas and Japanese cartoons. All of this melange is, of course, carefully dubbed into the national language (as are the many, mainly US, films which are screened). But even so, prominent intellectuals and tub-thumping politicians worry about cultural imperialism and fulminate about the defence of the national culture. The remaining 50 per cent of programming is strongly influenced in style and structure by the foreign imports, but is nationally produced. The last redoubt of national originality is the National Nightly News, devoted in the first instance to the doings of national political figures in the universally accepted ethnocentric manner.

Can it truly be said that the *content* of such communication is irrelevant to the audience? To take this view would commit Gellner to the more extreme versions of the new revisionism in communication studies outlined earlier. But he is actually arguing something different: namely, that the media function as a kind of hidden categorial system (in much the same way as many have argued that what matters about formal education is its 'hidden curriculum'). The invitation to identify with the national media culture is unavoidable, according to him. However, my example raises questions about *why*, after a certain point, we would want to call that media culture *national*. Say we increase the imports to 90 per cent (because of their cheapness and attractiveness), and the privatizing economy measures of the national government constrain the National Nightly News to become essentially a relay station for the international news agencies. Could the position then be sustained that only media mattered but the message did not? Presumably not. Gellner's model, while correct to argue that the very existence of national media matters for the marking of boundaries, nevertheless remains insensitive to the possibility that such markers are not set irrevocably in place, but that they may be suborned by the internationalizing tendencies of capitalist cultural production. (It is precisely such worries which lie behind the cultural imperialism debate – although, as we have seen, how the problems are to be formulated needs care.) For Gellner to stick to his own theory, the medium *can't* be the message; rather, the media have to a considerable extent to engage in communicative boundary maintenance by providing national contents as well as styles. But that still leaves open the role of mass communications in the reproduction of national culture and identity.

Imagining communities

In Gellner's theory 'national identity' emerges as a by-product of the formation of the nation-state, itself the outcome of a global trend impelled by 'industrialization'. It is not surprising then that the theory does not contain an account of the active construction of collective identity: indeed, the clear argument is that although nationalist intellectuals are in some quarters erroneously credited with inventing and diffusing nationalism, history (in the shape of industrialization) actually works behind their backs as the real transformer of the world. This is to overstate an important point, I think, as we shall see when examining the 'invention of tradition' approach.

   Benedict Anderson's recent contribution (1983) addresses the problem of national identity more directly, although again without actually employing those terms:

> In an anthropological spirit . . . I propose the following definition of the nation: it is an imagined political community – and imagined as both inherently limited and sovereign. It is *imagined* because the members of even the smallest nation will never know most of their fellow-members, meet them, or even hear of them, yet in the minds of each lives the images of their communion . . . The nation is imagined as *limited* because even the largest of them, encompassing

perhaps a billion living beings, has finite, if elastic boundaries, beyond which lie other nations . . . It is imagined as *sovereign* because the concept was born in an age in which Enlightenment and Revolution were destroying the legitimacy of the divinely ordered, hierarchical dynastic realm . . . Finally, it is imagined as a *community* because, regardless of the actual inequality and exploitation that may prevail in each, the nation is always conceived as a deep, horizontal comradeship. (1983: 15, 16)

These definitional contours clearly attempt to convey, with the broadest brush-strokes, the sense of nationhood as one looks outwards from within. The position, therefore, is quite centrally about the constitution of national identity. Anderson (1983: 15) consciously distinguishes his position from that of Gellner, whom he describes as 'so anxious to show that nationalism masquerades under false pretences that he assimilates "invention" to "fabrication" and "falsity", rather than to "imagining" and "creation"'. This strikes me as a rather trivial basis for disagreement, as the concept of 'invention' carries no such necessary connotation, as we shall see, nor indeed does that represent Gellner's position.

More important, perhaps, is the role assigned to language by each theory. In Gellner's model, the national language transmitted via the educational system is seen as central to the formation of national unity. For Anderson, the extensive consideration of *non*-European paths to nation-hood adds a complicating factor. For, as he points out, the administrative boundaries of ex-colonies become national boundaries. A national language in many instances is not a problem nor an objective to be striven for, as it is already *in situ*, part of the colonial heritage. His analysis of Latin American nation-state formation is an exemplary instance of this.

Whereas Gellner is primarily concerned with the transition from agrarian to industrial societies, Anderson's essay sets out to trace several distinctive paths to the 'imagined community'. In his argument concerning Europe he suggests that 'What, in a positive sense, made the new communities imaginable was a half-fortuitous, but explosive, interaction between a system of production and productive relations (capitalism), a technology of communications (print), and the fatality of human linguistic diversity' (1983: 46). Although the nation-building role of education appears in various cases, this is not given the same central status as in Gellner's theory. Rather, Anderson's central contention is that 'Print-language is what invents nationalism, not *a* particular language per se' (1983: 122). Thus, an element to highlight in his approach is the importance assigned to various means of communication in the construction of the imagined community, given the appropriate material conditions.

In Europe, Anderson argues, 'print capitalism' took vernaculars, standardized them and disseminated them through the market. This process provided the conditions for the creation of national consciousness. Following Walter Benjamin and Lucien Febvre, Anderson argues that mechanically reproduced print languages unify fields of linguistic exchange, fix languages and create new languages of power to replace sacred universalistic languages.

Anderson singles out the 'nationalist novel' (with its plot enacted in a recognized common space) together with the newspaper, with 'calendrical consciousness' as its principle of organization, as two of the arch vehicles for the formation of a national consciousness. By co-ordinating time and space, these, in *pre*-nation-state circumstances, may address an imagined national community prior to its actual formation. The newspaper, read as a kind of instant book, 'implies the refraction of "world events" into a specific world of vernacular readers' so that 'important to that imagined community is an idea of a steady, solid simultaneity through time' (1983: 63).

Anderson's theory offers a direct point of contact with the current preoccupations of media theory. Of particular note is his analogy of the taking of communion – the confines of the nation are inescapably implicit in the very categorizations used by the means of communication. Here, as noted earlier, is a point of convergence with Gellner. This relates back to a fundamental assumption mentioned above – namely, that irrespective of real divisions 'the nation is always conceived as a deep, horizontal comradeship'.

A further point concerns the question of temporality. For Anderson, the modern conception of time involves a break with Messianic, sacred time, replacing it with (in Walter Benjamin's phrase) 'homogeneous, empty time', measured by the clock and calendar. Here, he suggests, the concept of a 'sociological organism moving calendrically through homogeneous, empty time is a precise analogue of the idea of the nation' (1983: 31).

In some respects, Anderson's is a variant of the social communications approach, although it meets one important objection by assigning limits to the 'imagined community' of communicators by locating it *within* the social space of the nation-state rather than by attempting to define the nation by general and ultimately vacuous criteria such as efficiency and complementarity. Given the acknowledged importance of print communication it is exceedingly odd that Anderson does not push the argument further to take account of later, post-Gutenberg media technologies, and to try and examine their implications for the consciousness of nationhood. In terms of the discussion in Chapter 7, a prime instance would be a concern with audiovisual languages and the implications of their easy crossing of national boundaries.

This leads on to another, rather obvious point (though one apt to be missed by many high-culture sociologists). The newspaper is singled out for its insertion of the 'imagined community' into a simultaneous mode of address. But that has long been the effect of radio, and latterly of television. However, where Anderson mentions radio and television it is only in passing and to note that 'Multilingual broadcasting can conjure up the imagined community to illiterates and populations with different mother tongues' (1983: 123). Possibly. Others would argue, as for instance on the basis of the Canadian experience, that competitive multilingual broadcasting within the confines of a single state may under some circumstances reinforce separatist tendencies rather than cement identification with one overarching national entity (cf. Desaulniers, 1985; Raboy, 1985). To observe this is merely to say that Anderson's general approach is in principle capable of accommodating such qualifications. However, first, much more attention needs to be paid to the specific analysis of the various media; and second, the rather overworked Catholic metaphor of general communion in collective representations needs countering by a refreshingly sceptical measure of attention to the socially located sources of division, and the place of contending views of what properly makes up the field of national imagery.

To put this differently, Anderson's notion of the comunicative community is open to doubt. The boundedness of a given national imagery is one thing; *homogeneity* within those boundaries is quite another. In the terms already indicated here, we should better look to a process of continual reconstruction than to an accomplished fact. Gavin Kitching (1985) argues that Anderson's approach deals better with nationalism as passion than does Gellner's. Perhaps so. But on the *social distribution* of passion, it decidedly avoids the issue. In fact, I would suggest that it shares a similar shortcoming to Gellner's model (although richer in its attention to communicative practices): the structural point about how a national mode of address is first constituted (by education in the one instance, print capitalism in the other) is conflated in each case with the analytically separate question of how a national culture is continually redeveloped and the contours of national identity chronically redrawn.

'Time–space' and nation-state

In another recent contribution of note, Anthony Giddens has developed a position on the nation-state and nationalism in the first two volumes of his *A Contemporary Critique of Historical Materialism* (1981 and 1985). Giddens lays considerable emphasis upon the role of the concepts of time and space in social theory and elaborates upon these much more fully than does Benedict Anderson. Giddens' general position informs his discussion of the nation-state and of nationalism. A central point I wish to make in discussing his work is that although his conceptual scheme in principle allows him to theorize 'national identity', he does not do so, and he fails to make an important distinction between it and 'nationalism'.

First, a sketch of Giddens' general assumptions about 'time–space relations'. These, he argues, are to be portrayed as constitutive features of social systems, implicated as deeply in the most stable forms of social life as in those subject to the most extreme or radical modes of change' (1981: 30). His approach is based upon a *relational* conception of time and space:

The concept of *presence-availability* links memory (storage) and spatial distribution in the time–space constitution of social systems. All collectivities have defined *locales* of operation: physical settings associated with the 'typical interactions' composing those collectivities as social systems . . . The locales of collectivities are integrally involved with the structural constitution of social systems, since common awareness of properties of the setting of interaction is a vital element involved in the sustaining of meaningful communication between actors. (1981: 39)

This highly abstract characterization of the role of time and space in the constitution of given social systems permits Giddens to talk of 'locales' as diverse as offices and empires: a 'locale' is constituted by interactions in time and space. Clearly, within such an abstract scheme there is a place for the 'nation–state' as a given locale with its own subordinate 'regions'. Giddens goes on to characterize, in equally abstract terms, a 'society' or 'societal totality'. Here, he draws attention to four separate features: a social system in relation to a 'social space' or 'territory of occupation'; a legitimated series of prerogatives over occupied social space: the institutional clustering of practices among participants (which he says is especially important); and finally

an overall awareness, discursive and practical, of belonging to an inclusive community with a certain 'identity'. First, some accentuation of the term 'inclusive' is needed. A 'societal identity' tends to be an 'outer limit' of affiliation with others: it may often go wider than, although not necessarily be more strongly *felt* than, other more restricted group affiliations. Second, we have once more to avoid the necessary presumption of consensus: consciousness that a collectivity has a certain identity, and that one is a member of that collectivity, is not the same as according it normative approval. (1981: 45–6)

Here, again, is a highly generalized characterization of how to conceive of a 'societal identity'. It is an empty term in principle, employing the metaphor of 'space', which permits varying levels of inclusion and exclusion. The awareness of identity may be discursive (reflexive) or practical (involved in everyday life). Giddens does not indicate, however, precisely how those shifts take place nor what they imply for the articulation of identity. In this formulation (unlike Melucci's) collective identity is linked with a conception of sentiments, which are held to vary in an ultimately unpredictable manner. This opens up a problematic of the *mobilization of sentiments*, although Giddens does not signal it in quite that form. Finally, there is a useful distinction between, on the one hand an awareness of collective identity and, on the other, the creation of a consensus over collective actions.

This rather lengthy set of preliminaries has been necessary as Giddens is *par excellence* a conceptual definer, and the specific points made in relation to the nation–state exemplify the wider abstract scheme he employs. Giddens' starting point is that 'the emergence of the nation–state was integrally bound up with the expansion of capitalism' (1985: 12) and that it is to be distinguished from the absolutist state; it is a typically modern phenomenon of the past two centuries. In both of his texts he also distinguishes between the 'nation–state', the 'nation' and 'nationalism':

> What makes the 'nation a necessary element of the 'nation–state' . . . is not the existence of sentiments of nationalism (however strong these may be) but the unification of an administrative apparatus whose power stretches over precisely defined territorial bounds. 'Nationalism', by contrast, may be understood as symbols or beliefs which attribute a communality of experience to the members of a particular regional, ethnic or linguistic category – which may or may not be convergent with the demarcation of a nation–state. (1981: 13; cf. 1985: 116)

The spatial boundaries of the nation–state give form to the nation. Nationalism is seen as a cultural and psychological phenomenon. On this latter theme, the sentiments concerned are held to 'feed upon the rootlessness of an everyday life in which what Geertz calls the primordial sentiments of social reproduction, grounded in tradition, have become substantially disintegrated' (1981: 13). Giddens also notes the importance of mass identification with leaderships, an inherently ambiguous, 'Janus-faced' capacity to switch between benign and aggressive postures (cf. 1985: 215, 218).

The theme of identity (although never expressly labelled *national* identity, but rather, in effect, handled as the identity traits of *nationalism*) is developed at somewhat greater length in the second of the two volumes. Nationalism is modern by contrast with 'pre-existing forms of group identity' and relies significantly upon the formation of a national public sphere based upon print, which also allows 'the invention of history in some form or another' (1985: 212). A satisfactory framework, Giddens suggests, needs to take account of the political character of the nation–state, ideological characteristics associated with class domination, psychological dynamics and symbolic content. It is consistent with Giddens' overall approach, which lays emphasis upon the role of the production of ideas as a constitutive element in social reproduction, that he should consider nationalist intellectuals *à la* Herder to be important (1985: 216). The *content* of nationalist belief is characterized thus:

> Nationalism is the cultural sensibility of sovereignty, the concomitant of the coordination of administrative power within the bounded nation–state. With the coming of the nation–state, states have an administrative and territorially ordered unity which they did not possess before. This unity cannot remain *purely* administrative, however, because the very coordination of activities involved presumes elements of cultural homogeneity. The extension of communication cannot occur without the 'conceptual' involvement of the whole community as a knowledgeable citizenry. A nation–state is a conceptual community in a way in which traditional states were not. (1985: 219)

This passage fills in the more formal discussion of 'societal identity' quoted earlier with a specific 'nationalist' content. The 'cultural sensibility' of the national community is administratively bounded by the sovereign state. Such a cultural or 'conceptual' component is seen as an inescapable form of 'imagining the community' (to use Benedict Anderson's phrase, and to whose conception this is strikingly similar) and as *unity-conferring*: 'As the "moral component" of sovereignty, nationalist symbols provide a core of political discourse that significantly shapes both the rhetoric of national solidarity and of opposition' (1985: 221). The collective representations of the nation are inescapable by this account, love them or hate them. The established political boundaries *resolve* the problem of national identity, at least contingently, in a world of shifting players, by offering an irreducible point of reference.

One of the oddities of this account is that Giddens nowhere makes an explicit distinction between nationalism and national identity, but rather conflates the two. I should like to argue for the relevance of the distinction between them. Nationalism, one may agree, is a particular kind of doctrine, but the term tends to carry the sense of a community mobilized (in part at least) in the pursuit of a collective interest. National identity may be invoked as a point of reference without thereby necessarily being nationalistic. There are undoubtedly historical periods when the construction of a national identity may be part of a nationalist programme, and therefore involve a good deal of intellectual labour. However, once the political boundaries of the nation–state have been achieved, a national identity, with all the accompanying mythico-cultural apparatus, may be in place and is not necessarily identical with nationalism as such. It is strange that Giddens does not recognize the potential *variability* of what he identifies as the 'cultural sensibility' of nationalism in such or similar terms. For to do so would be entirely consistent with the way he describes the ambivalence of identification with leadership. Moreover, as pointed out, the mobilization of sentiments is also, at least implicitly, part of his problematic. However, the sole category of 'nationalism' is too large a receptacle to do justice to the range of variation of collective sentiments within the confines of the nation–state, and, in the contemporary context at least, 'national identity' as an analytical term is of potential utility.

Schools of invention

One process to which we need to direct explicit attention is that of the continuous defining and redefining of 'national identity'. Not surprisingly, much of the most illuminating work along these lines has been undertaken by historians, and to a certain extent by anthropologists too. In this section I should like to consider some examples and to examine their implications.

One way into the question is to play some of the evidence concerning the conscious manipulation of the counters of identity against the following argument by Ernest Gellner:

> Nations as a natural, God-given way of classifying men, as an inherent though long-delayed political destiny, are a myth; nationalism, which sometimes takes pre-existing cultures and turns them into nations, sometimes invents them, and often obliterates pre-existing cultures: *that* is a reality, for better or worse. Those who are its historic agents know not what they do, but that is another matter. (1983: 48–9)

As an attack upon essentialism, the position could hardly be better put. But there is an overstatement, surely, at the end. In the matter of constructing (inventing, as Gellner would say) new national identities, and the manipulating of existing ones, there is ample evidence of historic agents knowing full well what they do. They may not have invented *nationalism*, but that is distinct from inventing discourses upon *national identity*. Gellner's attack on the intellectualist theory of the origins of nationalism espoused by Elie Kedourie (1960) has gone overboard, and needs to be qualified.

One productive line of attack on the problem has recently come from Eric Hobsbawm and Terence Ranger and their collaborators in *The Invention of Tradition* (1983). This collection of empirical historical essays derives from an insight into the fact that while 'traditions' may certainly be of venerable duration they may also emerge 'within a brief and datable period . . . establishing themselves with great rapidity' (1983: 1). It is of more than passing interest to note that Hobsbawm, the Marxist historian, shares this perception with Edward Shils, a conservative sociologist, who, quite some years before, pointed to the identical phenomenon (although he did not explore it in empirical detail). Traditional belief, Shils observed, is not only that which is 'handed down' or 'a matter of passive reception of the given': 'There is a more active, seeking relationship to traditional belief which motivates recommendation and reception at least in part and which also appears in a more independent form. Traditions are sometimes sought for . . . "Renaissances" are the characteristic form of this rehabilitated tradition' (Shils, 1975: 192–3).

Of central interest for our purposes is Hobsbawm's hypothesis that 'invented traditions' following the Industrial Revolution flow from

> a sense of identification with a 'community' and/or the institutions representing, expressing or symbolizing it such as a nation . . . most of the occasions when people become conscious of citizenship as such remain associated with symbols and semi-ritual practices (for instance, elections), most of which are historically novel and largely invented: flags, images, ceremonies and music. (Hobsbawm and Ranger, 1983: 11–12)

Hobsbawm also draws attention to the way in which historical writing may contribute 'to the creation, dismantling and restructuring of images of the past which belong not only to the world of specialist investigation but to the public sphere of man as a political being' (1983: 13). This would seem to be something more than imaginings inspired by a *déformation professionnelle* as one or two illustrations may shortly demonstrate. Historiography, when viewed from the standpoint of producing interpretations of nationhood for broader diffusion and eventual collective consumption, is one form of cultural practice amongst many which elaborate and sustain conceptions of identity:

> The element of invention is particularly clear here, since the history which became part of the fund of knowledge or the ideology of the nation–state or movement is not what has actually been preserved in popular memory, but what has been selected, written, pictured, popularized and institutionalized by those whose functions it is to do so. (1983: 13)

This clearly raises questions about the specialized role of intellectuals in the process of imagining the national community – one which Giddens and Anderson, for instance, would consider of crucial significance. It is also important to recognize the distinction between 'popular memory' and codified official tradition as this carries considerable implications for research into the cultural processes concerned. It opens up the issue of *alternative* accounts of national identity, and the motivations, strategies and practices of various groups in producing these. As David Gross has recognized, the modern nation state is *the* institution *par excellence* which determines our representations of the past, and *a fortiori* of collective national identity. It provides a unified, secular time-frame which elapses within a unified (territorial) space. A 'political interpretation of time' is inherent in the very organization of the state, for it claims 'primary responsibility for remembering and interpreting the long span of time from the distant past to the present', exercising power through 'the manipulation of symbols, values and frames of meaning' (Gross, 1985: 65). It is against these deterministic contours that the game of 'alternatives' and 'resistances' must play itself out.

However, prior to the establishment of such national time–space frameworks there is room for a greater measure of definitional and counter-definitional contestation. In a brilliant essay, 'L'italiano' (in Bollati, 1983), Giulio Bollati has explored the construction of Italian national identity. He has done this through tracing the production of alternative images in the engaged historiography of the nineteenth century.

Bollati accepts Lévi-Strauss's view that social groups need to classify and that this is done by an emphasis upon *difference* and through negative and positive evaluations. This categorial structure not only works in relation to foreigners ('them') but also signals who should be considered one of 'us'. Bollati illustrates a crucial definitional process in nineteenth-century Italy during the shift from a pre- to post-unification historiography: there is a move from limited membership of 'the Italians' to broad membership. But the broadening of membership involved the construction of a particular, dominant image of 'the nation' and also entailed a move from a *cultural* to a *political* category – that of belonging to 'an ethnic community with an autonomous political personality' (Bollati, 1983: 43).

What had to be overcome in creating a unitary image was the perception of *due razze* or *due popoli* (one might ponder, with what ultimate success?). At the beginning of the nineteenth century *italianità* characterized the insiders; *italianitudine* labelled the residuum of the excluded. Bollati's argument is that at the turn of the century the advocates of the moderate Risorgimento recognized the need for 'Italians' to fight the French. The defence of *la patria* was a way of expanding the nation within an essentially socially conservative framework; the lower orders 'would have an identity and their own character, inasmuch as they learned them from their masters' (1983: 59). This approach clearly opens up the Gramscian problematic of cultural and ideological dominance in the articulation of the discourses of nationhood, one curiously absent from an avowed neo-Marxist such as Anderson.

A place for the newly 'included' had to be worked out, argues Bollati, and various prominent intellectuals and their coteries set themselves the task of constructing an acceptable version of national 'moral fibre'. After national unity had been achieved, the focus shifted much more to a concern with the image of the Italians as compared with that of other nations, especially those with strong industries. Here, Bollati touches upon the sources of an anti-utilitarian, institutionally conservative, anti-industrial culture in Italy. His argument is that the exaltation of peasants flowed into justifications of colonial adventurism in Africa, the national appeal for cannon-fodder in World War I and the anti-workerism of fascism.

Bollati's essay provokes a number of questions. For one, he places firmly on the agenda the conscious agency of intellectuals acting as the members of class fractions with definite interests. Related to this is the matter of definitional struggle amongst the nation-defining groups. It is not clear from Bollati's account *why* certain views prevailed or predominated; nevertheless, the crucial point is that the production of rival versions of national identity is seen as taking place upon a terrain of contestation. Furthermore, Bollati's approach is one that clearly has an analytical place for the means of communication. In a related essay, 'Il modo di vedere italiano' (in Bollati, 1983), he quite expressly directs attention to the reception and uses of photography in Italy, and raises questions about how the emphases of the host culture predisposed Italian photographers towards certain practices. Thus, he touches upon how Italian photography beame an archive of the picturesque, and the forms in which it represented central social institutions (especially the monarchy). In keeping with the Gramscian inspiration of his work, therefore, there is a culturalist framework for the analysis of national-identity construction which could helpfully be developed and applied in other contexts.

The same kinds of questions, this time about the construction of national identity in the United States, have been posed by Michael Kammen (1978). For him the issue is 'the comparative lack of shared historical interest in the United States, or the weakness with which *national* tradition – as opposed to particular ethnic, or religious, or regional traditions – has been felt, perceived and perpetuated' (1978: 3). Kammen suggests that 'collective notions of nationality' might be usefully explored by means of a cultural history which is especially attentive to the construction of national traditions in popular culture. At the centre of his argument is the thesis that the American Revolution lies at the heart of the feeling for tradition in the United States as, unlike the Civil War for instance, it is one historic moment which has never been repudiated by a significant segment of the population; it therefore provides 'a basic referent of collective identity' in S.N. Eisenstadt's phrase. In order to explore this theme Kammen has studied 'second-rate romances' and 'third-rate novels' of the post-revolutionary period, as well as historiography, memoirs and autobiography. In his emphasis upon 'symbolism and imagination' his approach converges with that of Benedict Anderson.

Out of this brief consideration of recent historical work arises the question of how to analyse 'traditions'. Kammen puts it well when he suggests that in part we are forced to deal with traditions in terms of the 'impermanence and changing uses of social memory'. We may reformulate this as the analysis of the *selector mechanisms* operating in the process of cultural reproduction which enable given versions of 'national memory' – and therefore of national identity – to be produced.

Concluding reflections

In spirit, this chapter and the previous one have been critical, but not, I hope, only negatively so. There is much to be learned from the work of others, and some systematic suggestions as to how we might in future approach the question of national identity will follow shortly. Without doubt, contemporary mediology, both academic and officially sponsored, has tremendous shortcomings. Whilst it talks of 'national identity', 'cultural identity', 'audiovisual space', and so on, it offers no clear conceptualization of the key terms in its discourse. The entire exercise seems to have an off-the-shelf character, in which terms function as signals for competing politico-economic projects rather than offering analytical purchase upon actual developments and their causes. That there is presently a demand for symbolic politics of this kind – whether it be to legitimate Euro-projects, Latino-projects or the contradictions of Unesco-ism – can hardly be doubted. The analysis in Chapter 7 demonstrates that the supply of work has been forthcoming, and that confusion is no serious disadvantage in research entrepreneurship. Between reliance upon an outmoded and discredited model of media effects and a trendy subjectivism, current mediology has not much to offer in shedding light upon the constitution of collective identity in general and national identity in particular.

The problem as conventionally understood needs to be stood on its head. So far, work on and argument about communicative and cultural processes makes gratuitous assumptions about the nation-state, national culture and national identity. All are taken to be unproblematic, and, as communications are the central concern, they are handled as residual categories. I propose we reverse the terms of the argument: let us begin with the problem of how national identity is constituted and locate communications and culture within *that* problematic.

In the above discussion a number of very general points have been endorsed in passing. By way of conclusion, I will bring them together in summary fashion. Clearly, they will need systematic elaboration in future work.

Theory

Recent developments, whether 'ethnic revivals' or new social movements, have provoked a demand for a theoretical grasp of the question of collective identity. A critique of recent literature on communications reinforces this, if anything. Relevant work has been forthcoming; however, for the most part, it has failed to conceptualize *national* identity as opposed to the identities of emergent collectivities within established nation–states. The parameters of the nation–state are taken for granted.

National identity

This is to be understood as a particular kind of collective identity. In other words, it is an identity constituted at a given strategic level of a society. In formal terms, to talk of national identity requires us to analyse processes of inclusion and exclusion. We are also obliged to consider the dialectic between internal and external definition. It has been suggested that the concept of national identity be distinguished from that of nationalism in order to open up a more discriminating way into the processes of mobilization of collective sentiment in the national context. This allows us to accommodate a range of variation which is otherwise obscured by a single concept.

An actionist perspective

I have suggested that an approach stressing collective action offers an appropriate starting-point for the analysis of national identity. Such a perspective requires us to see identity not as a prior condition of collective action but rather as a continually constituted and reconstructed category. To talk of collective identity requires the continuous action of an agent within a determinate set of social relations. It also requires us to take account of space and time.

Space

National identity is constructed within a definite social space. In the present context of a world system of nation–states the relevant confines for the reproduction of national identity are territorial and juridico-political givens. (We can, of course, complicate the picture by thinking of emergent national identities which involve a redrawing of existing national boundaries.) The social space occupied by the nation–state does not resolve the problem of how national identity is constructed: it merely sets a limit upon its possible elaborations. Within the social space, cultural space is where the elaboration of various cultural identities takes place.

National culture

The national culture is another phrase for national cultural space. In principle, the national culture is bounded by the territorial confines of a given nation–state. However, the 'national' characteristics are not given. National cultures are not simple repositories of shared symbols to which the entire population stands in identical relation. Rather, they are to be approached as sites of contestation in which competition over definitions takes place. We need to distinguish between historical phases in which national cultures are first being established and those in which problems of maintenance are pre-eminent. The national culture is a repository, *inter alia*, of classificatory systems. It allows 'us' to define ourselves against 'them' understood as those beyond the boundaries of the nation. It may also reproduce distinctions between 'us' and 'them' at the intra-national level, in line with the *internal* structure of social divisions and relations of power and domination.

Time

The elaboration of national identity is a chronic process. Of considerable importance is the relationship between the present of a national collectivity and its past. That relationship should be understood, at least in part, as an imaginary one, mediated by the continual, selective reconstitution of 'traditions' and of 'social memory'. These categories direct our attention to the role of cultural institutions and practices through which the chain of identity between past and present is forged. It also requires us to consider the special role of cultural producers as active constructors of national identity.

References

Anderson. B. (1983) *Imagined Communities: Reflections on the Origin and Spread of Nationalism*. London: Verso Editions and NLB.

Barth, F. (1969) 'Ethnic Groups and Boundaries', introduction to *Ethnic Groups and Boundaries*. Boston, Mass: Little, Brown; republished in *Process and Form in Social Life: Selected Essays of Fredrik Barth*, Vol. 1. London: Routledge & Kegan Paul, 1981. pp. 198–227.

Berger, P. and Luckmann, T. (1966) *The Social Construction of Reality*. New York: Doubleday.

Bollati, G. (1983) *L'Italiano: Il Carattere Nazionale come Storia e come Invenzione*. Turin: Einaudi; 2nd edn 1984.

de Swaan, A. (1985) 'In Care of the State: The Social Dynamics of Public Health, Education and Income Maintenance in Western Europe and the United States'. Typescript, University of Amsterdam.

Desaulniers, J.P. (1985) 'Television and Nationalism: From Culture to Communication', in P. Drummond and R. Paterson (eds), *Television in Transition*. London: BFI. pp. 112–22.

Deutsch, K.W. (1966) *Nationalism and Social Communication: An Inquiry into the Foundations of Nationality*, 2nd edn. Cambridge and London: MIT Press.

Gellner, E. (1964) *Thought and Change*. London: Weidenfeld & Nicolson.

Gellner, E. (1983) *Nations and Nationalism*. Oxford: Blackwell.

Giddens, A. (1981) A Contemporary Critique of Historical Materialism. London and Basingstoke: Macmillan.

Giddens, A. (1985) *The Nation–State and Violence (A Contemporary Critique of Historical Materialism*, Vol. 2). Cambridge: Polity Press.

Gross, D. (1985) 'Temporality and the Modern State', *Theory and Society*, 14 (1), January: 53–82.

Hobsbawm, E. and Ranger, T. (eds) (1983) *The Invention of Tradition.* Cambridge: Cambridge University Press.

Kammen, M. (1978) *A Season of Youth: The American Revolution and the Historical Imagination.* New York: Knopf.

Kedourie, E. (1960) *Nationalism.* London: Hutchinson; revised edn with 'Afterword', 1985.

Kitching, G. (1985) 'Nationalism: The Instrumental Passion', *Capital and Class*, 25, Spring: 98–116.

LaPierre, J.W. (1984) 'L'identité collective, objet paradoxal: d'où nous vient-il?', *Recherches sociologiques*, 15 (2–3): 155–64.

Mackenzie, W.J.M. (1978) *Political Identity.* Manchester: Manchester University Press.

Melucci, A. (1982) *L'Invenzione del Presente: Movimenti, Identità, Bisogni Individuali.* Bologna: Il Mulino.

Oriol, M. and Igonet-Fastinger, P. (1984) 'Recherches sur les identités: le retour paradoxal du sujet dans les sciences sociales', *Recherches sociologiques*: 'Identité Ethnique et Culturelle', 15 (2–3): 155–64.

Pistoi, P. (1983) 'Identità etnica e mobilitazione politica', *Rassegna Italiana di Sociologia*, 24 (1): 79–103.

Raboy, M. (1985) 'Public Television, the National Question and the Preservation of the Canadian State', in P. Drummond and R. Paterson (eds), *Television in Transition.* London: BFI. pp. 64–86.

Sciolla, L. (ed.) (1983) *Identità: Percorsi di Analisi in Sociologia.* Turin: Rosenberg & Sellier.

Shils, E. (1975) *Center and Periphery: Essays in Macrosociology.* London & Chicago: University of Chicago Press.

Smith, A. (1973) 'Nationalism: A Trend Report and Bibliography', *Current Sociology*, 21 (3): 5–185.

9

No Guide for the Perplexed: Collective Identities in a Changing Europe

Today we face an unprecedented challenge to long-standing patterns of cultural and political identity in Europe. The confrontation between two politico-economic systems that has characterized the post-war years has broken down before our very eyes. Nothing could have symbolized this more dramatically than the breaches – both literal and powerfully metaphorical – that appeared in the Berlin Wall in November 1989. None who have lived through the Cold War, and recall its chilling moments of high confrontation, could fail to be moved by the currents of democratization in Eastern Europe. However, by the same token, no one who remembers the disastrous circumstances that led up to the post-war partition of Europe could fail to be concerned about what kind of new order is to be constructed, and how.

The role of the news media has been of the foremost importance in relaying and interpreting the major developments of recent months: since last autumn and winter, 'Eastern' Europe has largely ceased to exist in its old political sense (that is, as a set of Soviet-dominated buffer states). Such headlong change poses a challenge of the first rank to the adequacy of our systems of communication as means for interpreting our socio-political environment. It also has major implications for the social role of intellectuals as interpreters of novel events and processes.

What is striking is how the relative opening up of the communication systems of most countries of the former Eastern bloc (as a consequence of political liberalization) has thrown contemporary media analysis into disarray. The analytical schemata founded upon the titanic ideological struggle between 'democracy' and 'totalitarianism' can no longer carry the punch they once had. A new and very practical task, that of tracking developments in the old Eastern bloc and of eventually coining conceptual frameworks appropriate to changed circumstances, has now come on to the research agenda. For instance, one of the most interesting processes to observe in the coming years will be the political, economic and cultural responses to the invasion of East-Central Europe by capitalist multi-media enterprises. Will a durable 'public sphere' be successfully established? How will emergent relations between market and state be regulated in the public interest? At a more general level, we shall eventually be called upon to theorize the communicative dimension of the novel transition from socialism to capitalism and its place in the creation of civil society.

The supply of relevant work will no doubt quite rapidly appear. Indeed, we already have our first, doubtless provisional, analyses of *glasnost* in the Soviet Union (cf. Goban-Klas, 1989; Graffy and Hosking, 1989; McNair, 1989). In the short term perpetual revision seems likely to be our fate, as may be illustrated by recent academic writing on countries such as Poland, Hungary and the GDR which in some cases was overtaken by events well before it was even published (cf., for example, Hanke, 1990; Jakubowicz, 1990). The time-scales of the academy will be inappropriate for some time to come. The reporter, the commentator, the pundit are those who hold the floor today and draw the outlines of our new interpretations. (The academic, of course, may – and does – readily assume one or more of these guises.)

As Europe undergoes its coming, highly complex transformation, our systems of communication (to be understood here in the broadest sense as including not just media, but the multifold socio-political networks that constitute European societies) are going to have an increasingly testing role to play. Some of the overarching, ready-to-hand stereotypes of yesterday have certainly lost their purchase (for instance, to talk today of the 'free world's mission' against 'communism' is decidedly *passé*), but there are plenty of other marks of distinction that are well fitted to our need to categorize, differentiate and make a kind of sense of an increasingly complex geopolitical cartography. And it is precisely this theme that I wish to pursue here in the shape of some reflections upon the question of collective identities.

Pressure points

The current, somewhat undirected vogue for reflecting on the concept of identity in political discourse clearly has its sources in perceptions of change. Amongst the factors pressing hard upon the post-Yalta configuration of Europe, with its decaying legacy of two ideologically opposed socio-political and economic systems, the following are of particular note:

- The accelerating (if at times uneven) attempt to bring about economic and political integration in the European Community, a process with implications not only for the economy and polity but also for culture.
- The complete disintegration of the socialist camp in the wake of the Gorbachev reform programme. The abandonment of the Brezhnev doctrine and internal decay amongst the ruling Communist parties opened space for a rather unpredictable measure of political pluralization (or at the very least, organized and legitimate opposition). During the course of 1990 we rapidly ceased to think *en bloc* any longer. The balance of forces and the pace of change in Poland, Czechoslovakia, Hungary, the GDR, Romania and Bulgaria have so far differed

considerably, and seem likely to continue doing so.

- In both East and West the question of the nation and its right to self-expression has forcefully re-entered the political agenda, although in different ways. The acceleration of European Community integration has provoked questions about national sovereignty and democratic representation. The disintegration of state socialism has produced a new ethnic assertiveness in the USSR (the Lithuanian attempt to secede crystallized the contradictions in the system) and has put on the agenda potential border disputes in East-Central Europe held in check until now by the post-war *pax sovietica*.
- To complicate matters further, the question of German reunification is now widely acknowledged to be the principal political issue in the construction of a new European order acceptable to NATO and the crumbling Warsaw Pact alike. The speed of the GDR's collapse surprised even the best-informed observers. However, it had nevertheless been entirely clear for several years that the *ultima ratio* of the new Soviet *Westpolitik* would inevitably bring in its train the German Question.

The issues provoked by these momentous changes, which challenge the skills of diplomacy and statesmanship in far-reaching ways, are both politico-economic and cultural. On the one hand, we are talking about a potential recasting of the structures of political and economic power in Europe, in ways that have wider, global implications. On the other, and this cannot be escaped, we must consider how we *think* about these structures and their interrelations. This will eventually require Europeans to reconsider the collectivities to which they owe allegiance, and the grounds of their legitimacy.

If we are to adopt new thinking for what, in the fashionable café Marxist phrase, are now called 'New Times' (Hall and Jacques, 1989) we shall have to engage in far-reaching processes of remembering and forgetting. We must remember what is common to European culture and society and we have to forget what has divided it. We may, of course, choose – as an alternative – to remember divisions and forget commonalities. I suspect that this course of resistance will be a rather powerful one for many, for it offers a form of reassurance at a time when navigation is rather difficult. At all events, however, for the purposes of self-disciplined analysis we must clearly attempt to ensure that the uses of memory and amnesia to construct new imaginings of the future, and the raw sentiments to which these are generally attached, attain some distance from one another. The task, then, is to remember and forget, but also to project, to imagine new alternatives and possibilities.

This rearrangement of established patterns of thought is a tall order, and particularly so as no one can be sure how far-reaching the process of change will be. There is already a great deal of projecting and imagining going on. Punditry abhors a vacuum. Euro-futurology (Eurology for short?) is all the rage. No self-respecting Eurological commentator can forbear to issue a sketch that tries to envisage 'Europe in the year 2000'. In one such projection in the London *Independent* newspaper, the German border 'has assumed the half-remembered air of a temporary aberration', Spain's GDP outstrips that of Britain as Gibraltar is returned, and Central Europe bears more than a passing resemblance to the Austro-Hungarian empire (Cottrell, 1989). The *Financial Times* offers a 'fantasy' of the year 2020 in which the following patterns of association are to be found: a 'United States of Western Europe', and a variety of 'Unions' variously denominated Central European, Scandinavian–Baltic, Balkan, Slavic and Turkic, together with a Caucasian Federation of Armenia and Georgia (Mortimer, 1990). The categorizing imperative is never far from the surface. In the 'Débats' section of *Le Monde*, to take another example, an SPD member of the Bundestag assures his French élite readers that in these post-nationalist times, it is the cultural moment of Germanity that matters. The world is heading towards a global identity, so:

> Today, we, the citizen-viewers, no longer live in a single state; all of us simultaneously live in other states and in other cultures. More and more, we are living in a kind of cultural collage. This now applies to most of the world's regions, and not to the Germans alone. (Duve, 1989)

We should not be seduced by this well-meaning line. The germ of truth, to be sure, lies in the importance of the means of communication in conveying images and interpretations of change for widely differing audiences. In these times of rapid political transformation, the importance of cross-national processes of communication has assumed a heightened import-ance, and the responsibilities of the interpreters of change have increased accordingly. But the post-modernist assumption in the *Le Monde* article that the citizen-viewer sees the world as a relativistic cultural collage is the one that I find utterly implausible. The interpretation of the message is not uniform. Whether or not the Oder–Neisse Line is recognized as durable may be treated with concern but relative equanimity in the United Kingdom or France but does not at all have the same resonances in Poland or the Soviet Union.

The European space, rather than offering a cultural collage, seems one in which many sharp assertions of national identity based upon divergences of interest are the order of the day: one has but to think of the secessionist movements in the Baltic states and their acute difficulties with the Soviet central state power, of the tendency to fragment into hostile constituent national groupings in Yugoslavia, of the lethal ethno-religious hatreds of the Caucasus or of the large Hungarian minority and its history of persecution in Romania. A post-nationalist German federation need not be the image for all our futures. For we are not all post-nationalists now.

Indeed, there could be no more telling index of how our sense of being European has become more complex and nuanced than the efflorescence of a new Euro-cartography. We are obliged to think of peoples and places whose existence has long been obscured by the crudely antagonistic grand design of the Cold War. Now maps abound designating actual and potential trouble-spots where ethnic and religious divisions have resumed their potency. In one such survey from the Atlantic almost to the Urals no less than forty-six locations were identified in the European 'patchwork of tensions' (cf. Ascherson, 1990). I will restrict myself to mentioning just two cases which have suddenly come into focus: the Silesians in Poland, whose 'German' identity has of late been rediscovered; and the new focus on religious divisions in which the claims of the United Catholic Church in the Ukraine have been reasserted against those of Russian Orthodoxy (Clough, 1990; Gott, 1990). There is little risk in predicting that given the continued messiness of European borders – when judged, that is, by the mythic nationalist criterion of a perfectly aligned polity and culture – there will be many strains inherent in the new European order.

Collective identities

In this turbulent context, an inescapable role for today's intellectuals is that of analysing the political, economic, social and cultural forces that mould collective identities, of which national identities are arguably the most important. As is well known, however, there is no *single* role for the intellectual, but rather a range of socially structured possibilities that is closely linked to the articulation of political and economic interests (cf. Schlesinger, 1982).

Within given states, class relations and political organization are of signal importance in defining the scope of intellectual activity. Between states, the fault lines of nationhood offer a prime source of identification and the political space for the elaboration of a national discourse. I would, nevertheless, stress that we should not conflate national identities with the boundaries of particular states, for polity and culture do not smoothly align with one another. States such as Britain and Spain, for instance, are multinational and contain significant identity-conferring regional differences, a fact of which one could hardly be unaware if resident, say, in Scotland or Catalonia. This dimension therefore adds a further complication. Besides, one must also not neglect the significance of supra-national, transnational and international bodies as locuses within which the articulation of intellectual projects takes place. It is precisely at such levels that many of the grand designs for the European future are being elaborated.

The Italian sociologist Alberto Melucci has essayed a definition of 'collective identity' along the following lines:

> Collective identity is an interactive and shared definition produced by several interacting individuals who are concerned with the orientations of their action as well as the field of opportunities and constraints in which their action takes place . . . Collective identity formation is a delicate process and requires continual investment. As it comes to resemble more institutionalized forms of

social action, collective identity may crystallize into organizational forms, a system of formal rules, and patterns of leadership. (1989: 34-5)

This stress upon the working out of cognitive and emotional processes within an opportunity-structure strikes me as apt. I would wish to add that collective identities are sustained by a dual process: one of inclusion that provides a boundary around 'us', and one of exclusion that distinguishes 'us' from 'them'. It is a common characteristic of social classifications to draw lines between 'friends', 'enemies' and 'neutrals' (cf. Schlesinger, 1988). Zygmunt Bauman (1990: 153) has pointed out that it is typical of the modern nation-state to seek to classify thus; and recalcitrant elements, such as the 'stranger' in our midst, pose a major problem where the quest for an homogeneous order is pursued. At the extreme, such classifying processes can be deadly (dehumanization of the Other and genocide being the limiting case) and, at the very least, they are often tenacious in ways that are far from trivial, as the Hungarian-born humorist George Mikes once somewhat poignantly observed:

> It is a shame and bad taste to be an alien, and it is no use pretending otherwise. There is no way out of it. A criminal may improve and become a decent member of society. A foreigner cannot improve. Once a foreigner, always a foreigner. There is no way out for him. He may become British; he can never become English. (1946: 8)

The pressure to assimilate, as Bauman (1990: 158) justly notes, entails regarding the alien or stranger as inferior, and may be seen as part of 'a declaration of war on foreign substances and qualities'. Mikes' insights into the peculiarities of the English do not prevent us from observing that very similar forms of categorization operate elsewhere in Europe: Theodore Zeldin's observations on France and its 'aliens' are a case in point (cf. Zeldin, 1985: ch. 26).

In the present context, as noted in the previous chapter, it is pertinent to consider several relevant principles for analysing collective identities. First, and the current pace of change reinforces the argument, we need to see such identities as *constituted in action* and as continually reconstituted in line with both an internal dynamic and external balances of force. As Alberto Melucci (1989: 25-6) has rightly argued, we need to see collective identities as an emergent feature of collective action.

Second, we should be aware of the *temporal dimension* through which the highly complex imaginary process of reconstituting traditions and of activating collective memories occurs (cf. Hobsbawm and Ranger, 1983; Namer, 1987; Schama, 1987). The anthropologist Mary Douglas (1987: 70) has observed: 'Public memory is the storage system for the social order. Thinking about it is as close as we can get to reflecting on the conditions of our thought.' The key questions, then, are what we as members of collectivities socially forget and what we remember – and why.

Third, we also need to think *spatially*. This can also be complex, for collective identities need not tidily conform to a model of territorial concentration and juridico-political integrity. Witness, for instance, the nations and ethnic groups that aspire to have states, those that straddle the boundaries of states, those that survive as diasporas.

These rather general observations bear upon contemporary European reality and its interpretation. Post-war socio-political space has been divided into alignments of Friends and Enemies, with broad labels of difference attached: Democracy vs Totalitarianism; Capitalism vs Communism; East vs West. Of course, these simplistic verities clouded internal differences within the two great camps and made pariahs within each of those who hankered for something substantially different (although, certainly McCarthyism and the Gulag cannot be equated). The weight of post-war international politics suppressed claims to commonality and abolished the idea of a Centre in a Europe divided into West and East, Good and Evil.

Discourses on Europe

The processes of political and economic change currently under way are producing competition at the level of political discourse, and it is here, in the fashioning of new interpretations, that the intellectuals (together with the mass media that diffuse their arguments and frameworks) have a major contribution to make. With different force, and with different appeal depending on where we are situated in the European mosaic, we are being asked to 'imagine' or visualize a number of different Europes. This process is likely to accelerate and intensify. There are several distinctive fields in which debate is taking place, although they clearly interrelate.

Inside the European Community, there has been a conflict, now apparently beginning to be resolved, it would seem, between minimalism and maximalism. The *locus classicus* of minimalist discourse is British Prime Minister Margaret Thatcher's by now notorious Bruges speech, in which she said: 'the European Community is *one* manifestation of . . . European identity. But it is not the only one. We must never forget that east of the Iron Curtain peoples who once enjoyed a full share of European culture, freedom and identity have been cut off from their roots' (Thatcher, 1988: 3). These words were spoken before the revolutionary changes that began to reshape the erstwhile East in 1989. As Budapest, Prague, Warsaw and Berlin once more begin to assume their places in a wider European constellation, one may reflect that, although what Mrs Thatcher said was true, it was certainly not innocent. In her view, a loosely affiliated Europe, wider than the projected Single Market of 1992, may both reclaim the East and give Britain a wider stage on which to play – and keep her distance. (This view was reiterated in yet another set-piece address, at the Aspen Institute in August 1990: Thatcher, 1990). For Mrs Thatcher and those, who, as she does, stress national sovereignty, the key principle of 'willing and active co-operation between independent sovereign states is the best way to build a successful European community'. There is an interesting (but hardly surprising) conflation here between state and nation at the same time as it is insisted that nationhood, national customs, traditions and identity be maintained against 'some identikit European personality' and 'super-state' (Thatcher, 1988: 5).

Although this minimalist view in defence of national sovereignty and cultural integrity commands some support, it now seems unlikely to prevail against the forces for integration ranged across EC Europe. In April 1990 a further major step in pursuit of the integrationist vision was undertaken when President Mitterrand and Chancellor Kohl proposed accelerating the drive towards political union. Precisely what this means in terms of institutional development is open to question, and the eventual outcome will be the product of much horse-trading (cf. Butt, 1990). Nevertheless, it is not too far-fetched to suppose that the national-state level will become less important as an instance of sovereignty and decision-making in the coming years. In part, behind this latest push lies the need to create a viable framework for containing the enlarged German state as a result of the absorption by the Federal Republic of the GDR.

EC maximalism envisages a 'social Europe' or Euro-welfare-state offering an opening, it seems increasingly likely, to an integrated political and defence community. Spokesmen for this point of view present a different image of the future from that of the homogenizing 'identikit Europe'. Jacques Delors, President of the European Commission, for instance, has talked in homely terms of the creation of a 'European Village'; whereas, for his part, Felipe González, the Spanish Prime Minister, has gestured towards a 'European space'.

It must be said that the precise constitution of this 'space' remains in need of detailed specification. Certainly, since the 1980s there has been an effort (largely bureaucratically inspired by Brussels) to find a cultural character for the Twelve, most notably under the label of a 'European audiovisual space', defined in many respects against the importation of US television programmes. As is now dramatically apparent, EC media space *tout court* increasingly occupies the territories of the former East as well, so in many respects that project will have to be rethought.

Indeed, one may expect the redefinition of a 'European cultural space' to be one of the most popular intellectual and bureaucratic pastimes of the coming years, and a lucrative source of work for consultants and researchers. Nor can this rest with the regulation of broadcasting and the cinema alone, for it will eventually have to deal with culture in all its manifold shapes. Recently, we have also begun to hear about the 'European economic space' which is to be the consequence of a renegotiated set of trading relations between the European Community and the European Free Trade Association. Naturally, such a reconfiguration of economic space also will have inevitable political and cultural consequences (cf. Cornelius and Milner, 1990).

European collective identities have also been deeply bound up with

European collective security and insecurity: consequently, NATO and the Warsaw Pact have functioned as symbolic counters defining the nominal allegiances of millions. It is only to be expected, therefore, that the processes of redefinition noted above have also been at work in the field of defence in analogous ways. Although given considerable play, particularly in the élite media, the detailed nature of such thinking really makes it part of the province of the specialist rather than placing it at the heart of political marketing. The general public is more aware of the grand gestures and proposals concerning troop reductions and nuclear weaponry that make it feel either safer or more vulnerable than of the nuances of policies and institutions.

What is now becoming steadily clearer, though, is the growing interconnection between strategic defence thinking and other broader political designs. For instance, in calling for a new European 'architecture', NATO Secretary-General Manfred Wörner has taken the national question on board as one of the central issues that the Atlantic Alliance needs to address if stability is to be achieved. A new political order in Europe, he argues, needs to be one that 'makes national frontiers much less significant, while respecting self-determination and national sovereignty; one that fosters economic integration thereby giving all nations a vital stake in common prosperity and an interest in moving together politically; one that equally provides for democracy and human rights in all states' (1990: 10).

This shows a due sense of the interpenetration of culture, economy and polity, at the same time, of course, as staking out a future for NATO – which others, such as CND's Bruce Kent (1990), have questioned fundamentally, arguing for new ways of establishing common security. During the past decade or so, it has been the anti-nuclear movement that has been most explicitly aware of the cultural consequences of our wider defence arrangements. Now, as NATO and the Warsaw Pact begin to reshape, the profound impact of the familiar co-ordinates of Cold War political identity on our thinking is being thrown more and more into relief. If the old enemy less and less constitutes a widely perceived threat, however, this does not imply the disappearance of all foes. Rather, the conditions for a *displacement* of perceived threat have been met by current developments, and this too is likely to have cultural consequences in perceptions of those who compete with the new, enlarged Europe on the world stage. At this time of writing, the Gulf Crisis of 1990 has shifted attention away from Europe, and raised with great sharpness the issue of so-called 'out-of-area' deployment of NATO forces.

Of late, a second field of discourse has intersected with debates internal to the EC in the shape of the Soviet call for a 'Common European Home' or, according to the vagaries of translation, a 'Common House of Europe'. This is a particularly interesting metaphor which implies, in Ernest Gellner's phrase (1983), a common political roof over our heads. To date, taken as an image, the Common Home has been more emotive than programmatic, though attempts have been made by Soviet spokesmen to fill it with some content: for instance, an all-European security system and co-ordinated action over the environment, energy and communications. But it must be said that the House still has no foundations, let alone a roof on top or furniture inside. Despite these defects, it is plainly a slogan that has stirred the political imagination as others have tried to appropriate it. In one such echo from the West, Jacques Delors has said that he shares this vision; in yet another, James Baker, US Defense Secretary, has opined that the New Europe of the Freedoms holds the key to the European House of the Future. In short, there has been growing competition in the realm of post-Cold-War discourse.

The demise of the Brezhnev doctrine has led to its replacement by another, the new Sinatra doctrine ('I did it my way . . .') in the phrase coined by the Soviet Foreign Ministry spokesman, Gennady Gerasimov. This has been represented as a corner-stone in the construction of the Common Home. However, whereas to date detachment from the Soviet embrace has become possible for the states of the Eastern bloc, even semi-detachment within the confines of the USSR remains an unresolved problem, although as more and more Soviet republics declare themselves to be sovereign states the day of reckoning can hardly be far off.

From East to Centre?

Of all the new Euro-fantasies, it is particularly striking that, thus far at least, Central Europe has merited most discussion as a political space, and even as a moral project. Until very recently the debate has been profoundly shaped by opposition to Soviet rule, and has been carried out mainly in Czechoslovakia and Hungary (and to some extent Poland) by sections of the intelligentsia. Across the old Iron Curtain interest has also been shown in Austria and the Federal Republic. At the heart of the debate has been the question of what kind of political and cultural space can define itself between Germany and Russia, what future relations (given the initially hypothetical, but now real, withdrawal of Soviet power) should be developed with the West and the East, and whether there is a distinctive Central European identity at all (cf. Schöpflin and Wood, 1989). Until late 1989 the debate has really been one about the projection of possibilities. Beyond these, as Timothy Garton Ash (1989: 188–9), one of the most perceptive and sympathetic commentators on the region, has observed, there is a need for a 'dispassionate and rigorous examination both of the real legacy of historic Central Europe – which is as much one of divisions as of unities – and of the true conditions of present-day East Central Europe – as much one of differences as of similarities'. Recent change has meant that confronting the past and working out the future are now unavoidable, as has been noted by the Czechoslovak President, Václav Havel (1990: 18–19).

The new rhetorics offer more comfort than the old but they also obscure many problems of socio-economic and political reorientation. The reform process in the East may be seen as a relative historic victory for bourgeois democracy and capitalist efficiency. Not all would formulate it thus. Sir Ralf Dahrendorf (1990: 36), taking a leaf out of the Popperian manual, has argued that East-Central Europe has 'shed a closed system in order to create an open society, *the* open society to be exact, for while there can be many systems, there is only one open society'. Apart from tending to idealize Western democratic practice as the embodiment of rationality, this flattering self-portrait of our social order side-steps the question of its political economy, and neglects to consider how 'the open society' might look viewed from the outside. It has relevantly been pointed out (Pohoryles and Kinnear, 1989) that in latterly becoming fixated with the crisis of the East, we are apt to forget that the West is hardly problem-free. Poverty, unemployment, inequality, racism, homelessness and unresolved political differences still exist. The global capitalist economy is still subject to cyclical fluctuations; and, in a world in which we are compelled to recognize our interdependence, we cannot ignore how the North–South divide and major ecological problems are likely to shape our future. In short, the West may have won the post-war *Kulturkampf*, but it remains far from invulnerable.

Returning more directly to the question of collective identity, one might note that the emergent so-called Europe of the Freedoms is one in which one is also freer to migrate (as has been most dramatically demonstrated by the flight from the GDR in 1989). Large-scale population movements (which engender increased socio-economic demands upon host countries and associated political problems) have a tendency to put defensive conceptions of national and cultural identity on the political agenda. Racism and discrimination against incomers are ever-present dangers.

The optimistic expectations currently held about the impact of systemic change in the East lead one to take seriously pertinent questions, posed by the Polish sociologist Jerzy Mikulowski-Pomorski (1988), about whether there really are common 'European values' and whether the collapse of communism in the East will bring about the long-awaited 'convergence' of systems. Extensive experience of totalitarian rule, he argues, has produced a decline in political and civic morality: the lack of a public sphere and of a vital civil society, in other words, and no settled habit of tolerating the strains of political difference. As may already be seen, the political evolution of the former states of the Eastern bloc is far from uniform, and we shall have to keep an open mind about what kinds of governments and political cultures will follow the first wave of fully democratic elections. Dahrendorf (1990: 96) has rightly urged caution here, noting that while citizenship can be built by legislation and supporting policies, the 'creative chaos of organizations, associations and institutions is not as easily built', and that civic virtues such as civility and self-reliance 'cannot be built at all'; they have 'to grow . . . and will not grow in a season or even a parliamentary period . . . a generation is needed at least'. In sombre vein, Timothy Garton Ash (1990: 56) has observed that, to varying extents, in Czechoslovakia, Hungary and Poland, whose progress is crucial for all post-Communist states, 'one can see the seeds of an authoritarian temptation'.

Certainly, as the more far-sighted of Western politicians have realized, the transformation of the East, and its 'normalization' according to the liberal-democratic canon, will not come cheap. For political stability will have to be bought by relative economic improvement. Ultimately, fine words aside, one could be forgiven for thinking that the questions will be posed more in terms of interests and the costs and benefits engendered by entry to the Common Home (ultimately, an all-ecompassing EC?) than of arguments about political and cultural virtue. The Scottish political commentator Neal Ascherson has noted that the European house has always had an upstairs and a downstairs, and that the current disposition of economic strengths and weaknesses will ensure that the servants' quarters remain well occupied.

One expected benefit for the East, the Hungarian sociologist György Csepeli (1984) has argued, and this well before the developments of 1989, would be the *modernization* of forms of national identity within a wider European space, a shift from *Gemeinschaft* to *Gesellschaft*. However one evaluates this proposition, it seems certain that the ethnic factor will remain extremely important, although one voice has questioned this of late, in a very specific way. Eric Hobsbawm suggests that in the late twentieth century nationalism is 'no longer a major vector of historical development' (1990: 163). His main point is that nationalism no longer provides a principle for political restructuring or offers a global political programme. Underlying this argument, *inter alia*, are assumptions about the globalization of the world economy rendering the national economy an instance incapable of sovereign regulation, and a progressivist teleology which sees current manifestations of nationalism as essentially negative reactions to population movements and 'future shock'.

The debate on globalization is becoming increasingly ramified, and in the present context no more than a few pertinent points can be made in response to Hobsbawm. First, although obviously one must accept that the traditional model of the sovereign nation-state has been modified by processes of globalization (cf. Held, 1989), in the light of German unification, and its unforeseeable consequences for the EC, a little caution would be well advised before writing off the nationalist project altogether. Second, within the EC, despite economic convergence, the basic rights and duties of citizenship remain within the purview of the nation–state, which shows no immediate signs of supersession in this regard (cf. Dahrendorf, 1990: 124–6). Third, it is important not to underestimate the continuing weight of states as articulators of national culture, and thus as still exceptionally important focuses of collective identification (cf. Smith, 1990).

Although today one might increasingly plausibly speak of a European 'family of cultures' that 'consists of overlapping and boundary-transcending cultural and political motifs and traditions' (Smith, 1990: 187), one should nevertheless take seriously Csepeli's observation that expectations of a United States of Europe on the North American model come up hard against the resilience of the national question. The historical preconditions in the Old World clearly do not match those in the New. In Csepeli's terms the United States is an 'inorganic' nation, that is, one juridically defined, in which the myth of consanguinity simply cannot work, given the nation's basis in successive waves of diverse immigration. Europe, by contrast is utterly congested with historical memories in which nationhood plays a central role. Thus, 'Unity of what kind, for whom and on what terms?' are the questions to be posed.

Boundaries of belonging

One of the odder risks of interrogating debates about 'Europeanness' in this way is to be accused of Eurocentrism. This point came home when I presented an earlier version of this chapter to an audience that contained many Latin Americans. Aware of this, I had taken the precaution of excusing the focus on Europe as driven by a consuming interest in exploring something close to home. It seemed obvious to me that my kind of treatment of the topic would inevitably be interpreted as problematizing rather than as celebratory. Not entirely so. The reaction was instructive: namely, to ignore the explanation and to warn that such preoccupations may tend to exclude others. Underlying this was a practical perception: namely, that the current wave of Europhoria places at further risk the heavily indebted South, as investment flows into developing Eastern Europe.

There is one issue that I particularly wish to raise, namely the question of inclusion and exclusion, or, putting it differently, where Europe stops. In the recent debate about Central Europe, the focus has been upon whether or not Russia can rightly be seen as 'European'. One may expect this matter to remain on the agenda, and it is certainly interesting to note that the lines of exclusion drawn up by Milan Kundera in the well-known article that initiated this discussion in 1984 (Kundera, 1984) have latterly found an echo in the thinking of one of Britain's leading military historians, Sir Michael Howard, expressed in a recent lecture to the International Institute of Strategic Studies in London:

> 'Central Europe' consists of lands once part of Western Christendom; the old lands of the Habsburg Empire, Austria, Hungary and Czechoslovakia, together with Poland and the eastern marches of Germany. The term 'Eastern Europe' should be reserved for regions which developed under the aegis of the Orthodox Church: Bulgaria and Romania and the 'European' parts of the Soviet Union. It is these old nations of Central Europe that we must welcome first and most warmly into our European commonwealth, and ultimately into the European Community. (Howard, 1990: 19)

The outer waiting-room, it would appear, is a likely way of euphemizing rejection or marginalization. One should take ideas seriously when they quickly translate themselves from a debate in the literary journals into the thinking of military commentators. The theme has also been addressed by Sir Ralph Dahrendorf in his recent reflections on Europe's revolutions, where he offers different grounds for excluding the Russians. Apostrophizing his Polish correspondent, he says: 'the European house which you and I want to turn into our common home ends where the Soviet Union, or whatever succeeds it, begins' (Dahrendorf, 1990: 13). The grounds offered are that the former hegemonic power should keep its distance, that the Soviet Union is still a developing country and that Europe should consist of small and medium-sized countries, so 'a superpower has no place in their midst' (1990: 112). These differ from those above, but the message is the same, and clearly one whose volume one may expect to grow steadily, in a variety of permutations.

Lines of inclusion and exclusion also criss-cross the relations between Islam and Europe (whether East, West or Centre). Unquestionably, this problem too will have to be confronted in a variety of arenas. As Akbar Ahmed (1990: 22) has justly commented: 'There are signs that some of the free-floating hostility directed against communism over the last decades will move towards Islam.'

In Britain, the emergence of Islam as a politico-cultural force offering a potent source of collective identification for sections of the Asian community was latterly crystallized by the Salman Rushdie affair. As is well known, sections of the British Muslim community were mobilized against the novelist Rushdie in the wake of the Ayatollah Khomeini's denunciation as blasphemous of his novel *The Satanic Verses*; the effect of this edict was to sentence him to death and send him into hiding under police protection, where he still remains (cf. Appignanesi and Maitland, 1989). This episode raised central questions of cultural identity, with the dominant view proclaiming Islamic fundamentalism to be an eruption of an alien tradition within the body politic. Compelled by the need to defend its public space, much of the intelligentsia rallied round the threatened writer in a defence of the liberal conception of authorship, which certainly (and rightly) sees the cultural producer as needing to be free from the threat of intimidation or violence.

But that is only part of the story. Having provided a focus for the accumulated resentments of the Muslim community at the discrimination and marginalization that it has suffered, the Rushdie case has also cystallized a much wider problem, namely how the international politics of Islam may at times be articulated inside Western polities.

This question is by no means unique to the United Kingdom. After the US bombing of Tripoli and Benghazi in 1986, Muslims living in Belgium engaged in organized protest. In a study of this event and its coverage by the news media, Dassetto and Bastenier (1987: 119) have commented: 'That an expression of collective identity may today take on religious forms openly cuts across the usual conception we have of the socio-political game.' One should add that the usual conception may not last indefinitely.

Behind these tensions lies the sensitive question of labour migration into the more affluent Western European states and the establishment within the wider societies of ethnic subcultures with highly distinctive communal identities. In the near future, the EC is likely to have to face dealing with Turkey's manifest desire for accession. As Christie Davies points out (1989: 24), 'the Turkish politicans who come and knock on Europe's door to ask for entry will have to face a powerful and deep-rooted set of anti-Turkish sentiments, many of very ancient origin, held by their European neighbours'. This issue poses with considerable sharpness the question of the relation between 'Europeanness' and Islam.

The matter also assumes greater significance at a time when Pope John Paul II and other leading figures in the Catholic Church argue that 'Christianity is at the very roots of European culture' (cited in Kettle, 1990: 14) and that 'Europe has no identity without Christianity' (cf. Koenig, 1989: 23). The denunciation of materialism and the evocation of Christian spirituality as a solution to Europe's identity crisis in the wake of 'the death of Marxism' have also come from Anglican quarters (cf. Booth, 1990). One can only conjecture how future relations between the various Christian denominations and between Christians and the non-Christian faiths who are excluded from these projections will evolve.

Outside the EC, in the Soviet Union's Muslim regions and in Yugoslavia too, the question of Islamic religio-ethnic separatism has come to the surface, with potentially far-reaching consequences for those states. No doubt the already rich field of 'orientalist' representations of threat and difference will become even further developed, to embrace more systematically the Muslim worlds both outside Europe's confines and within (cf. Said, 1981).

Finally, we should also not overlook the growing evidence of rising anti-semitism in some countries of Eastern Europe, where the liberalization of politics has given rise to the most visceral forms of overt prejudice. Nor is the West immune. The deeply symbolic disinterment of a body and the defacement of graves in France's oldest Jewish cemetery at Carpentras has sent shock waves throughout the Jewish communities of France, and beyond. Other Jewish cemeteries in France and cemeteries and synagogues in Britain have been desecrated in campaigns inspired by Nazi ideology. In this context one could be forgiven for taking the primordial more seriously than the postmodern.

Closing remarks

One can only close *pro tempore*, rather than conclude. The field with which this chapter has dealt remains extraordinarily volatile, with the unavoidable and no doubt beneficial results of continual revision in one's thinking.

From all that I have said, it is certain that our systems of communication are going to bear a heavy weight in the coming years and those who communicate through the public media a correlative responsibility to ensure that we interpret the times with finesse, tolerance and accuracy. As for the moot question of European identity, one can predict with calm conviction that this will provide an arena for a great deal of ideological contestation in the years to come. It is also an issue that is bound to provoke much theoretical, analytical and empirical work in the human sciences.

I suggested earlier that for the purposes of analysis we have to set sentiment aside. This is difficult of course, given the lived relation that we bear to what is being observed and written about. At root, I cannot but feel that if we are to navigate our way with success through the whirlpools of collective identity, there is no alternative to developing a thoroughgoing pluralism of structures in the Europe of the future, one that recognizes multi-ethnicity, multiculturalism and the multi-faith society as indispensable elements in a new order. At the moment one says this, one is also bound to accept that it is the profound diversity of the proposed Common Home that is striking rather than its similarities.

References

Ahmed, A. (1990) 'Jeans for You, Robes for Me', *Guardian*, 5 July.

Appignanesi, L. and Maitland, S. (1989) *The Rushdie File*. London: Fourth Estate.

Ascherson, N. (1990) 'Old Conflicts in the New Europe', *Sunday Review, Independent on Sunday*, 18 February.

Bauman, Z. (1990) 'Modernity and Ambivalence', *Theory, Culture and Society*, 'Global Culture', 7 (2–3), June: 143–69.

Booth, A. (1990) 'A Gap Karl Left to God', *Guardian*, 16 April.

Butt, R. (1990) 'Political Union in Europe', *New European*, 3 (2–3), Summer/Autumn: 45–51.

Clough, P. (1990) 'We Want to Be Germans Again', *Independent*, 7 March.

Cornelius, A. and Milner, M. (1990) 'EFTA Nations Queue Up to Find their Place in Brave New World of the Super Market', *Guardian*, 6 March.

Cottrell, R. (1989) 'Europe in the Year 2000', *Independent*, 30 October.

Csepeli, G. (1984) 'An Inorganic Nation', *Annales Universitatis Scientiarum Budapestinesis de Rolando Eötvös Nominatae*, Separatum, Sectio Philosophica et Sociologica, XVIII (Budapest): 131–44.

Dahrendorf, R. (1990) *Reflections on the Revolution in Europe. In a Letter Intended to Have Been Sent to a Gentleman in Warsaw, 1990*. London: Chatto & Windus.

Dassetto, F. and Bastenier, A. (1987) *Media U Akbar: Confrontations autour d'une Manifestation*. Louvain-la-Neuve: CIACO.

Davies, C. (1989) 'Time to Talk Turkey', *New European*, 2 (2), Summer: 22–4.

Douglas, M. (1987) *How Institutions Think*. London: Routledge.

Duve, F. (1989) 'Qui pose la question allemande?', *Le Monde*, 'Débats', 26 October.

Garton Ash, T. (1989) *The Uses of Adversity: Essays on the Fate of Central Europe*. Cambridge: Granta Books; London: Penguin.

Garton Ash, T. (1990) 'Eastern Europe: Après le Déluge, Nous', *New York Review of Books*, XXXVII (13), 16 August: 51–7.

Gellner, E. (1983) *Nations and Nationalism*. Oxford: Blackwell.

Goban-Klas, T. (1989) 'Gorbachev's Glasnost: A Concept in Need of Theory and Research', *European Journal of Communication*, 4 (3): 247–54.

Gott, R. (1990) 'Faith, Fear and Fury', *Guardian*, 8 January.

Graffy, J. and Hosking, G.A. (eds) (1989) *Culture and the Media in the USSR Today*. Basingstoke: Macmillan.

Hall, S. and Jacques, M. (eds) (1989) *New Times: The Changing Face of Politics in the 1990s*. London: Lawrence & Wishart.

Hanke, H. (1990) 'Media Culture in the GDR: Characteristics, Processes and Problems', *Media, Culture and Society*, 12 (2), April: 175–93.

Havel, V. (1990) 'The Future of Central Europe', *New York Review of Books*, XXXVII (5), 29 March: 18–19.

Held, D. (1989) 'The Decline of the Nation State', in Hall and Jacques (1989). pp. 191–204.

Hobsbawm, E. (1990) *Nations and Nationalism since 1789: Programme, Myth, Reality*. Cambridge: Cambridge University Press.

Hobsbawm, E. and Ranger, T. (1983) *The Invention of Tradition*. Cambridge: Cambridge University Press.

Howard, Sir M. (1990) 'Escape from History', *Guardian*, 13 March.

Jakubowicz, K. (1990) 'Musical Chairs? Poland and its Three Public Spheres', *Media, Culture and Society*, 12 (2), April: 195–212.

Kent, B. (1990) 'Vision of a New Europe', *New European*, 3 (2–3), Summer/Autumn: 13–16.

Kettle, M. (1990) 'John Paul's Grand Design for Europe', *Guardian*, 27 April.

Koenig, Cardinal F. (1989) 'Europe's Spiritual Guidelines', *New European*, 2 (1), Spring: 20–3.

Kundera, M. (1984) 'The Tragedy of Central Europe', *New York Review of Books*, 26 April.

McNair, B. (1989) 'Glasnost and Restructuring in the Soviet Media', *Media, Culture and Society* 11 (3), July: 327–49.

Melucci, A. (1989) *Nomads of the Present: Social Movements and Individual Needs in Contemporary Society*. London: Hutchinson Radius.

Mikes, G. (1946) *How to Be an Alien*. London and New York: Wingate.

Mikulowski-Pomorski, J. (1988) 'The Idea of "One Europe"', *Innovation*, 1 (4–5): 785–98.

Mortimer, E. (1990) 'When the Lion Lies Down with the Lamb in 2020', *Financial Times*, Special Report: East Europe in Ferment, 24 January.

Namer, G. (1987) *Mémoire et Société*. Paris: Méridiens Klincksieck.

Pohoryles, R. and Kinnear, R. (1989) 'Europe – a Political Concept? Tasks of the intellectuals in East and West in a Period of Growing Uncertainty'. Paper presented to the conference on 'Universities Today and Tomorrow – their Role in the Integration of Europe', Rabka, 15–21 September.

Said, E. (1981) *Covering Islam: How the Media and the Experts Determine How We See the Rest of the World*. New York: Random House.

Schama S. (1987) *The Embarrassment of Riches: An Interpretation of Dutch Culture in the Golden Age*. London: Fontana.

Schlesinger, P. (1982) 'In Search of the Intellectuals: Some Comments on Recent Theory', *Media, Culture and Society*, 4 (3), July: 203–23.

Schlesinger, P. (1988) 'Kollektive Identitäten, Freunde, Feinde', *Innovation*, 1 (1): 102–15.

Schöpflin, G. and Wood, N. (eds) (1989) *In Search of Central Europe*. Cambridge: Polity Press.

Smith, A.D. (1990) 'Towards a Global Culture?', *Theory, Culture & Society*, 7(2–3), June: 171–91.

Thatcher, M. (1988) The Prime Minister's speech in Bruges, September.

Thatcher, M. (1990) 'On Shaping a New Global Community'. Speech made by the Prime Minister to the Aspen Institute, in Aspen, Colorado, USA, 5 August.

Wörner, M. (1990) 'The Atlantic Alliance in the Nineties: Cornerstone of a New European Security Structure', *New European*, 3 (1): 8–14.

Zeldin, T. (1985) *The French*. London: Collins Harvill.

Index